GOING POSTCARD

Before you start to read this book, take this moment to think about making a donation to punctum books,
an independent non-profit press

@ https://punctumbooks.com/support

If you're reading the e-book, you can click on the image below to go directly to our donations site. Any amount, no matter the size, is appreciated and will help us to keep our ship of fools afloat. Contributions from dedicated readers will also help us to keep our commons open and to cultivate new work that can't find a welcoming port elsewhere. Our adventure is not possible without your support.
Vive la open-access.

Fig. 1. Hieronymus Bosch, *Ship of Fools* (1490–1500)

GOING POSTCARD: THE LETTER(S) OF JACQUES DERRIDA Copyright © 2017 by the Authors and Editor. This work carries a Creative Commons BY-NC-SA 4.0 International license, which means that you are free to copy and redistribute the material in any medium or format, and you may also remix, transform and build upon the material, as long as you clearly attribute the work to the authors (but not in a way that suggests the authors or punctum books endorses you and your work), you do not use this work for commercial gain in any form whatsoever, and that for any remixing and transformation, you distribute your rebuild under the same license. http://creativecommons.org/licenses/by-nc-sa/4.0/

First published in 2017 by dead letter office, BABEL Working Group
an imprint of punctum books, Earth, Milky Way.
https://punctumbooks.com

The BABEL Working Group is a collective and desiring-assemblage of scholar–gypsies with no leaders or followers, no top and no bottom, and only a middle. BABEL roams and stalks the ruins of the post-historical university as a multiplicity, a pack, looking for other roaming packs with which to cohabit and build temporary shelters for intellectual vagabonds. We also take in strays.

ISBN-13: 978-0-9985318-7-8
ISBN-10: 0-9985318-7-1
Library of Congress Cataloging Data is available from the Library of Congress

Book design: Vincent W.J. van Gerven Oei

GOING POSTCARD
THE LETTER(S) OF JACQUES DERRIDA

Edited by
Vincent W.J.
van Gerven Oei

TABLE OF CONTENTS

J. Hillis Miller
Glossing the Gloss of "Envois" in *The Post Card* · · · 11

Michael Naas
Drawing Blanks · · · · · · · · · · · · · · · · · 43

Rick Elmore
Troubling Lines:
The Process of Address in Derrida's *The Post Card* · · 59

Nicholas Royle
Postcard Telepathy · · · · · · · · · · · · · · · · 65

Wan-Chuan Kao
Post by a Thousand Cuts · · · · · · · · · · · · · 69

Eszter Timár
Ateleia/Autoimmunity · · · · · · · · · · · · · · · 83

Hannah Markley
Philately on the Telephone:
Reading, Touching, Loving the "Envois" · · · · · · · 95

Éamonn Dunne
Entre Nous · · · · · · · · · · · · · · · · · · · 115

Zach Rivers
Derrida in *Correspondances*:
A Telephonic Umbilicus · · · · · · · · · · · · · · 129

Kamillea Aghtan
Glossing Errors:
Notes on Reading the "Envois" Noisily · · · · · · · 161

Peggy Kamuf
Coming Unglued · · · · · · · · · · · · · · · · · · 171

James E. Burt
Running with Derrida · · · · · · · · · · · · · · · 179

Julian Wolfreys
Perception–Framing–Love · · · · · · · · · · · · · 185

Dragan Kujundžić
Envoiles: Post It · · · · · · · · · · · · · · · · · 197

Vincent W.J. van Gerven Oei
Postface · 217

***

About the Contributors · · · · · · · · · · · · · · 227

ABBREVIATIONS

PC: Jacques Derrida, *The Post Card: From Socrates to Freud and Beyond,* trans. Alan Bass (Chicago: University of Chicago Press, 1987); *La carte postale: de Socrate à Freud et au-delà* (Paris: Flammarion, 1983). Page numbers after the slash refer to the French edition.

Other abbreviations particular to individual chapters are indicated in the footnotes.

J. Hillis Miller

Glossing the Gloss of "Envois" in *The Post Card*

The Post Card invites glossing of all sorts. It is an immensely complex and rich text, one of Derrida's most fascinating and challenging. *La carte postale* is full of specific historical and personal references that will puzzle many readers. Many formulations and allusions are enigmatic or counter-intuitive. They need explanatory glossing. Derrida uses just about every rhetorical device and figure of speech in the book. You name it, it is there (*il y a là*): puns (*calembours*), metaphor, metonymy, synecdoche, catachresis, apostrophe, prosopopoeia, hyperbole, prolepsis, analepsis, ellipsis, paradox, aporia, and of course a constant pervasive destabilizing irony. How can you tell when this joker is telling the truth or speaking straight, if ever?

"Envois," moreover, is full of complex wordplay that is not exactly "figurative" in the usual sense. This wordplay is often not easily translatable from French to English. One tiny example: In the last entry for February 1979, Derrida writes: "La séance continue, tu analyse ça comment? Je parle grammaire, comme toujours, c'est un verbe ou un adjectif?" ("*La séance continue*, how do you analyze that? I'm talking grammar, as always, is it a verb or an adjective?" [*PC*, 178/193]) Derrida here plays on an untranslatable ambiguity on whether "continue" in the French is verb or an adjective. In the first case, the locution would mean: "The session continues." In the second, "The continued session." It makes a lot of difference which way you read it, as a duck or as a rabbit, as in the famous Gestaltist diagram that oscillates unpredictably before the viewer's eyes between those two animals. The reader (you! [singular]) will note the second person singular pronoun in "tu analyse ça comment?" This is an example of the endless play on the difference between "tu" and "vous" that pervades the "Envois."

You(!), dear reader, can easily imagine a glossed *La carte postale* that would be immensely longer than the original. If the glosses were marginal, the result might be like one of those Renaissance glossed Bibles or theological treatises in which the margins on both sides and at the bottom are filled with glosses on specific points of a few lines of the original text. The glosses are much longer than the glossed text.

I presume, however, that before glossing a given text, it is helpful to decide just what sort of text it is. That is not so easy to decide for the "Envois" in *The Post Card*. My remarks here will focus on that apparently limited and presumably answerable question. To what genre does "Envois" belong? "La loi du genre" ("The Law of Genre"), a wonderful essay in *Parages* on Blanchot's récit, *La folie du jour* (*The Madness of the Day*), begins by asserting firmly that genres should not be mixed:

> Genres are not to be mixed.
> I will not mix genres.
> I repeat: genres are not to be mixed. I will not mix them.
>
> (NE PAS MÊLER les genres.
> Je ne mêlerai pas les genres.
> Je répète: ne pas mêler les genres. Je ne le ferai pas.)[1]

Is this a constative assertion or a performative speech act, followed by a promise? Derrida of course goes on to break his promise and also to show that Blanchot extravagantly mixes

---

[1] Jacques Derrida, "The Law of Genre," in *Acts of Literature*, ed. Derek Attridge, 221–52 (New York & London: Routledge, 1992), 223; "La loi du genre," in *Parages*, 249–87 (Paris: Galilée, 1986), 251.

genres. Nevertheless, it sounds like a sensible idea that a given text should have an ascertainable genre and that decisions about appropriate glosses should be made on the basis of that certainty. Let me see if I can do that.

***

"Envois" appears from many clues to be autobiographical, to be made up of real letters, and to be full of representations of events that did actually take place. I can testify that the episodes that mention me really did happen as Derrida describes them. Of course I might be lying, even though I swear I am telling the truth, giving accurate testimony.

Paul de Man and I *did* go year after year to pick Derrida up after his flight from Paris and take him to one or another of the Yale residential colleges where he was to stay while giving his annual five-week seminar series. It is the case that Derrida, after we met him at the arrivals gate, used to go to make a phone call to someone or other. (Perhaps his wife? Who knows? He never said. None of our business.)

It is the case that Derrida and I visited on one occasion Joyce's tomb in the cemetery next to the zoo in Zurich. We did encounter on our walk back through the cemetery the gravestone of one Egon Zoller, "der Erfinder des Telefonographen," the inventor of the ticker tape, or of some device to turn telephone signals into graphic ones that can be printed out. A ticker-tape machine is carved on Zoller's tombstone with tape going from alpha to omega. We both stood for several minutes contemplating this tombstone. It fascinated Derrida (me too), partly because he was working at that time on communication technologies, a big topic in *The Post Card*. At Derrida's request I asked a Zurich friend to take a photograph of this gravestone and send it to Derrida. I heard recently that this photo is still among his *Nachlaß*. We looked for the grave of Peter Szondi but did not find it, as one of the "postcards" says.

It is a fact that during one of Derrida's visits to Yale I took him sailing on Long Island Sound in my 18.5 foot Cape Dory

Typhoon, the "Frippery." I did not tell Derrida, however, that the "Small Craft Warnings" were up for strong wind and waves. We had no great difficulty with those, however, and returned safely to the mooring up the river in Branford.

I have in my possession a precious original of the post card from the Bodleian showing Plato, absurdly, instructing Socrates in what to write (or to erase). Whoever writes those postcards in *The Post Card* spends much time, as you readers will know, exuberantly trying to interpret this enigmatic graphic. The postcard writer says Jonathan Culler and Cynthia Chase took him to the Bodleian to let him discover the postcard for himself. Cynthia Chase sent me my exemplar on June 10, 1977. In tiny but quite legible handwriting she begins by mentioning her wonderful essay on George Eliot's *Daniel Deronda* (referred to by "Derrida" in *The Post Card*). It had just been accepted by PMLA, the *Publications of the Modern Language Association*. She then goes on to say, "Derrida was here last week to talk informally in Jonathan's seminar, where he began in very slow but precise English, and spoke about parisitage and the more amusing features of his lengthy response to Searle in a forthcoming *Glyph*." This seems to confirm that the account in *The Post Card* of Derrida's discovery of the postcard in the Bodleian is historically accurate. It really did happen just as that particular post card says it did. Here are recto and verso of my postcard. You can see from the postmark that it was in truth sent from Oxford on June 10, 1977. The postmark on the recto has what seems to be the beginning of the word "Remember." Remember what? The rest is cut off. It seems a provocative exhortation:

GLOSSING THE GLOSS OF "ENVOIS" IN *THE POST CARD*

GREETINGS

June 9

Dear Mr Miller,

I reviewed my Daniel Derrida essay and Mr Schaefer approved the new version and will put it in PMLA next again. I'm so pleased. Thank you for encouraging me to make the attempt. It would be especially nice if Maggie Ferguson's essay comes out that issue too.

Would you be my superviser for talking Derrida's lectures as a course in the fall? He will be doing Heidegger and Beyond the Pleasure Principle. I'm at the need while writing recent papers to study Freud properly. Derrida was here last week to talk informally in Jonathan's seminar where he began in very close but precise English, and spoke about Parrastage and for more amusing features of his lengthy response to Searle in a forthcoming Glyph. Have a nice Summer

Cynthia Chase

POST CARD

ADDRESS

J. Hillis Miller,
Chairman
English Department
Yale University
New Haven,
Conn. 06520
USA

AIR MAIL

BODLEIAN LIBRARY, OXFORD See p. 68
Socrates and Plato, the frontispiece of Prognostica
Socratis basilei, a fortune-telling book. English, 13th
century, the work of Matthew Paris.
MS. Ashmole 304, fol. 31v

Those external confirmations, my own and Cynthia Chase's, lead me to believe that other episodes in the "Envois" are "true to life" too. A drunk did wander around the phone booth on one occasion while "Derrida" was trying to make a call. Someone did phone him collect at home claiming to be "Martini Heidegger." He did encounter an American graduate student, perhaps Avital Ronell, and suggest to her that she write her PhD dissertation on the telephone in modernist literature (Proust etc.): "and then asking the question of the effects of the most advanced telematics on whatever would still remain of literature. I spoke to her about microprocessors and computer terminals, she seemed somewhat disgusted. She told me that she still loved literature (me too, I answered her, *mais si, mais si*), Curious to know what she understood by this" (*PC*, 204). That "me too, [...] *mais si, mais si*," is wonderfully ironic. "*Mais si*" is a more or less untranslatable French idiom that is positive and negative at the same time, something like, "Yes. But nevertheless. But nevertheless," or colloquially, "Yeah, but."

I associate this interchange with the unnamed American graduate student, which I believe to have occurred "in the real world," with a passage a few pages earlier. That passage is of great importance for me. It leads me to endless reflection. In it "Derrida" asserts that "an entire epoch of so-called literature, if not all of it, cannot survive a certain technological regime of telecommunications (in this respect the political regime is secondary). Neither can philosophy, or psychoanalysis. Or love letters" (*PC*, 197). Literature, philosophy, psychoanalysis, and love letters will be destroyed by the computer, the Internet, email, and those other features of our present (2012) prestidigitalization that Derrida could not yet foresee in 1977: email, Facebook, Twitter, iPhones, iPads, Kindle, etc.

Whether or not what Derrida says is really the case as hyperbolically as he says (the complete disappearance of these four forms of discourse) is an immense question, but Derrida gets an A+ for prophetic insight. His very first interview, out of hundreds given over his life time, was in 1968 for a now long-defunct journal called *Noroît*. It was called "Culture and écriture. La proliferation des livres et la fin du livre." That puts our present situation in 2012 in a nutshell. The printed book industry is thriving, but even so Amazon since 2011 has been selling more e-texts than printed books. I take it Derrida in 1968, long before e-texts became common, meant by "livre" a printed book that you can hold in your hand and read by turning physical paper pages.

I conclude from these examples that it seems easy to decide that *The Post Card* belongs to the genre of confessional autobiography and needs to be glossed as such. You would do that by adducing as much factual and contextual information as possible, as I have done with a few examples. Doing this will make the text more perspicuous and more believable as truth-telling testimony.

***

Matters are not quite so simple, however, as a little more attention to the text of *The Post Card* will show. Derrida gave me my copy of the French original. He has charmingly, but a little alarmingly, added to the title of the first section, "Envois": "à Hillis, à Dorothy," as though all those post cards were addressed and sent to us. "Telepathy" is a section of "Envois" that was mysteriously omitted and then published separately. There is a long story to tell about that omission and about "Telepathy" itself. I have tried to tell that story in *The Medium is the Maker: Browning, Freud, Derrida and the New Telepathic Ecotechnologies*.[2] My little book is an extended gloss on a section of "Envois," "Télepathie," that is present there only in its ghostly absence, though published separately. Does an omitted section of "Envois" deserve a gloss for readers of "Envois"? I think the answer must be yes, but the mind boggles at the thought of glossing a spectral absence/presence. As you readers of "Telepathy" will know, Derrida claims in

---

2 J. Hillis Miller, *The Medium is the Maker: Browning, Freud, Derrida and the New Telepathic Ecotechnologies* (Brighton: Sussex Academic Press, 2009).

that essay that a postcard, in part because it is open for anyone in the world to read who comes upon it, makes any one who intercepts it as it travels through the postal system into the person, the "you [*tu*]" for whom the postcard is intended. The reader, whoever he or she might be (Hillis, or Dorothy, or whoever), is transmogrified into the addressee of the postcard.

That is what I mean by "alarmingly"! I'm not at all sure I want to be transformed into the person those postcards in the "Envois" invoke into being by a magic telepathic or hypnotic hocus pocus, by an irresistible "transfer" in the psychoanalytic sense. I just want to go on "being myself," thank you very much. Part of me, however, knows that each of those poems, novels, and other texts I have read and taught and written about for so many years, including *La carte postale,* has dispossessed me, turned me, at least temporarily, into someone other than myself, perhaps into someone of a different gender. In reading Eliot's *Middlemarch* I become Dorothea Brooke or the personified narrator, "George Eliot" "himself." In reading Gerard Manley Hopkins's poems, prose works, and letters I become Hopkins. In reading *The Post Card* I become the person "Derrida" addresses as "tu." (The reader needs always to remember how much is lost in translation when *La carte postale* is turned into *The Post Card.* Derrida, for example, as I have said, in the "Envois" section carries on a complex play between French second person singular and second person plural, *tu* and *vous*. English makes no such distinction. I shall return to this.)

Nevertheless, the reader wonders just whom these so circumstantial-sounding letters were really meant for, to whom they were originally destined as *envois,* sendings, to whom they were mailed. Surely, in spite of the discretionary total absence of any proper names, these are real love letters sent by a male named Jacques Derrida to some never-named intimate female beloved. Derrida's short untitled preface, however, dashes all our hopes for a certain identification of either sender or addressee, as I shall show. A preface is a species of anticipatory gloss. My gloss in this essay will focus on glossing that gloss. Prefaces are usually intended, like glosses, to guide or orient the reader for the proper reading of the text to come. Derrida's preface, in this case, however, only makes matters more complicated and puzzling, as I shall show.

***

Let me take the "Envois," for the moment, as perhaps an example of yet another venerable genre, not an autobiography, but an epistolary novel. In one place within "Envois" Derrida claims to have had just this genre in mind as a set of conventions to parody, as well as the detective story, yet another genre. "Envois," he writes, will be "a kind of false preface, once again. Which, while parodying epistolary or detective literature (from the Philosophical Letters [by Voltaire, 1733] to the Portuguese nun [*Letters of a Portuguese Nun, 1669,* believed to be fictions composed by Gabriel-Joseph de La Vergne, comte de Gulleragues], from the *liaisons dangereuses* [1782, by Choderlos de Laclos] to Milena [Franz Kafka, *Briefe an Milena*, 1952]), would also obliquely introduce my speculations on Freudian speculation" (*PC*, 179). I suppose "Envois" is a kind of detective story in the way it hides the mystery of just who the sender(s) and receiver(s) of these letters are and just what romance the letters covertly reveal. That gives two more possible genres for "Envois": novel in letters and detective story.

It is easy to identify the generic laws of the epistolary novel, from Richardson, Marivaux, and Rousseau in the eighteenth century on to more recent examples. These laws are a special case of the standard conventions of the Western novel from *Don Quixote* to Ian McEwan. Those conventions, for either sort of novel, are a version of what Derrida, notoriously, called "logocentrism." Logocentrism is a coherent system of concepts or presuppositions that centers on the notion of the *logos*. *Logos* is a multivalent word in Greek meaning Being, transcendent and simultaneously immanent ground, discourse, word, mind, ratio, rhythm. Jesus is the *Logos* in Christian theology. He is the second person of the Trinity, both transcendent and immanent deity, the God/man in whose name the creation was created and is upheld in being.

In the case of the conventions of the Western novel, whether epistolary or not, the stress is especially and in manifold ways on the unity of the self, subject, or ego. The Western novel assumes that the selves of the author, narrator, and characters are unified and remain the same through time, however much they may evolve. A not so latent sexism assumes that authors and narrators are most likely male. Some form of intersubjective communication, however limited it may be in some novels, is presumed. A good novel tells a unified story with a beginning, middle, and end. Within the fiction of a given novel, it is possible to understand the other person, to some degree at least, and to sympathize with him or her. The pleasure of reading novels is to a considerable degree the pleasure of an intimate access to the interiority of other (fictive) persons such as we do not have in "real life."

Marian Evans became a novelist when she adopted a male pseudonym and called herself George Eliot. Her *Middlemarch* (1872), that prototypical Victorian novel, is told by an imaginary male narrator who has telepathic insight into the minds and feelings of the imaginary characters, both male and female, and can speak for them in that logocentric form of narration, free indirect discourse. The narrator transfers that telepathic knowledge to the reader. George Eliot's narrator speaks in the third person past tense for what Dorothea Brooke and all the other characters are presumed to have experienced in the past and in the first person, present tense. Though the characters evolve through time, the cores of their selfhoods remain the same. The name "Dorothea" goes on referring to something unified and perdurable. Dorothea's insight into other people is at first limited and laughably mistaken, as in her radical misreading of her first husband, Mr. Casaubon. Gradually she learns to read others more accurately and to sympathize with them. That change leads to the happy ending and makes it possible.

An epistolary novel differs from novels like *Middlemarch* in having, typically, no overt narrator. Nevertheless, the presence of a supervising and ordering consciousness is implied in the way the letters are put in a sequence that tells a unified story. A vestigial narrator is implied, in some cases, in the identification of the sender and receiver of each of the letters in some impersonal, exterior, notation. An example is that belated epistolary short story by Henry James, "A Bundle of Letters" (1879). I say "belated" because the eighteenth century was the heyday of the epistolary novel in Europe. Relatively few were published in the nineteenth century, though hardly a Victorian novel exists that does not cite at least one or two letters. An example of the latter convention is the inclusion of letters in the novels of Anthony Trollope. The sender and receiver of each letter in James's "A Bundle of Letters" are labeled by some impersonal external authority: "Miss Miranda Hope in Paris to Mrs. Abraham C. Hope at Bangor Maine"; "From Mrs. Violet Ray in Paris to Miss Agnes Rich in New York," and so on. The letters are dated. They are arranged (by that effaced narrator) so as to tell a latent story. The letter-writers' unity of selfhood in an epistolary novel is indicated by the way they are signed and by the unity of a personal style that the author invents for them. James has evident fun in imitating what he imagines to be the epistolary style of Miss Miranda Hope, an intelligent young woman from the exceedingly provincial town of Bangor, Maine, traveling alone in Europe, e.g., "I guess we don't know quite *everything* at Bangor."[3] Though hardly a novel of either sort from *Don Quixote* on does not in one way or another challenge the assumptions I have been identifying, the regime of logocentrism remains relatively sovereign, relatively untouched, except in special notorious cases like *Don Quixote* itself or like *Tristram Shandy*.

In Derrida's "Envois" every single one of the conventions I have named is defiantly, exuberantly, systematically, and overtly transgressed, except for the dating of each entry, a convention

---

3 Henry James, "A Bundle of Letters," in *Lady Barbarina, The Siege of London, An International Episode, The Pension Beaurepas, A Bundle of Letters, The Point of View*, The New York Edition of Henry James, vol. 14 (New York: Charles Scribner's Sons, 1907–9), 481.

he obeys. The reader cannot tell for a given entry who is writing and to whom, or whether a single "je" wrote them all to a single "tu," since neither salutation nor signature is ever given. Moreover, the assertion that these long entries are all being written on numerous postcards seems extremely unlikely. At a minimum of four postcards a page it would take over a thousand postcards at least for the whole of the "Envois," something highly implausible. See how few words Cynthia Chase was able to get on the postcard from the Bodleian she sent me, even with her miniature handwriting.

The letters in "Envois" are punctuated by seemingly random breaks of 52 characters each, so that parts do not even make grammatical sense. If these are supposed to be love letters, all the learned discussion of Plato, Socrates, Freud, psychoanalysis, the history of the postal system, the constant word play and use of obscure allusions, etc., seems an exceedingly odd and probably ineffective way to say, "I love you," in spite of the constant circumstantiality of detail about the writer's or writers' daily activities that might plausibly make up part of "real" love letters. I say Derrida's defiance of conventions is "exuberant" to bring into the open Derrida's evident ironic joy in subverting logocentric expectations. Just in case you might not notice this for yourself, the unnamed preface, or, as I have called it, proleptic gloss, makes these wholesale transgressions explicit.

***

That anticipatory gloss of four pages, which I shall now partly gloss, is an exceedingly odd and even exasperating document, for a commonsensical person like me, someone who wants univocal certainty. That makes me what Derrida calls in this foreword a "*bad*" reader" (*PC*, 4). What characterizes a bad reader, according to Derrida, is an impatient desire for certainty, for knowing ahead of time what to expect. I cite the whole wonderful paragraph because it is so splendid a description and de(con)structive analysis of the sort of reader that is certain to get "Envois" wrong through what John Keats called, in a letter to Bailey, a "hunger […] after Truth":

> Because I still like him, I can foresee the impatience of the *bad* reader: this is the way I name or accuse the fearful reader, the reader in a hurry to be determined, decided upon deciding (in order to annul, in other words to bring back to oneself, one has to wish to know in advance what to expect, one wishes to expect what has happened, one wishes to expect (oneself)). Now, it is bad, and I know no other definition of the bad, it is bad to predestine one's reading, it is always bad to foretell. It is bad, reader, no longer to like retracing one's steps. (*PC*, 4)

The canny reader (you!) of this distinctly insolent paragraph (who would want to be a *bad* reader, even if Derrida says he likes them?) will note that Derrida begins by saying that he foresees the impatience of the *bad* reader, but ends by saying it is always bad to foretell. He does what he forbids, perhaps by an unavoidable law. You must have some sort of expectations in order to be able to read at all. You may also remember, perhaps on a re-reading (praised here as an escape from bad reading), that the famous postcard from the Bodleian of plato dictating to Socrates, that begat the whole of "Envois," is from a fortune-telling book of the thirteenth century, by one Matthew Paris, *Prognostica Socratis basilei*. The "Envois" proper have a lot to say about the ambiguities of fortune-telling, of prognostication. Psychoanalysis is a form of fortune-telling, with Dr. Sigmund Freud as the all-knowing telepathic medium receiving postcards from the patient's unconscious and from the future.

I say the post card of plato (small "p" on the postcard) and Socrates "begat the whole of *Envois*." Derrida says just that in an entry of 9 March 1979, in what follows the entry about epistolary and detective fiction already cited: "The entire book, accordion astrologies of post cards, would initiate into speculation via the reading of Sp [Socrates/plato]. Finally that is all there would be, everything would come back and amount to the patient, interminable, serious and playful, direct or detoured, literal of figurative description of the Oxford card" (*PC*, 179). That gives you yet another genre. The whole of "Envois," from beginning to end, is nothing but a glossing of that postcard, a reading of it, or annotation of it. It is certainly the case that Derrida has a wonderful time imagining different readings of the somewhat sinister or even obscene intercourse that he finds to be going on between Socrates and plato. Just what, for example, is that long cylindrical object sticking out from under Socrates's right leg?

In its scrupulous care for the significance of graphic detail, "Envois" resembles (in parody perhaps) yet another genre: the learned essay in art historical interpretation of a graphic artwork, for example the endless essays reading Dürer's *Melencolia I* or the learned quarrels over Van Gogh's paintings of shoes. (Are they female peasant shoes, as Heidegger claimed in a famous sentimental passage about peasant life, or are they the artist's own shoes?)

***

The first sentence of the preface gives the reader a distinctly anomalous genre for the "Envois" to add to those I have already identified. It is the first of many proposed genres: "You might read these envois as the preface to book that I have not written" (*PC*, 3). There is an odd genre for you! Derrida (I don't know what else to call whoever wrote these words; he speaks as an "I," a "je," throughout what you might call a preface to the preface or a proleptic gloss)... Derrida, you will note, does not say that the "Envois" is the preface to a book he just never got round to writing. He says, "Vous pourriez lire ces envois comme la préface d'un livre que je n'ai pas écrit": "You (second person plural: any "you" whatsoever) *might* [*pourriez*] read these sendings as a preface to an unwritten book [*PC*, 3/7]. It is up to you to decide whether or not to do so. It's a free country, and I'm not going to make up your mind for you."

Here, already, it has taken me a paragraph to gloss the grammar and rhetoric of the very first sentence. If I were to go on like this, which you will be happy to know I shall not, a truly monstrous interminable gloss would result.

Derrida goes on to say that the unwritten book would have "treated that which proceeds from the *postes, postes* of every genre, to psychoanalysis." He makes this more precise by adding: "Less in order to attempt a psychoanalysis of the postal effect than to start from a singular event, Freudian psychoanalysis, and to refer to a history and a technology of the *courrier*, to some general theory of the envoi and of everything which by means of some telecommunication allegedly *destines* itself" (*PC*, 3). The problem of course is that the "Envois" do in great detail just what he says the unwritten book would have done. This is especially the case if you include the mysteriously omitted section on "Telepathy," not to speak of the six essays added after the "Envois." These are primarily on Freud, though one is the splendid and definitive put-down of Lacan, "Le facteur de la vérité." What Derrida calls the preface to an unwritten book is in fact that book itself, in a species of what Derrida calls "invagination," the outside becoming the inside, the preface the text proper, in a perpetual oscillation.

Having proposed that you can, if you like, consider the "Envois" as the preface to an unwritten book, "Derrida," if that is who it is, goes on to say that he does not know whether reading them "is bearable" ("est soutenable") (*PC*, 3/7). "Soutenable" means "bearable" all right, but it has, to my ear, an overtone, of "sustainable," "able to be carried on," as in "sustained discourse." The "Envois" may be both unbearable to read and impossible to read in a sustained fashion.

***

"Derrida" then proposes yet another genre for the "Envois" that you might wish to consider: "You might consider them, if you really wish to (*si le cœur vous en dit*, if the heart tells you to do so), as the remainders (*les restes*) of a recently destroyed correspondence" (*PC*, 3/7). You can do so if you really want to, but I do not authorize your choice. In any case, the remainders of a recently destroyed correspondence is another odd genre, to say the least. "*Reste*" or "*restes*" are key words in Derrida, as I have elsewhere shown.[4] The word "restes" always has an overtone of dead body, "remains," as well as of archived writings, *Nachlaß*, as in the double word "corpus," corpse and body of writings.

Derrida goes on to say that what we read in the "Envois" is just what is left over, what remains, of a much more extensive correspondence, much of which has been "destroyed by fire or by that which figuratively takes its place, more certain of leaving nothing out of the reach of what I like to call the tongue of fire, not even the cinders if cinders there are [*s'il y a là cendre*]" (*PC*, 3). What could be "more certain" than fire? A shredder? Derrida tells in one place in "Envois" the story of how at some time in the past he took a huge correspondence in his car and first tried unsuccessfully, beside the Seine, to tear it into illegible scraps and throw it in the river. It would have taken far too long. He then drove to a suburb of Paris that was unfamiliar to him and burned the whole collection beside the road. What a wanton act of vandalism! I know of nothing like it except Henry James's burning of *his* accumulated correspondence.

Much later in "Envois" "Derrida" describes circumstantially the process whereby he decided which parts of the correspondence to destroy, which parts to save by typing them on his electric typewriter for publication in the book you are now reading. He observes that the rule of leaving out everything private, everything that would identify the sender and receiver, was unworkable, since everything was both private and at the same time relevant to the general project of the "Envois" and of his desire to make a book open to everyone. "Before all else I wanted, such was one of the destinations of my labor, to make a book—in part for reasons that remain obscure and in part for other reasons that I must silence" (*PC*, 5). That phrase about "leaving nothing out of reach of what I like to call the tongue of fire" is of course completely double-faced, or fork-tongued.

---

4 J. Hillis Miller, "Derrida's Remains," in *For Derrida*, 72–101 (New York: Fordham University Press, 2009).

A tongue of fire is totally destructive. You speak about the way "flames licked the roof of the burning house." At the same time that "tongue of fire" speaks, as in the tongues of fire that in the *Book of Acts* in the New Testament settled on the apostles at Pentecost and gave them the gift of tongues, the ability to speak all languages so that they might spread the Gospel through all the world: "And there appeared unto them cloven tongues like as of fire, and it sat upon each of them. And they were all filled with the Holy Ghost, and began to speak with other tongues, as the Spirit gave them utterance" (Acts 2:3–4).

As for intending to destroy even the cinders of the conflagrated parts of the correspondence, if cinders there are [*s'il y a là cendre*]: a cinder may be dead ash, or it may hide a secret glow ready to burst into flame again. The reference is to another extremely enigmatic book by Derrida, *feu la cendre* (1982; 1987, apparently written in 1971). The title of the Italian translation by Stefano Agosti links this book to "Envois": *ciò che resta del fuoco,* "what remains of a fire." A cinder is what remains of a fire, just as "Envois" is what remains of a destroyed correspondence.

Feu la cendre is a meditation on a phrase that Derrida says has been haunting him for fifteen years: *il y a là cendre*. To gloss just the preface to "Envois" you would perhaps need also to gloss the whole of *feu la cendre,* another virtually interminable task. Just part of the leitmotif, *il y a là,* is extremely difficult to translate, though, or perhaps just because, it is idiomatic French. Literally it means "it has there there," nonsense in English. *Il y a* is the French equivalent of German *es gibt,* or of English "there is" or "there are." "There are/is some[thing] there." "Cinder there is, there is, there, cinder."[5]

Derrida plays on the complexities of his phrase in the strange and enigmatic dedication to *feu la cendre*. He gives the dedication the strange and ominous name of "Animadversiones." I am included as a dedicatee (to my great honor) along with several others, listed in carefully non-hierarchical alphabetical order,

---

5   Jacques Derrida, *Cinders,* ed. and trans. Ned Lukacher (Lincoln and London: University of Nebraska Press, 1991), 21.

and followed by "d'autres," "among others." An animadversion is in modern French or English "hostile criticism" or "a critical or censorious remark." Really? Does Derrida mean he is making a hostile criticism of us, or that we are doing so with him. Neither makes good sense. Happily, however, the first meaning given in the *OED* for "animadversion" is neutral: "the turning or directing of the attention." "Animadversiones," moreover, is neither French nor English, but the nominative, accusative, or vocative plural of the Latin word, *animadversio*, which means initially perception, observation, paying attention to, that is, "turning the mind toward." Only secondarily does the word mean punishment, censure, or blame. Peter Ramus wrote in 1543 a book called *Aristotelicae animadversiones*. The word *animadversiones* has the meaning in biblical studies of commentary or gloss on a particular problematic word or passage in the Bible. So Derrida most probably intends no more than to name, in dedicatory acknowledgment, turnings of his mind toward, paying attention to, those who have read him or whom he has read ("their reading, "leur lecteur"), to his benefit. I rather like, however, trying to take *animadversiones* as somehow vocative. "O *Animadversiones*" might be an apostrophe addressed by Derrida to those who have turned their minds toward his work, that is, the dedicatees. My tentative glossing of *animadversiones* is a good example of how Derrida habitually says much in little by way of word play and of how that much in little is likely to be puzzling or contradictory, perhaps even "undecidable."

I cite below part of these animadversions, since the part I cite links with the idea in "Le facteur de la vérité" in *The Post Card* that since a letter may always not reach its destination, it never does. The first part of the dedication asserts, in a way that echoes the preface to *The Post Card*, that writing absents itself from its author as soon as it is written, resulting in the "effondrement extrême de la signature" ("the extreme disintegration of the signature"). You wrote it, but you cannot sign it. The second paragraph is also counter-intuitive: "Que la lettre soit forte en cette seule indirection, et de toujours pouvoir manquer l'arrive, je n'en prendrai pas prétexte pour m'absenter à la ponctualité d'une dedicace: R. Gasché, J-J. Goux, J.-C. Lebensztejn, J.-H. Miller, d'autres, il y a là cendre, reconnaîtront, peut-être, ce qui intervient ici de leur lecture. Décembre 1971" ("Though the letter gains strength solely from this indirection, and granted that it can always not arrive at the other side, I will not use this as a pretext to absent myself from the punctuality of a dedication: R. Gasché, J. J. Goux, J. C. Lebensztejn, J. H. Miller, others, cinders there are [*il y a là cendre*], will recognize, perhaps, what their reading has contributed here. December 1971") (C, 14/30).

This entire "dedication" has always made me more than a little uneasy, greatly honored as I am by it. What in the world, for example, does Derrida mean by adding that "il y a là cendre" after our names, in all its ambiguity or undecidability as a locution? Does he mean that those named or perhaps just their names are the dead cinders of past friendships, or that his writings have never reached us as their destination, that we haven't really ever understood a word of what he has written (a distinct possibility), or does he mean that the names are live coals that might burst into cloven tongues of flame if breathed upon by a dedication or even by an animadversion. "De leur lecture" is also undecidable in meaning. It could mean the dedicatees' reading of Derrida, or it could mean Derrida's reading of what they have written, perhaps including what they have written about his writing. You must decide that for yourself, dear reader, though I incline to the latter, since it hardly makes sense that my solitary reading of Derrida in those far-off days could have contributed anything to *feu la cendre*.

That some positive reading ought to win the day over the negative implications of "animadversion" is suggested not only by Derrida's almost forty years of generosity and friendship for me, but also by the dedication he inscribed in the copy of the 1987 reprint of *feu la cendre* he gave me in Laguna Beach in 1987: "pour Hillis/(la dedicace, depuis plus de 15 ans, est/ dans le livre)/affectueusement/Jacques./Laguna Beach, 6/avril 1987." He means, I think, that the book was apparently first written, with the dedication, more than fifteen years before the revised printing of 1987. Here, in case you doubt my word, is a scan of the kind inscription:

> pour Hillis
> (la dédicace, depuis
> loi de 15 ans, est
> dans le livre)
> affectueux souvenir
> Jacques.
> Laguna Beach, le 1 avril 1987

feu la cendre

***

I am now beginning to be seriously anxious. I have somewhat partially glossed in almost twenty-four pages only about two-thirds of the first page of the unnamed "preface" to "Envois," and I have by no means yet got to the most important part of that preface, for my purposes of genre-identification. Clearly I must pick up the pace or I'll never reach even a provisional answer to my initial apparently simple and straightforward question, "To what genre does 'Envois' belong?"

After having said that "Envois" is the remains of a destroyed correspondence, Derrida goes on to say that to say that is to say too much or too little, since "it was not one (but more or less) nor very correspondent. This still remains to be decided" (*PC*, 3). This is another example of the putting in question of any kind of presumed or decidable unity. It is more or less than a single correspondence and it does not successfully correspond to boot.

He then asserts that the partial saving was "due to a very strange principle of selection" (*PC*, 3). This "due to" and "saved" raises the ghost of the word "registered." All three are postal words, as in "postage due," or "registered mail." After having said that only part of the correspondence was "saved" Derrida adds an odd parenthesis: "(j'entends murmurer déjà 'accusé' comme on dit de réception).". Sure enough, the phrase "accuser [signaler] réception" means to give notice that one has received something,[6] so Alan Bass's translation is correct: "I already hear murmured 'registered,' as is said for a kind of receipt" (*PC*, 4/8). The saved part of the conflagrated correspondence is registered in the sense that the recipient has confirmed receipt by returning a receipt. I suppose that means that "Derrida" may have kept a tally of the remains or registered them by typing them out, as he evidently did in preparing the manuscript for publication. If they were actually sent, by the way, how come he has them and has the right to burn some and save some by some secret principle of selection or filtering? He speaks of "the grate, the filter, and the economy of sorting" ("la grille, le crible, l'économie du tri") (*PC*, 4/7). "To filter fire?" he asks, but continues: "I have not

---

6   *Le Petit Robert*, 15b.

given up doing so" (*PC*, 4). What a monstrous mélange of mixed metaphors, as bad as mixed genres!

Derrida then says that he finds the principle of selection he has used "questionable." Well, why did he use it then? He goes on to say, "I rigorously do not approve of this principle. [I wish he would say what that principle of selection was! Why not tell us outright?] I denounce it ceaselessly [Really? Where?], and in this respect reconciliation is impossible" (*PC*, 4). Reconciliation of whom with whom or with what? Another extremely odd sentence follows: "But it was my due to give in to it [j'ai *dû* y céder: 'I *had* to give in to it'], and it is up to you to tell me why" (*PC*, 4). Why can he not tell us why himself? This question raises in me a cascade of questions, not helpful answers to the question of the genre of "Envois" or directions for how to read it.

A separate one sentence paragraph follows that puts the ball definitely in the reader's court: "Up to you [*toi*, first person singular] first. I await only one response and it falls to you" (*PC*, 4). How in the world can you decide on the basis of the slender evidence Derrida gives? He puts the you, the addressee, that is, me the reader, in an impossible position. I have the responsibility to decide when there are no solid facts on the basis of which to decide. How can you know whether he was or was not right to destroy what he did destroy if we can no longer see and read the destroyed parts and do not know what the principle of selection was?

***

The next paragraph suggests yet another genre for "Envois." It can be taken as an extended apostrophe, an interpellation of the you that reads. Derrida in effect says: "You decide. You must decide." In an apostrophe the speaker breaks off the constative discourse and turns to address some "you" directly, someone either present or absent, as in Cicero's direct address to Catilina. "O" is often the sign of an apostrophe, though only in the translation in this case: "Quo usque tandem abutere, Catilina, patientia nostra!" ("When, O Catiline, do you mean to cease abusing our patience?") Apostrophe is closely associated with prosopopoeia. An apostrophe personifies the "you" to whom it is addressed, as in Wordsworth's apostrophe in "The Boy of Winander": "ye knew him well, ye cliffs and islands of Winander." "Thus I apostrophize," writes Derrida. "This too is a genre one can afford oneself, the apostrophe. A genre and a tone. The word—apostrophizes—speaks of words addressed to the singular one, a live interpellation (the man of discourse or writing interrupts the continuous development of the sequence, abruptly turns toward someone, that is, something, addresses himself to you), but the word also speaks of the address to be detoured" (*PC,* 4). The last phrase reminds the reader that apostrophe involves a turning away as well as a turning toward. Cicero turns away from his primary audience to address Catilina directly rather than making a reasoned argument for Catilina's condemnation to that primary audience, the Roman Senate. The whole of "Envois" can be taken as a huge extended apostrophe. That possibility is kept before the reader by the pervasive use of direct address ("tu") in the letters. If Derrida is right to say that an intercepted letter or post card turns the accidental reader into the "you" to whom the missive is addressed, then any you as reader of "Envois" becomes the apostrophized addressee of the letters, with all the responsibilities to respond and decide that Derrida so much insists on.

Then follow that paragraph about the bad reader (already discussed) and then several more paragraphs about the way he indicates in the text something of any length left out of a given letter by a 52 character space, though he swears he no longer remembers the long calculations that led to this "clever cryptogram": "If I state now, and this is the truth, I swear, that I have totally forgotten the rule as well as the elements of such a calculation, as if I had thrown them into the fire, I know in advance all the types of reaction that this will not fail to induce all around" (*PC,* 5). Derrida claims to be like someone who has carefully protected a file or a memory disk with a password and then has destroyed and completely forgotten the password. That certainly can happen, but nevertheless (*mais si!*), I as bad reader find myself muttering, in an apostrophe to the dead, "Come on, O Jacques, you can't expect me to believe that!"

***

Then at last follow the paragraphs that perhaps interest me most in this short preface. This is the sequence that resolutely dismantles, or, dare I say, "deconstructs," for "Envois" at least, all the logocentric narratological certainties about the separate unities of author, narrator, and characters I began by briefly summarizing. Derrida says in no uncertain terms that you cannot be certain who or how many different persons is/are writing these letters or whether the destined recipients are one or more persons, whether the author of the whole thing (presumably Jacques Derrida) is one person or many, whether any given "I" or "you" is male or female, or both, whether the sender is the same as the writer, or the receiver the same as the destined recipient. Even "Derrida" swears that he does not know. Here, nevertheless, is what "Derrida" says, in one of his most intransigent disaffirmations, or assertions of dispossession, of disappropriation. You must, I think, take him at his word:

> Who is writing? To whom? And to send, to destine, to dispatch what? To what address? Without any desire to surprise [Uh huh; there's a denegation for you!], and thereby to grab attention by means of obscurity, I owe it [there again is that notion of debt, of obligation, of what is due, as in "postage due"] to whatever remains of my honesty to say finally that I do not know. Above all I would not have had the slightest interest in this correspondence and this cross-section, I mean in their publication, if some certainty on this matter had satisfied me. (*PC,* 5/9)

This is an extravagant and implausible confession of ignorance, of uncertainty. It's implausible because he has told you, the reader, that he has removed the names of addresser and addressee, along with other evidence of what hidden love story lies behind these letters. Nevertheless, he must have known these facts, and he is not likely to have forgotten them. Now he wants to claim that the law of adestination is such that he really does not know who is writing and to whom in what remains of this destroyed correspondence, a correspondence that is not one (unified) and not correspondent. Perhaps the partial burning of the correspondence frees what remains of its ties to its original circumstances and makes the remains float in the air, so to speak, or perhaps lie dormant in some dead letter repository such as Melville makes much of in "Bartleby the Scrivener," a work known to Derrida. He uses the postal phrase "left unclaimed" ("laissé pour compte") in the first of the letters in the "Envois" proper (*PC*, 7/11).

Derrida then goes on to say that this radical uncertainty is not only disagreeable, but also even tragic. It is "tragic" presumably because it deroutes all the certainties and calculated distances on which ethical decision and responsible interpersonal relations depend, not to speak of that coherent reading of the text that you as a student of literature, or perhaps as a teacher of literature or as a writer about literature, depend. How far would you get if you said, "I haven't the slightest idea what this text means or how to talk or write sensibly about it." How could this publication be justified if it was just made up of a collective shrugging of shoulders in despair?

> That the signers and the addressees are not always visibly and necessarily identical from one *envoi* to the other, that the signers are not inevitably to be confused with the senders, nor the addressees with the receivers, that is with the readers (*you* [*toi*] for example), etc. — you will have the experience of all this, and sometimes will feel it quite vividly, although confusedly. This is a disagreeable feeling that I beg every reader, male and female, to forgive me. To tell the truth, it is not only disagreeable, it places you [*vous*; note he says "you" the reader, not the imaginary persons in the story] in relation, without discretion, to tragedy. It forbids that you regulate

distances, keeping them or losing them. This was somewhat my own situation, and it is my only excuse. (*PC*, 5/9)

"Well, OK," you say to yourself. "I can take that as a kind of elaborate set of fictional uncertainties achieved by leaving out signatures and proper names, but I am certain at least of one thing: Jacques Derrida himself wrote this preface and uses 'I' and 'me' with calm certainty, as though these pronouns indubitably refer to one singular person whose given name was Jacques (actually 'Jackie' when he was a child in Algiers) Derrida." The final paragraph of the preface seems reassuringly to confirm this, or at least somewhat reassuringly, since the opening of this final sentence is a little uneasy-making: "Accustomed as you [*vous*] are to the movement of the posts and to the psychoanalytic movement, to everything that they authorize as concerns falsehoods, fictions, pseudonyms, homonyms, or anonyms, you will not be reassured, nor will anything be the least bit attenuated, softened, familiarized, by the fact that [...]" (*PC*, 5–6/9–10). Not at all reassuring. Psychoanalysis and the movement of the posts (not to speak of all the fabrications of fictional selves these days by politicians, by email, by Facebook, and so on) have made us all suspicious readers, on the lookout for falsehoods, fictions, etc. We are unwilling to assume that anyone is who she or he says they are. Nevertheless, what follows "by the fact that" seems to make a wholesale reversal: "by the fact that I assume responsibility for these *envois*, for what remains, or no longer remains, of them, and that in order to make peace within you [*vous*] I am signing them here in my proper name, Jacques Derrida" (*PC*, 6/10). A date (7 September 1979) follows on the next line in a parody of legal confirmation of a signature.

"Whew!" you say, "At least one thing is certain. Jacques Derrida was one single person and took responsibility for having written the whole of 'Envois,' even the parts left out, burned away." This certainty is reinforced in my copy of the French original that Derrida dedicated to me and to my wife. (See scan above.) He also signed his first name on the last page of the preface in his own unmistakable handwriting, or perhaps it is the work of a cunning forger. Here is a scan of that:

> 10   LA CARTE POSTALE
>
> *au mouvement psychanalytique, à tout ce qu'ils autorisent en matière de faux, de fictions, de pseudonymes, d'homonymes ou d'anonymes, vous ne serez pas rassurés et rien ne sera le moins du monde atténué, adouci, familiarisé par le fait que j'assume sans détour la responsabilité de ces envois, de ce qui en reste ou n'en reste plus, et que pour faire la paix en vous je les signe ici de mon nom propre, Jacques Derrida*[1].
>
> *le 7 septembre 1979*

Alas, even this certainty is dashed by a footnote to that printed signature at the end of the preface. Note that small superscript 1. The appended footnote, with its characteristic cheerful Derridean irony, takes away even the residual unification of Jacques Derrida the putative author that has momentarily reassured you or me as readers:

> I regret that you [*tu*] do not very much trust my signature, on the pretext that we might be several. This is true, but I am not saying it in order to make myself more important by means of some supplementary authority [as when a critic, theorist, or philosopher says, for example, "we shall show" rather than "I shall show." Derrida habitually uses this professorial "we."]. And even less in order to disquiet. I know what this costs.

> You [*Tu*] are right, doubtless we are several, and I am not as alone as I sometimes say I am when the complaint escapes from me, or when I still put everything into seducing you [*à te séduire*]. (*PC*, 6/10)

That might add yet another genre. The "Envois" are an attempt to seduce you, that is, me, as the reader, any reader, of "Envois."

***

My apparent search has been for an answer to the question, "To what genre does 'Envois' belong?" I need to know this in order to know how to gloss it and what to gloss. Far from reaching certainty about this, I have instead encountered, in what Derrida himself says in the "preface," a long series of possible but incompatible genres. Far from obeying his own command not to mix genres, Derrida mixes genres big time. "Envois" may be a disguised autobiography, or the remains of a destroyed correspondence, or the preface to a book he has not written, or an extended interpretation of that post card from the Bodleian, or an extended gloss of that unwritten book, or a strange apostrophe to you the reader, or an attempt at seducing that you, or a history of the postal system in its relation to psychoanalysis, or an epistolary novel, or a detective story. In the end, to your dismay, "Derrida" is saying that it is up to you to choose which genre it is, to take responsibility for that choice and to gloss on that basis.

If Derrida is right to say that something is literature if it is taken as literature, that there is no "essence of literature," no distinctive linguistic markings that justify you to say "This is a literary work,"[7] it follows that you are to a considerable degree free to assign a genre to any text you gloss, teach, read, or interpret.

---

7 Derek Attridge, "'This Strange Institution Called Literature': An Interview with Jacques Derrida," trans. Geoffrey Bennington and Rachel Bowlby, in *Acts of Literature*, ed. Derek Attridge, 33–75 (London and New York: Routledge, 1992), 73.

Each choice would determine what and how to gloss. You would gloss differently if you took "Envois" as an extended apostrophe rather than as a somewhat disguised autobiography.

I myself lean toward taking "Envois" as belonging to a genre that had, in 1980, when *La carte postale* was published, only recently been given a name, and that Derrida himself does not suggest: the so-called post-modern novel. That sort of novel, from proto-post-modern narratives by Beckett, Borges, and Woolf (especially *The Waves*) down through more recent work by Pynchon, Doctorow, Delillo, McEwan, Coetzee, et al., has had as one of its goals a wholesale putting in question, not just in theory but also in practice, of those logocentric assumptions about the unitary selfhood of author, narrator, and characters, and those assumptions about intersubjectivity, that formed the standard conventions of the novel from Defoe to Conrad. Though those conventions were always in one way or another problematized in any given novel from *Don Quixote* on, nevertheless they had a considerable degree of sovereign authority over readers' expectations. Postmodern novels take material from the real world and even from the life of the author to create a non-realistic fictive world of one sort or another that questions unitary selfhood and the coherence of beginning, middle, and end in a narrative. Putting the "Envois" in that context and taking it as a post-modern novel would make possible productive choices about what to gloss in that text.

Deer Isle, Maine
July 14, 2012, revised August 28, 2016

J. Hillis Miller

J. Hillis Miller
UCI Distinguished Research Professor Emeritus
Departments of Comparative Literature and English
University of California
Irvine, CA 92697
Jhmiller@uci.edu
949–824–6722; 207–348–6696; 207–359–6535

Home addresses. Please use one of these for postal communication.

Early April to Early November:

697 Sunshine Road
Deer Isle, ME 04627
USA

207–348–6696

Early November to Early April:

293 Reach Road
Sedgwick, ME 04676
USA

207–359–6535

Michael Naas

Drawing Blanks

The reader of *The Post Card* is surely to be excused for drawing a blank from time to time. It's not easy going — a Derrida text rarely is — and "To Speculate — on 'Freud'" and "Le facteur de la vérité" are among Derrida's most challenging works. But patience and rereading almost always have their rewards when it comes to Derrida. However difficult these essays may be at first glance or at a first reading, they are not impenetrable, as some have wanted to pretend, and multiple readings almost always yield a coherent if not convincing reading of Freud or Lacan on themes such as repetition, legacy, language, the unconscious, or the relationship between psychoanalysis and philosophy. Even if the reader winds up drawing a blank now and again, the goal nonetheless remains and should remain to interpret and to understand, in a word, to *gloss* — the argument as well as the rhetoric, the organization as well as the themes, everything from the theses that are put forward to the language and terms used to support them. To arrive at a *reading* of these works — that should remain the goal of every reader who enters the ring or the arena of interpretation, every reader who agrees to going postcard.

When it comes to the "Envois," however, something else seems to be at work. More prosaic, comprehensible, sometimes even pedestrian — at least on their surface — the envois display another sort of blank, one drawn not by the reader but by the author or author/editor of these envois. Unlike the blanks drawn by the reader of the essays of *The Post Card,* the blanks of the *en-*

vois are marked *as blanks* and so have to be read as such. Like a text written in invisible ink, these blank spots or white blotches on the page seem to erase what was once there, making invisible what was once visible — and then making this very invisibility itself visible for a stretch of some 52 spaces. Derrida speaks of these blanks in this way in his preface to *The Post Card*:

> Whatever their original length, the passages that have disappeared are indicated, at the very place of their incineration, by a blank of 52 signs   and a contract insists that this stretch of destroyed surface remain forever indeterminable. In question might be a proper name or punctuation mark, just the apostrophe that replaces an elided letter, a word, one or several letters, in question might be brief or very long sentences, numerous or scant, that occasionally were themselves originally unterminated. Obviously I am speaking of a continuum composed each time of words or sentences, of signs missing from the interior, if it can be put thus, of a card, of a letter or of a card-letter. For the totally incinerated *envois* could not be indicated by any mark. I had first thought of preserving the figures and the dates, in other words the places of signature, but I gave it up. […] As for the 52 signs, the 52 mute spaces, in question is a cipher that I had wanted to be symbolic and secret — in a word a clever cryptogram, that is, a very naïve one, that had cost me long calculations. If I state now, and this is the truth, I swear, that I have totally forgotten the rule as well as the elements of such a calculation, as if I had thrown them into the fire, I know in advance all the types of reaction that this will not fail to induce all around. (*PC*, 4–5)

Derrida's comments help clarify the artifice of these blanks, Derrida's art of drawing blanks — the "contract" he would have drawn up with himself in order to publish these quasi-autobiographical *envois,* these "remainders," as he writes earlier, "of a recently destroyed correspondence" (*PC*, 3). It is not that the text was already "there," printed or formatted, already laid out in page proofs, as it were, and that 52 characters were then erased — whited out — at strategic places throughout the envois. No, a blank of 52 characters was inserted each time to efface anything from a single character — a single letter or punctuation mark — to short or very long sentences. The 52 characters thus impose a kind of measure or regularity on what is irregular and of unequal measure. Beneath the blanks of equal length are — were — texts of unequal length that have become through their erasure equally unreadable.

As for the location of these blanks, they can be found, it would seem, more or less anywhere in an envoi or sentence. Looking at just the first three envois, those of 3 June 1977 (*PC*, 8–9), we see that the 52 blank spaces can be found at what appears to be the *beginning* of a sentence ("   we have asked each other the impossible, as the impossible, both of us."), the *middle* of a sentence ("Never taken, in sum, the time to write you what I would have wanted, it has never been left to me, and if I write you without interruption   I will have sent you only cards."), the *end* of a sentence ("Even if they are letters and I always put more than one in the same envelope   "), and even at the *beginning and end* of a sentence ("   I love all my appellations for you and then we would have but one lip, one alone to say everything   "). If there is a rhyme or reason for the placement of these blanks, it will take a mighty clever reader to discover it.

As for the *content* of the blanks, the text or writing that has been blotted out, Derrida gives us some indication of this in the preface — though only in general and as a sort of temptation for interpretation: "a proper name or punctuation mark," he says. Presumably, most of these blanks were drawn, as we say, to protect the innocent, or to protect their author, as a way of practicing or exercising discretion by concealing a proper name, an identifying mark, or a compromising detail. What is blanked out could be a name, a date, a place, or a declaration of some kind, and unless there is some key or code for deciphering these blanks — a hypothesis that would need to be demonstrated — the reader is condemned each time to frustration, that is, to drawing or redrawing blanks.

In the "Envois," drawing blanks is thus not a preliminary stage on the way to a fuller understanding, something to be overcome in principle if not in fact. It is an essential element of the text and an unavoidable experience of reading. The blanks in the program are, as it were, part of the program, part of the text, interruptions of meaning that ultimately cannot be parsed or filled in, lacunae for which no reader can compensate or make amends. It is one of the reasons why Derrida writes on the first page of *The Post Card,* "As for the 'Envois' themselves, I do not know if their reading is bearable" (*PC,* 1).

Not unlike what are called by grammarians "irrecoverable ellipses," these blanks do not suggest or convey some hidden or absent or implicit meaning (as in Diderot's line to Sophie Volland cited at the outset of *Memoirs of the Blind,* "wherever there will be nothing, read that I love you"); they erase or incinerate meaning — with no promise of recovery or return. Unlike the blanks drawn by the reader of the essays, the blanks of the "Envois" — the letters, words, names, phrases, or sentences that have been, for whatever reason, effaced or erased, excised or incinerated — must *remain* blank in principle and not only in fact. We can only ever guess — we can never *know* — what was written there, what event is being recalled, what names invoked. In these "open letters," there is something that will remain forever closed. Assuming that no trace of what was once written there remains to be discovered in the archive — drafts of these letters *before* the insertion of blanks, at IMEC or at Irvine — these blanks will continue to resist our reading, and Derrida's death in October 2004 will have forever drawn a veil over even the *promise* of one day discovering their secret. What was once secret to Derrida alone, and yet still able to be revealed while he was still living, will have become with his death forever concealed — *like a crypt.*

One thus cannot know what is contained in these crypts, and even speculation about them is dangerous, prone to all kinds of phantasmatic projections. As for this word crypt, it seems justified by Derrida's own reference to a "clever cryptogram" that would have governed the making of these blanks of 52 spaces. While it is impossible, therefore, to discover what is in or behind these crypts, it is hard not to ask about the nature of the crypt itself, to ask, for example, "What is a crypt?," a question that Derrida himself asked just a year before the first of the envois, in 1976, in his forward to Nicolas Abraham and Maria Torok's *The Wolf Man's Magic Word: A Cryptonymy*.[1] Derrida begins that essay: "What is a crypt? What if I were writing on one now?" ("*Fors*," ix) This theme of the crypt will have been central to much of Derrida's work from at least *Glas* (1974) onward. To cite just the first of many references to crypts in *Glas*, especially since it — and the letter of Genet folded within it — seems to bear an uncanny relation to the situation of the *envois*: "You are still *on the stairway*, on the way to a crypt that always expects you to come in advance of just what it seems to conceal. 'It was then that we began to exchange the love letters in which we spoke of ourselves […]. He signed his first letter 'Illegible,' as a matter of caution, and I began my reply with 'Dear Illegible'" (*G*, 33b).[2]

The blanks drawn throughout *The Post Card* are, it would seem, so many *crypts*, where names and places and who knows what else have become illegible, erased or effaced, or else locked away, sealed from the inside, as it were, with no possibility of ever being revealed. But, again, it seems appropriate to ask, since Derrida asks this not once but several times throughout "*Fors*," "What is a crypt? Not a crypt *in general*, but *this* one, in its singularity, the one I shall keep coming back to?" ("*Fors*," xiii) The first answer to this question would obviously have to be that every crypt defies the generality of the "What is…?" or *ti esti*

---

[1] Jacques Derrida, "*Fors*: The Anglish Words of Nicolas Abraham and Maria Torok," in Nicolas Abraham and Maria Torok, *The Wolf Man's Magic Word: A Cryptonymy*, trans. Barbara Johnson (Minneapolis: University of Minnesota Press, 1986), xi–xlviii. The essay initially appeared in French in 1976; henceforth, "*Fors*."

[2] Jacques Derrida, *Glas*, trans. John P. Leavey, Jr., and Richard Rand (Lincoln: University of Nebraska Press, 1986). First published by Éditions Galilée in 1974; henceforth, *G*.

question. As Derrida argues on the same page: "it *remains* that the question 'What is a crypt?' can no longer, it seems to me, be posed" ("*Fors,*" xiii).

And yet certain traits of the crypt remain to be deciphered, even glossed. For example, still in "*Fors,*" and right on the next page, after again posing the "What is…?" question, Derrida gives us something of an answer: "What is a crypt? No crypt presents itself. The grounds [*lieux*] are so disposed as to disguise and to hide: something, always a body in some way. But also to disguise the act of hiding and to hide the disguise: the crypt hides as it holds" ("*Fors,*" xiv). And then a couple of pages later: "What the crypt commemorates, as the incorporated object's 'monument' or 'tomb,' is not the object itself, but its exclusion, the exclusion of a specific desire from the introjection process. […] The crypt is the vault of a desire" ("*Fors,*" xvii).

These passages are illuminating, clarifying, at the same time as they multiply the difficulties and ambiguities. To do full justice to this question of the crypt—something that is beyond the ambitions of this modest reading of the blanks of *The Post Card*—would involve, clearly, a reading of Derrida's entire relationship to psychoanalysis, a rethinking, for example, of the nature of the unconscious, of desire, loss, introjection and incorporation, the distinction between mourning and melancholy, and so on. Let me instead underscore just a few traits of the crypt in relationship to the passage from *The Post Card* that I have been following here. We will then see, I think, how these blanks—these crypts—communicate in a subterranean way with not only the essays of *The Post Card* but Derrida's corpus more generally.

The first essential trait of the crypt is that it is not natural. In *The Post Card* Derrida emphasizes, as we already saw, that the blanks he drew were the result of a "contract." In "*Fors,*" he says even more forthrightly with a nod toward Heraclitus: "A crypt is never natural through and through, and if, as is well known, *physis* has a tendency to encrypt (itself), that is because it overflows its own bounds and encloses, naturally, its others, all others" ("*Fors,*" xiv). The crypt is thus never purely and simply natural but the place, the contrived, artificial, non-natural, always historically determined place, where a desire or a force becomes encrypted, entombed, sealed away by a process wherein nature folds back on itself, as it were, after a detour through language and history.

Second, if the crypt passes always by way of encryption, it is itself mute or is itself a place of mute forces. Again in *The Post Card* Derrida speaks of "the 52 signs, the 52 mute spaces," and in "Fors" he writes: "The violence of the mute forces that would thus be setting up the crypt does not end with the trauma of a single unbearable and condemned seduction scene — condemned to remain mute" ("*Fors*," xv). This muteness is related, clearly, to secrecy, to the need for keeping or remaining silent, the need for these remains to remain silent: "'Secrecy is essential,' whence the crypt, a hidden place, a disguise hiding the traces of the act of disguising, a place of silence" ("*Fors*," xvii).

Third, and perhaps most obviously, the crypt is always related to death — even as it always calls into question the very notions of life and death and the limit between them: "the cryptic place is also a sepulcher," and "the inhabitant of a crypt is always a living dead, a dead entity we are perfectly willing to keep alive, but *as* dead, one we are willing to keep, as long as we keep it, within us, intact in any way save as living" ("*Fors*," xxi). If the blanks of the "Envois" are indeed crypts, well beyond the artifice of the 52 blank spaces, well beyond, therefore, the controlled and calculated intentions of their author, they also conceal a "living dead" that cannot, by definition, make it into a text or into consciousness without having to declare itself living *or* dead but never both at once. To try to fill in these blanks or open these crypts would thus be nothing short of a violation of their very logic or force: "To track down the path to the tomb, then to violate the sepulcher: That is what the analysis of a cryptic incorporation is like" ("*Fors*," xxxiv). This line alone goes a long way to explaining Derrida's resistance to a certain psychoanalysis, to one that does not know, for example, how to leave the crypt intact, or how to think a genuinely radical unconscious, or how to fail to mourn.

The crypt is, therefore, a sepulcher — or an urn — containing remains that have been buried or burned, incinerated. This would be yet another trait of the crypt: it is not just the place where a body is buried but the site of an incineration. In a passage from the preface to *The Post Card* where we find encrypted, as it were, the name of this other text on the crypt that we have been reading ("*Fors*"), as well as a signature phrase from the end of *Dissemination* ("*il y a là cendre*"), Derrida says that the envois are like the remains of a correspondence recently destroyed by fire:

> You might consider them, if you really wish to, as the remainders of a recently destroyed correspondence. Destroyed by fire or by that which figuratively takes its place, more certain of leaving nothing out of the reach of what I like to call the tongue of fire, not even the cinders if cinders there are [*s'il y a là cendre*]. Save [*fors*] for a chance. (*PC*, 3)

If the *envois* are like what remains after a fire, then the blanks are like what is still smoldering or burning within them — disrupting their order and their logic and so introducing incalculability into their numbers and their chronology. For the crypt, like the blank, is ultimately incalculable — a fifth characteristic of the crypt. Even if the blanks of *The Post Card* are the result of calculation, each time exactly 52 characters, what is burned or buried there is beyond calculation. Derrida writes in "Shibboleth," another important text on the crypt: "[T]here is something of a crypt, one that remains incalculable; it does not conceal a single, determinate secret, a semantic content waiting behind the door for the one who holds a key. If there is indeed a door, […] it does not represent itself in this way."[3]

---

[3] Jacques Derrida, "Shibboleth: For Paul Celan," in *Sovereignties in Question: The Poetics of Paul Celan,* trans. Joshua Wilner, revised by Thomas Dutoit (Bronx: Fordham University Press, 1995), 33; henceforth, "S." This essay is dated October 14, 1984.

Sixth, the crypt — like the blank — always raises the question of singularity and repetition. While what is encrypted is always absolutely singular and unique, absolutely unrepeatable, in order for that uniqueness to be read, in order for it to be encrypted, precisely, it must appear in a series. Unique, unrepeatable, unreadable, the crypt must be readable as what is each time unreadable, repeatable as what is each time unrepeatable, in a series with other singularities that always resist serialization — just like a date, the seventh and final trait of the crypt that I will follow here, the seventh and final seal of the crypt to be opened.

It is no coincidence — or rather, it is in order to think *coincidence* otherwise, at the intersection, as always, of nature and chance — that the *envois* are each time preceded by a *date*. The date at once marks the *envoi*'s singularity, its absolute uniqueness, that which will remain incalculable and unrepeatable about a unique event or encounter, and the place where that event is put into relation to another — into a calendar or a journal with 52×7 days, as a way of ordering, precisely, unique events that have no "natural" order. The crypt — like the date — seems to mark the place where the incalculable repeats itself and thus becomes calculable, the place where the unique and unrepeatable event encounters itself and so gets repeated.

In "Shibboleth" again, a text written seven years after the first *envoi,* Derrida treats the question of the date in a way that is very similar to the way he treated the crypt. He asks, for example, "What is a date? Do we have the right to pose such a question, and in this form? The form of the question 'What is…?' is not without provenance" ("S," 14). The date, like the crypt, seems to resist the "What is…?" question of classical ontology insofar as it too marks a singularity that cannot be gathered under any concept other than that of singularity. And, like a crypt, a date is not purely natural. Hence Derrida in "Shibboleth" uses the same Heraclitus he used to speak of the crypt to speak, seven years later, of the date.

> It is necessary that, in a certain manner, the unrepeatable divide itself in repeating itself, and in the same stroke encipher or encrypt itself. Like physis, a date loves to encrypt itself. It must efface itself in order to become readable, to render itself unreadable in its very readability. For if the date does not suspend in itself the unique marking that connects it to an event without witness, without other witness, it remains intact but absolutely indecipherable. ("S," 15)

To think the date we thus need to rethink everything associated with the crypt. Notice in the following passage from "Shibboleth" the way in which Derrida brings together the date and the crypt through the themes of uniqueness or nonrecurrence, repetition, unreadability, incineration, and ash: "Consumption, becoming-ash, burning up or incineration of a date: on the hour, in the hour itself, at each hour. This is the threat of an absolute crypt: nonrecurrence, unreadability, amnesia without remainder, but nonrecurrence *as* recurrence, *in* recurrence itself" ("S," 46). It is as if the crypt were always dated and the date were always a kind of crypt.

To return to the place from which I set out, it can be said that the blanks of *The Post Card* remain — like a crypt — unreadable, secret, not only in fact but already in principle, beyond all hermeneutical or interpretative keys. Each time, it remains unique, each time — that is, repeatedly — it is unreadable, undecipherable. To cite "Shibboleth" again:

> The crypt remains, the *shibboleth* remains secret, the passage uncertain, and the poem unveils a secret only to confirm that there is something secret there, withdrawn, forever beyond the reach of hermeneutic exhaustion. A non-hermetic secret, it remains, and the date with it, heterogeneous to all interpretative totalization. ("S," 26)

What the blanks of *The Post Card* "signify," in the end, is not or not only that a determinate content has been lost but that there is something incalculable and unreadable, a blank, precisely, even there where there is no blank, a crypt that encrypts itself even in those places where there is no "obvious" crypt. What remains in *The Post Card*, then, are the remains of a correspondence—one that is dated and pockmarked by blanks or crypts that will have made visible an invisibility that haunts the visible as well. The crypt encrypts itself not just in the blanks but in all those places where a singular event is marked. In other words, what the blank makes visible is that there is a drawing of blanks within writing itself, an incineration of the remains from within, a crypt even in those places—especially in those places—where names are recalled and dates are given. To cite "Shibboleth" one final time:

> [T]he experience of ashes in the incineration of the date, from within the experience of the date *as* incineration. The latter will no longer designate, in this place, the *operation* at times decided on or rejected by whoever asks himself whether or not to proceed with the cremation, with the destruction by fire, leaving no remains other than ashes, of this living being or of this archive. The incineration of which I speak takes place prior to any operation, it burns from within. ("S," 41–42)

What remains, then, are the remains of a correspondence and a certain relationship between the unreadable and the readable, between remains and what remains, between incalculable ashes and the calculable spaces—each time 52.

But why the number 52—since the "choice" of number was, after all, Derrida's, a choice imposed upon him perhaps by other factors but one that was more or less freely taken up by him and used as an ordering principle? The first thing to note about 52, the first thing that Jacques Derrida would have no doubt noted, is that 5 and 2 add up to 7, not just the number of days in a week but the number of letters in both "Jacques" and "Derrida". The number 7 was thus important to Derrida for reasons of both the name and the date—and for the fact that it is typically on the seventh day of life that a Jewish boy is given his secret name during the ritual of circumcision. Some 14 years after the publication of *The Post Card* (1980), Derrida in *Archive Fever* (*Mal d'archive*) (1994) cites the beginning of a letter from Jakob Freud to his son, Sigmund, that recalls this fact: "Son who is dear to me, Shelomoh. In the seventh in the days of the years of your life the Spirit of the Lord began to move you and spoke within you: Go, read my Book that I have written and there will burst open for you the wellsprings of understanding, knowledge, and wisdom."[4] But one does not need to go out twice 7 years from *The Post Card* in order to learn of the importance of the number 7 (*sept*) for Derrida. Already near the very end of the "Envois," Derrida speaks most eloquently about his own "set theory" — his *sept* theory or theory regarding the number sept. After a blank of 52 spaces, we read:

and on the card's itinerary, short pause, you encounter Aristoteles: the male who begins to have sperm at twice 7 years, the gestation of fish that corresponds to a period divisible by 7, the death of newborns before the 7th day and this is why they receive their name on the 7th, and the foetus that lives if it is expulsed at 7 months, and not at 8 months, etc., so only circumcision was missing from this history of animals. The first telephone number in El-Biar, the unforgettable one I had told you, 730 47: in the beginning was a seven, and at the end, and in the middle 3 + 4, and it turns around zero, the central. (*PC*, 254)

And then, just a bit later, at the beginning of the penultimate envoi, as if the number 7 and the 52 blanks were crypts for an unnameable god: "7, my god   "
(*PC*, 255).

---

[4] Jacques Derrida, *Archive Fever*, trans. Eric Prenowitz (Chicago: University of Chicago Press), 1996, 23; henceforth, *AF*. First published in French as *Mal d'archive* by Éditions Galilée in 1995. Derrida dates this text "Naples, 22–28 May 1994."

As for 52, which is not, alas, divisible by 7, it is a natural choice insofar as it recalls the return of the year after a 52 week cycle, a "natural" number, therefore, that is nonetheless culturally determined, at once dating and dated, determined, in some sense, by nature *and* by chance, a good number, then, for the total number of cards in a deck—like the kind Derrida's mother Georgette would have used to play her favorite game of poker. Between the cycle of the year and the cards of a deck, between nature and chance, calculability and incalculability, it is surely not by chance that the number 52 should be found at the center of a work whose letters or postcards are both the random remains of a correspondence and a carefully ordered sequence of cards dealt out chronologically from 8 June 1977 to 30 August 1979.

But the number 52 must have been important to Derrida for other reasons as well, since *The Post Card* would not be the last time he would use the number 52 as an ordering device. Seven years after the French publication of *The Post Card*, Derrida published, in 1987, a short text on architecture entitled "Fifty-two Aphorisms for a Foreword," a text which begins with this aphorism on the aphorism: "1. The aphorism decides, but as much by its substance as by its form, it determines by a play of words."[5] And then seven years later again, in 1994, in the writing of his important essay "Faith and Knowledge," Derrida would divide his text into 52 numbered parts, 52 unequal sequences.[6]

The number 52 thus seems to have imposed itself upon Derrida in a rather unique way. In the preface to *The Post Card*, Derrida says that he "had wanted [this number] to be symbolic and secret—in a word a clever cryptogram, that is, a very naïve

---

5 Jacques Derrida, "Fifty-Two Aphorisms for a Foreword," trans. Andrew Benjamin, in *Psyche 2: Inventions of the Other*, eds. Peggy Kamuf and Elizabeth Rottenberg, 117–26 (Stanford: Stanford University Press, 2008), 117.

6 Jacques Derrida, "Faith and Knowledge: The Two Sources of 'Religion' at the Limits of Reason Alone," trans. Samuel Weber, in *Religion*, eds. Jacques Derrida and Gianni Vattimo, 1–78 (Stanford: Stanford University Press, 1998). Though this text was not completed and signed until April 1995, it was first presented at a conference on the Island of Capri in February 1994.

one, that had cost [him] long calculations." But he then goes on to say, to confess or to feign to confess, that he has "forgotten the rule as well as the elements" of the calculation that got him to 52. He wanted it to be a "cipher" for him alone, it seems, "symbolic and secret" only for him, a "clever cryptogram" that would be readable only by him, which is no doubt why it was necessary for him too to forget it. For it to become a crypt, it would have to be, like all crypts, forever unreadable for him as well as for us.

The cipher, the crypt, must remain forever indecipherable. And yet Derrida tells us enough about the cipher in general to allow us to speculate a bit, to calculate, to try to make an educated guess not about each and every blank but at least about the principle of 52 that marks the headstone of each. As Derrida writes, for instance, in "Shibboleth": "The date (signature, moment, place, gathering of singular marks) always operates as a *shibboleth*. It shows that there is something not shown, that there is ciphered singularity: irreducible to any concept, to any knowledge, even to a history or tradition" ("S," 33). Since Derrida relates the "ciphered singularity" here to the *date*, which is, as we have seen, always absolutely singular, each time absolutely unique, repeatable as unrepeatable, we might speculate that the number 52 also encrypts a date, one close or dear to Derrida, the sum, in sum, of a birth date—July 15, 1930, that is, 7 + 15 + 30—a date, a crypt, "symbolic and secret," that would be absolutely unique, like every other date, and that would return, like the year, every year in an anniversary.

But this is, of course, just speculation, since all we can do today is speculate—speculate and then perhaps wonder with regard to Derrida what Derrida in *Archive Fever* once wondered about Freud:

> We will always wonder what, in this *mal d'archive*, he may have burned. We will always wonder, sharing with compassion in this archive fever, what may have burned of his secret passions, of his correspondence, or of "his life." Burned without him, without remains and without knowledge. With no possible response, be it spectral or not, short of or beyond

a suppression, on the other edge of repression, originary or secondary, without a name, without the least symptom, and without even an ash. (*AF,* 101)

We will always wonder about the blanks he will have drawn. But if those blanks are also always the source of our wonder or our compassion, then perhaps we must learn not to fill them in but to draw them ourselves, poetically.

Rick Elmore

Troubling Lines: The Process of Address in Derrida's *The Post Card*

There is a line in *The Post Card* that has always bothered me. Now, to be clear, I do not hate this line. It does not keep me up at night. I do not have to suppress the urge to burn the book every time I read it. But I have never understood its phrasing or placement. It is, for me, in tension with the constellation of claims and concepts around which it circulates. This line comes in the second entry marked 6 June 1977 (*PC*, 16–17/20–22). In this passage, Derrida gives a reading of the postcard that inspires his text. One will recall that the image on this card is of Socrates seated at a writing desk, pen in hand, with a smaller Plato standing behind him, seemingly dictating. Derrida spends the majority of this passage analyzing a number of the peculiarities of this image (the positioning of the figures, the fact that it is Socrates writing and not Plato, the seeming confusion of master and pupil, teacher and student, etc). In the middle of this analysis, however, Derrida interjects the following statement, apparently in response to the question, "[t]o whom do you think he [Socrates] writes?" Derrida states, "[f]or me it is always more important to know that [to whom one writes] than to know what is being written; moreover I think it amounts to the same, to the other finally" (*PC*, 17/21). This is the line that has always troubled me, particularly because of the privilege it grants to knowledge of addressees over that of content. Allow me to elaborate.

In this line, Derrida claims an epistemological privilege of the *who* of a letter over its *what*. It is more important, he contends, to know the addressee of a letter rather than its content. What I find initially troubling about this claim is that it resonates a little too closely with a certain history of privileging the subject at the expense of the object. This resonance is extended with the introduction of an identity between addressee and content. According to the final clause of Derrida's assertion, knowledge of a letter's addressee is ultimately identical to knowledge of its content — they, in the end, "amount to the same." The mixture of these two claims, that, on the one hand, there is a certain epistemological privilege of the addressee and, on the other, that ultimately addressee and content form an identity, suggests that even in their identity content is somehow subordinate to its addressee. They are identical. And yet, the addressee remains supreme. It is this double logic of identity and privilege that, for me, moves this claim in the direction of an idealism that, at least since Hegel, would mark *the what* as subservient and, ultimately, reducible to *the who*. Such idealism is, of course, one of the targets of Derrida's critique of logocentrism, where the ideological superiority of speech, voice, *logos,* and the Enlightenment subject is put in question precisely by the figure of writing. Thus, it seems odd that Derrida would endorse the epistemological privilege of the addressee over the written text, the privilege of *the who* of a letter over its *what,* and, ultimately, the subordination of *the what* to *the who*. The oddness of this claim is furthered by the fact that it does not seem readily explained.

There is little in the context of the passage in which this claim emerges that directly speaks to it. Derrida's statement neither answers the question that precedes it, concerning to whom Socrates might write, nor is it developed in the remainder of the passage. In addition, it seems impossible to justify this privilege purely on the grounds of otherness, since, insofar as otherness forms the identity between addressee and content, it cannot, simultaneously, serve to justify the epistemological privilege of the addressee. In fact, this claim reads like a methodological interjection, as though, having asked the question of Socrates' intended audience, Derrida simply wanted to remind us of his general approach to such issues: "don't forget," he seems to be saying, "I prefer knowledge of addressees to that of content." Yet, while there is little in this passage that directly explains the privilege afforded to the addressee, there is at least one additional element with which it is at odds, namely, the issue of violence.

The passage in question begins with a discussion of the violence involved in the act of addressing. Derrida writes:

> [O]ut of this atrocious exclusion that we make of all of them — and every possible reader. The whole world. The worst of "final solutions," without limit, this is what we are declaring, you and I, when we cipher everything [*chiffrant tout*], including our clothes, our steps, what we eat, [...] write, "signify," etc. And yet the opposite is not less true. All those left out have never been so alive [...]. (*PC*, 16/20–21)

The stakes of deciding whom one will address, in the broadest sense, always involves the risk of violence. The selecting of one addressee over another, the encoding of a message to a specific audience, effectively excludes an entire world of other readers, an act that Derrida associates with the holocaust. When one addresses a letter, one engages in a process of exclusion and violence, which, in principle, has no limit to its destructive force. Hence, addressing necessarily involving the risks of violence, exclusion, death, and annihilation. Yet, while these risks remain necessarily immense and irreducible, they also remain, at root, indecipherable.

Although the process of addressing contains the possibility of the worst kinds of violence, it does not guarantee violent ends. Rather, the indecipherability of this process means that those excluded may, in fact, not be harmed at all. They may, on the contrary, be made more alive than ever, insofar as they remain outside the classificatory grasp of this logic. Hence, selecting an addressee involves both the denial and extension of life: the ultimate affirmation of life and its absolute negation. What seems particularly powerful about this claim is the way in which it highlights, in its indecipherability, the stakes of this process.

The addressing of a letter is not, for Derrida, merely an act of inclusion or exclusion. It is an action that encodes the very determinations of inclusion and exclusion, violence and nonviolence, and, most radically, life and death. Insofar as every act of addressing involves both the denial and extension of life, this process also clandestinely demarcates the border separating life from death, living from non-living. Those to whom one addresses a letter are inscribed on the side of life, while those excluded remain, in some sense, indeterminate in relation to life and death. This inscription and indeterminacy introduces the notion that while every addressing marks a possible moment of violent exclusion, a determination of life, and a demarcation of who or what can be counted among the living, this inscription is also necessarily put into question by this process. Hence, addressing inscribes and destabilizes the categories of life and death, living and non-living, animate entity and inanimate object. It marks a certain definition of life while suggesting that there could always be "life" outside this definition. Hence, to return to the question of a letter's addressee and its content, what Derrida's analysis shows is that it is precisely the border between addressee and content, *who* and *what,* that is put in play by this logic. It is in this context that one must, I think, reevaluate Derrida's claim concerning the privilege of addressees.

Although the logic of Derrida's argument suggests that fundamentally at stake in the process of address is a determination of the categories of living/non-living, addressee/content, who/what, the epistemological privileging of the addressee seems to bypass this logic. There is little evidence on which to justify Derrida's claim concerning the privilege of the addressee, insofar as it is the process of addressing that, for him, establishes and destabilizes the distinction between addressee and content as such. It is this radical possibility that grounds the fascinating claim that those excluded in the act of address are, indeterminately, alive and dead, utterly animate or totally inanimate. However, it is also this possibility to which the question of identity and otherness alludes, as such an identity destabilizes the superiority of the addressee. The inability to absolutely differentiate addressee from content, the always active confusion between living/non-living, who/what undermines the privilege of the addressee. Hence after this analysis, I return to the impasse with which this gloss began: unwilling to simply throw this line out and yet unable to justify it. Faced with this impasse, I think it is more important to hang on to the radical implications of Derrida's discussion of addressing. It is more important to follow out the logic of address as establishing the determination of what it means to be "alive," since this concern is at the heart of Derrida's critique of logocentrism and the logic of deconstruction generally. Thus, the troubling line remains troubling. It remains at odds with the critical thrust of everything Derrida has to say in this passage concerning violence and the logic of address. And yet, perhaps one can take some comfort in its obstinate persistence, in this line's refusal to square up or back down. Perhaps one can take comfort in the thought that there is something important about lines that refuse clear explanation, as this refusal entices us to continue to think. After all, it seems to me that there is perhaps nothing more fundamentally Derridean than that.

Nicholas Royle

Postcard Telepathy

How construe commentary on a postcard that is specifically figured as "a pictorial performative which never ends" (*PC*, 98/108) — especially if it must reckon, at the same time, with that fragmentary phantom supplement published later as "Telepathy"[1]? I have been trying to read a bit of one of your postcards, one of several dated 6 June 1977 (I note in passing that my own record of that day reveals that I too was in Oxford, and in the evening went to watch *Yellow Submarine* — Oxford can be a lonely place on a Monday night):

> What is going on under Socrates' leg, do you recognize this object? It plunges under the waves made by the veils around the plump buttocks, you see the rounded double, improbable enough, it plunges straight down, rigid, like the nose of a stingray, to electrocute the old man and analyze him under narcosis. You know that they were both very interested in this paralyzing animal. Would it make him write by paralyzing him? All of this, that I do not know or do not yet want to see, also comes back from the bottom of the waters of my memory, a bit as if I had drawn or engraved the scene, from the day that, in an Algiers lycée no doubt, I first heard of those two. Do people (I am not speaking of "philosophers" or

---

[1] Jacques Derrida, "Telepathy," trans. Nicholas Royle, in *Psyche: Inventions of the Other*, vol. 1, eds. Peggy Kamuf and Elizabeth Rottenberg, 226–61 (Stanford: Stanford University Press, 2007).

of those who read Plato) realize to what extent this old couple has invaded our most private domesticity, mixing themselves up in everything, taking their part of everything, and making us attend for centuries their colossal and indefatigable anaparalyses? (*PC*, 18/23)

Anaparalyses: is it you? Perhaps you imagine I am invoking the name of a woman, the figure of Derrida's nonexistent daughter, Anna Paralyses. In any event, it is a question of the reserves opening up in the wake of this bizarre portmanteau neologism, as if coming back up from the bottom of the waters of memory. Paralysis analysis. Analysis of paralysis, analysis as paralysis. Paralysis up or back (*ana-*). Anaparalysis as paranalysis. Irreducibly pluralized. Anasemic.

Much has been said about the 52 spaces on the page and the effects of disjunction produced, but the sting of the envois is there at every turn, comma, word. Even more perhaps than "Circumfession," it is a bewildering practice of touching, or almost touching, and evading. Rather than seek to multiply the examples, let's try to repose, just for a little while, on this weird numbing of all analects.

It is all about the ray. Or at least its nose (*la nez d'une torpille*). (But what kind of nose? And when is a nose a nose? So many nose stories in Derrida, starting perhaps with the question of being on the "scent" of the trace in *Of Grammatology*[2]: another interminable work of commentary deconstructing commentary to be sniffed out there.) Just prior to this moment he has been talking about the multiple erections, the impression of Plato "getting an erection in Socrates' back," and the assortment of the "phallus sheaf, the points, plumes, pens, fingers, nails and *grattoirs*" (*PC*, 18/23). But this torpedo (also called in English the cramp-fish, the cramp-ray, and the numb-fish) — let's not get completely marinated in a discussion of the law of genre,

---

2 Jacques Derrida, *Of Grammatology*, trans. Gayatri Chakravorty Spivak (Baltimore: Johns Hopkins University Press, 1976), 162; *De la grammatologie* (Paris: Les Éditions de Minuit, 1967), 233.

genus and species, translation of fish between one language and another, what kind of *narkē* Plato or Socrates had in mind and whether it would have had a nose like the one Derrida sees in the fortune-telling postcard picture — this fish is nose-down, erection tomb, miming Socrates' writing instrument or (undecidably) figuring as the thing to be imitated.

And when Derrida observes that "you know that they were both very interested in this paralyzing animal," you know that he is recalling, among other things, that passage in "Plato's Pharmacy" in which he talks about "the Socratic *pharmakon*" in *Meno* 80a–b: "Socrates' pharmaceutical charms provoke a kind of *narcosis*, benumbing and paralyzing into aporia, like the touch of a sting ray (*narkē*)."[3] It is one of the countless examples of analectic shock, quasi-magical transmission between texts, a postcard telepathy that, in this case, carries on as if unseen through the waters all the way up into "the ray that therefore I am."

---

3 Jacques Derrida, *Dissemination*, trans. Barbara Johnson (Chicago: Chicago University Press, 1981), 118.

Wan-Chuan Kao

Post by a Thousand Cuts

> *Le 8 juin 1977*
> *L'émission de sens ou de semence peut être rejetée (tampon, timbre et retour à l'envoyeur). Imagine le jour où, comme je l'ai déjà fait, on pourra envoyer du sperme par carte postale, sans passer par un chèque tiré sur quelque banque du sperme, et que ça reste assez vivant pour que l'insémination artificielle donne lieu à fécondation, voire à désir [The emission of sense or of seed can be rejected (postmark, stamp, and return to sender). Imagine the day, as I have already, that we will be able to send sperm by post card, without going through a check drawn on some sperm bank, and that it remains living enough for the artificial insemination to yield fecundation, and even desire.]* [1]

At the turn of the twentieth century, foreign visitors to China could purchase postcards with photographs or illustrations of "Chinese tortures" (*les supplices chinois*) and mail them home. The particular artifact in figure 1, sent from China to France in 1912, depicts a man being executed by *lingchi* (凌遲 "slow slicing," or "death by a thousand cuts"). This postcard is one iteration of the West's persistent horror at and fascination with *lingchi*. Another example is a post-execution photograph of dismembered body parts reproduced in Henry Norman's *The Peoples and Politics of the Far East in 1895* (fig. 2).[2] As histori-

---

1 *PC*, 24/29.
2 Henry Norman, *The Peoples and Politics of the Far East* (London: T. Fisher Unwin, 1895).

Fig. 1. A postcard of *Les Supplices Chinois* (1912), as reproduced in Shouxiang Chen, *Jiu meng chong jing: Fang Lin, Bei Ning cang Qing dai ming xin pian xuan ji* (1989). © Guangxi mei shu chu ban she. By permission.

ans point out, foreign military occupation of Beijing following the Boxer Rebellion allowed Europeans, especially those able to afford a camera, to roam the country more or less at will. Images of *lingchi* executions began to circulate as curiosities and mementos — especially in the form of postcards — in Europe.³

Photographs of *lingchi,* such as those printed on postcards, would leave Georges Bataille both terrified and enraptured, as he confessed repeatedly his obsession with the "young and seductive [*jeune et séduisant*] Chinese man" (fig. 3), most famously in his 1961 book *The Tears of Eros* (*Larmes d'Eros*) but also throughout the 1940s.⁴ Bataille writes in *Inner Experience* (*Expérience intérieure*):

> I focused on the photographic image — and sometimes just my memory of it — of a Chinese man who must have been

---

3 Timothy Brook, Jérôme Bourgon, and Gregory Blue, *Death by a Thousand Cuts* (Cambridge: Harvard University Press, 2008), 22, 29–32.

4 Georges Bataille, *Inner Experience,* trans. Leslie Anne Boldt (Albany: State University of New York Press, 1988), 120; *The Tears of Eros,* trans. Peter Connor (San Francisco: City Lights Books, 1989).

Fig. 2. *China: "Death by the Thousand Cuts,"* as reproduced in Henry Norman, *The Peoples and Politics of the Far East* (1895).

tortured within my own lifetime. I had several prints of this torture representing successive stages. By the end of it, the figure twists away, his chest flayed out, his arms and legs cut off at the knees and elbows. His hair standing on end, hideous, haggard, striped with blood, beautiful as a wasp.[5]

What attracts Bataille is the apparent ecstatic expression on the victim's face, with his eyes turned up, head thrown back, and trembling lips that bare the teeth. For Bataille, photographs of lingchi function as a medium, a meeting place of eroticism and religious ecstasy through terror.

The turn-of-the-century *lingchi* postcards and photographs conjure up, for me, an image of cannibalistic Mongols drawn by Matthew Paris in his thirteenth-century *chronica maiora* (fig. 4). (Are not illuminated manuscripts postcards from the past?) Medieval Mongols, it turns out, have everything to do with Bataille's photographs of *lingchi*. While the origin of *lingchi* remains ob-

---

5 The translation is by Bill Burgwinkle in Bill Burgwinkle and Cary Howie, *Sanctity and Pornography in Medieval Culture: On the Verge* (Manchester: Manchester University Press, 2010), 32.

Fig. 3. The lingchi of pseudo-Fuzhuli, as reproduced in Georges Bataille, *Tears of Eros* (1989). © City Lights Books. By Permission.

scure, the practice is probably dated to the tenth-century Liao dynasty of the Khitans in the Central Asian steppes. The Mongols' Yuan Dynasty, in fact, was the first Chinese regime that codified *lingchi* into law; the execution method was listed as one of the Five Punishments in the penal code.[6]

Bataille's insight into the commingling of horror and ecstasy, pain and pleasure, is facilitated by a postal system from the East; through photographs of *lingchi,* he completes the geo- and temporal-circuit of love. The postal relay systems of the Orient — in both the Near and the Far East — were legendary institutions that frequently earned the admiration of the West in the Middle Ages and beyond. Marco Polo, for instance, meticulously detailed in his *Travels* the lavish hostels that played host to foreign ambassadors and merchants in the fabled city of Cambaluc (current day Beijing) during the reign of Kublai Khan. Emanating from the imperial center was a network of post-stations that

---

6 Brook et al., *Death by a Thousand Cuts,* 73–74.

Fig. 4. Matthew Paris, *Chronica majora*. Corpus Christi College, MS. 16, fol. 167r. © The Master and Fellows of Corpus Christi College, Cambridge. By permission.

served the messengers in the Great Khan's efficient postal system. At every post (*yizhang* 驛站), called *yam* (from the Mongolian *jamci*, Chinese *zhanchi* 站赤), was a "palatial hostelry" worthy of royalties.⁷ While, strictly speaking, post-stations were not necessarily hostels or inns, the two became intertwined in the *yams* spread throughout the medieval Mongol empire.

Curiously, the Mongolian *yam* was also understood by some medieval travelers from the West to mean a "manager of postal relay stations."⁸ The term denotes both a body and an architectural structure. The polysemy of the medieval *yam* uncannily anticipated Derrida's deconstructive play with the postal. The narrator of *The Post Card*, under the sign of "Jacques Derrida," sees himself as resembling "a messenger from antiquity [...] a runner, the courier of what we have given one another" (*PC*, 8). As Alan Bass points out, Derrida fully explores the rich ambiguity and polyvalence of the term *poste*, which derives from the

---

7   Marco Polo, *The Travels of Marco Polo*, trans. Ronald Latham (New York: Penguin Books, 1958), 151.
8   For instance, William of Rubruck referred to yams as "the men stationed at intervals of a day's journey for the reception of envoys," in *The Mission of Friar William Rubruck: His Journey to the Court of the Great Khan Möngke 1253–1255*, trans. Peter Jackson (London Hakluyt Society, 1990), 166. See also Wan-Chuan Kao, "Hotel Tartary: Marco Polo, Yams, and the Biopolitics of Population," *Mediaevalia* 32 (2011): 43–68, at 52.

Fig. 5. Matthew Paris, opening of a fortune-telling tract. Oxford, Bodleian Library MS. Ashmole 301, fol. 31v. © Bodleian Libraries, University of Oxford. By permission.

Latin *ponere,* meaning "to put, to place," and is linked to the word *position.* The French *la poste* denotes mail, while le poste can mean a position to be held, like a soldier's post, or a station (*PC,* xxv–xxvi). The word's complex associations and histories are also evident in Marco Polo's *Travels.* In both the original Franco-Italian version of Rustichell and in the first French translation in 1310, *poste* is used to designate the Mongol *yam.*[9]

Derrida's interest in all things postal derives from a particular postcard that he came across by chance in the Bodleian Library,

---

9   See Marco Polo, *Milione: Le divisament dou monde. Il milione nelle redazioni toscana e franco-italiana,* ed. Gabriella Ronchi (Milan: Mondadori, 1982), 130; and Marco Polo, *La description du monde,* ed. Pierre-Yves Badel (Paris: Livre de Poche, 1998), 244–45.

one that reproduced, for retail purchase, a detail of Matthew Paris' illumination depicting Plato and Socrates (fig. 5). What intrigues Derrida are the positions of Socrates and Plato in relation to each other in the image: Plato stands *behind* a seated Socrates, who, instruments in hands, is ready to mark a blank parchment page. The scene both affirms and upends Western philosophy's assumed origins, teleologies, directions of communication, and the interplay between the spoken and the yet-to-be-written (or is it *pictured*?) words.

As staged, Derrida's obsession with this postcard shares many affective and spiritual parallels with that of Bataille and his photographs of *lingchi*. First, both men experience moments of ecstatic epiphanies in their respective encounter. Like Bataille before the photograph of a *lingchi* victim, Derrida records his reactions to the postcard: "I stopped dead, with a feeling of hallucination [...] and of revelation at the same time, an apocalyptic revelation" (*PC*, 9). Second, for both, these revelatory moments are inseparable from eroticism. Derrida reads the postcard as "obscene," for he sees "Plato getting an erection in Socrates' back and [...] the insane hubris of his prick, an interminable, disproportionate erection traversing Paris's head like a single idea and then the copyist's chair" (*PC*, 18). The medieval writing desk becomes a giant phallus; the encounter between Socrates and Plato, homoerotic. Compare this to Bataille's own phallic moment in the midst of his meditation upon the image of the Chinese *lingchi* victim:

> [S]uddenly, I felt myself become an erect penis. [...] Like a torture victim, I had to have my eyes turned up and my head thrown back. In this state, the cruel representation of the torture victim, of the ecstatic gaze, of the bloody bare flanks, gave me a lacerating convulsion: a spurt of light crossed through my head from bottom to top as voluptuously as the passage of semen through a penis."[10]

---

[10] Georges Bataille, *Guilty*, trans. Stuart Kendall (Albany: State University of New York Press, 2011), 188.

Whereas Bataille's vision climaxes in an imploding inner death as a metamorphosis of the self into an ejaculatory conduit, Derrida's reverie culminates in a fantasy of the posthuman postcard as a reproductive organ from the future that, like a pollinator, would instantly inseminate the recipient upon contact: "Imagine the day, as I have already, that we will be able to send sperm by post card [...] and that it remains living enough for the artificial insemination to yield fecundation, and even desire" (*PC*, 24).

Ecstasy, Wayne Koestenbaum explains, is a condition outside of stasis: "The word 'ecstasy' comes from the Greek *eksta*, stem of *existanai*, 'put out of place.' *Histanai* means to place. The Greek *ekstasis* incorporates *stasis*, from *sta-*, the base of *histanai* (stand)."[11] Etymologically, *ecstasy* implies a state of exile from the usual place. Hotel, Koestenbaum suggests, is ecstasy's territory precisely because it is a spatial and temporal displacement from home. I would add that the positionality of *ecstasy* reveals it to be fundamentally a postal experience.

There is a bit of Derrida in Bataille, and there's a bit of Bataille in Derrida. Between the two of them, there is a lot of Matthew Paris. Unwittingly, the two engage in a male collaboration via the scenes and histories of violence depicted on postcards. In addition to ecstatic epiphany, homoerotic discharge, and heightened self-reflexivity in Bataille and Derrida, there are a few more visual cross-inseminations between their respective fetishes. Michael Camille has observed that Socrates' hat (fig. 5), which Matthew Paris uses throughout his repertoire to indicate the pagan status of medieval Jews and unbelievers, is strikingly curled and "eastern-looking."[12] We see a similar hat on the head of the cannibalistic Mongol soldier in Matthew's other illustration (fig. 4), and also a modified version of the headgear worn by Manchu executioners in Bataille's *lingchi* photo (fig. 3). The

---

11 Wayne Koestenbaum, *Hotel Theory* (New York: Soft Skull Press, 2007), 50.
12 Michael Camille, "The Dissenting Image: A Postcard from Matthew Paris," in *Criticism and Dissent in the Middle Ages*, ed. Rita Copeland, 115–50 (Cambridge: Cambridge University Press, 1996), 127.

instruments held by Socrates — the stylus and the scraper — also resonate visually with the axe in the Mongol cannibal's hands, as well as with the blade held by the Manchu executioner, poised before it touched the naked flesh of the victim. That image of the blade entering the flesh, Bataille recounts, is "so great a horror" that it faithfully lays bare your nature, "what you are."[13] Derrida's Socrates is not only a pagan but also an Easterner, a Mongol, and an executioner in the act of laying bare a different nature upon a parchment skin.

If I have been attempting to chart a genealogy here, I want to dramatize (à la Bataille), post (à la Derrida), and picture (à la Matthew Paris) different deliveries, addresses, senders, and recipients. That is, different postcards, ecstasies, and scenes of horror. What if Bataille had received the Bodleian postcard of Matthew Paris' Socrates and Plato? And what if Derrida had stumbled across a postcard of a Chinese *lingchi* execution? These are the essential pair in the chiasmus: Socrates and Plato; the executioner and his victim; and Derrida and Bataille. As Bataille meditates upon the Socrates/Plato postcard, who is the executioner? Socrates with an oriental hat? Who is the sacrificial victim? Plato, or the blank parchment? And with whom will Bataille have a direct ecstatic union? As Derrida faces the *lingchi* postcard, there is the Chinese victim's prick and the executioner's blade. But in this scene, who stands behind whom? Who is displacing whom? Positionality is a postal ecstasy.

Koestenbaum argues that hotel existence is an uncanny suspension above groundedness: "To be *in hotel* is to float."[14] When in a hotel, one does not stay but stray. The guest at a hotel needs to "check in" and, though not always necessary, "check out." The postcard is a time-space compression of the hotel experience. Upon delivery, the recipient gazes and touches it, front and back. Moreover, the recipient uses the postcard to hallucinate, to arouse, to climax, to disembody, to inseminate, and to ecstasize. Are these not hotel activities? In other words, to behold a

---

13 Bataille, *Guilty*, 33.
14 Koestenbaum, *Hotel Theory*, 7.

postcard is to check into and then check out of the hotel experience. To be in possession of a postcard is not to stay but to stray, float, and suspend. Hotel time is the time of abeyance, or, as Derrida might put it, the time of the postal: "the Postal Principle as differential relay, that regularly prevents, [and] delays" (*PC*, 54). Hotel, Koestenbaum reminds us, is the desired elsewhere; "a communication from a hotel comes from nowhere."[15] The postcard is the technology that makes possible the simultaneity of the elsewhere, the nowhere, and the here.

A postcard is a hotel text. The *lingchi* photocard (fig. 1) is a talisman of magical thinking, or rather, magical feeling. Bataille's responses — as *envois* — are symptomatic of his impulse to collapse medieval technology of hagiography, with its figurations of eroticized saints in pain, and modern *dispositif* of enchantment. The young Chinese man on the 1912 postcard is a courier of history: his is a dismembered body of the cannibal, the messenger, the criminal, and the saint. And might we not arrive at a similar understanding of Derrida's reading of the Plato/Socrates postcard, simply substituting the proper noun "Derrida" for "Bataille," and "Plato/Socrates" for the dying Chinese beauty?

In his postal narrative, Derrida recounts how he stumbled across the Matthew Paris postcard in Oxford's Bodleian Library. The encounter was nothing short of serendipity. As for Bataille, his claim that he had received a photo of *lingchi* from his analyst, Dr. Adrien Borel, remains unsubstantiated in the correspondence between them. It is possible that Bataille accidentally discovered, on his own, an image of *lingchi* execution in the Bibliothèque nationale in December 1934.[16] The archive, then, is simultaneously the birthplace and burial ground of postcards. Derrida desires "to reassemble an enormous library on the *courier,* the postal institutions, the techniques and mores of telecommunication, the networks and epochs of telecommunication throughout history — but the 'library' and the 'history' themselves are precisely but 'posts,' sites of passage or of relay

---

15 Ibid., 10.
16 Brook et al., *Death by a Thousand Cuts,* 233.

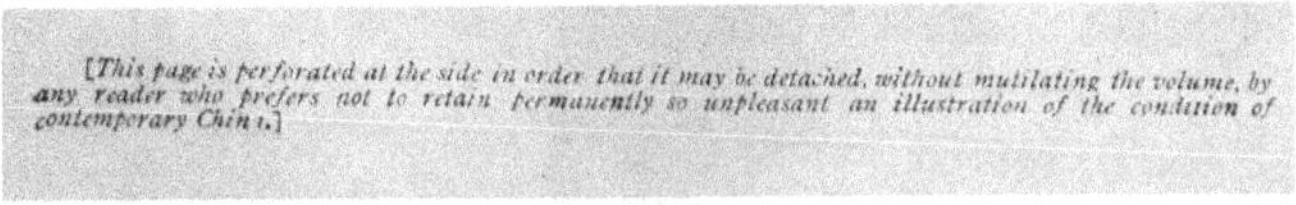

> [This page is perforated at the side in order that it may be detached, without mutilating the volume, by any reader who prefers not to retain permanently so unpleasant an illustration of the condition of contemporary China.]

Fig. 6. Detail. *China: "Death by the Thousand Cuts,"* as reproduced in Henry Norman, *The Peoples and Politics of the Far East* (1895).

among others" (*PC*, 27). For him, and for Bataille as well, libraries and histories are already yams and hotels, places and artifacts of magical thinking.

I want to close by returning to Henry Norman's photograph of a Chinese *lingchi* execution (fig. 2). The page where the photo is located is perforated at the inner edge, and the caption reads: "This page is perforated at the side in order that it may be detached, without mutilating the volume, by any reader who prefers not to retain permanently so unpleasant an illustration of the condition of contemporary China" (fig. 6). Perhaps this is what Socrates would have written in Matthew Paris's imagining (fig. 5). Maybe Matthew's Socrates is also attempting to perforate the parchment in front of him, making a postcard out of Western philosophy. As for Norman, the desire to protect his book from mutilation is premised on the mutilation of a page. Each tiny puncture on the page is a prick. Or, as Roland Barthes would call it, each piercing is a *punctum* (point): a detail, a "mark of *something*" in a work of art that provokes "a tiny shock" in the viewer and overwhelms its perception.[17] Note that in Bataille's formulation, the punctum is the point before ecstasy, and the projection of the point is the act of affective devotion.

As devotion, the monastic practice of *compunctio cordis* (piercing of the heart) blossomed into the tradition of the Charter of Christ in both literature and the visual arts in the late Middle Ages. In an illumination of the Charter of Human Redemption on folio 23r of British Library MS. Add. 37049 (fig. 7), the wounds of Christ are almost indistinguishable from the words of the poem. Words and wounds become *puncta*, pricks,

---

17 Roland Barthes, *Camera Lucida: Reflections on Photography*, trans. Richard Howard (New York: Hill and Wang, 1981), 49.

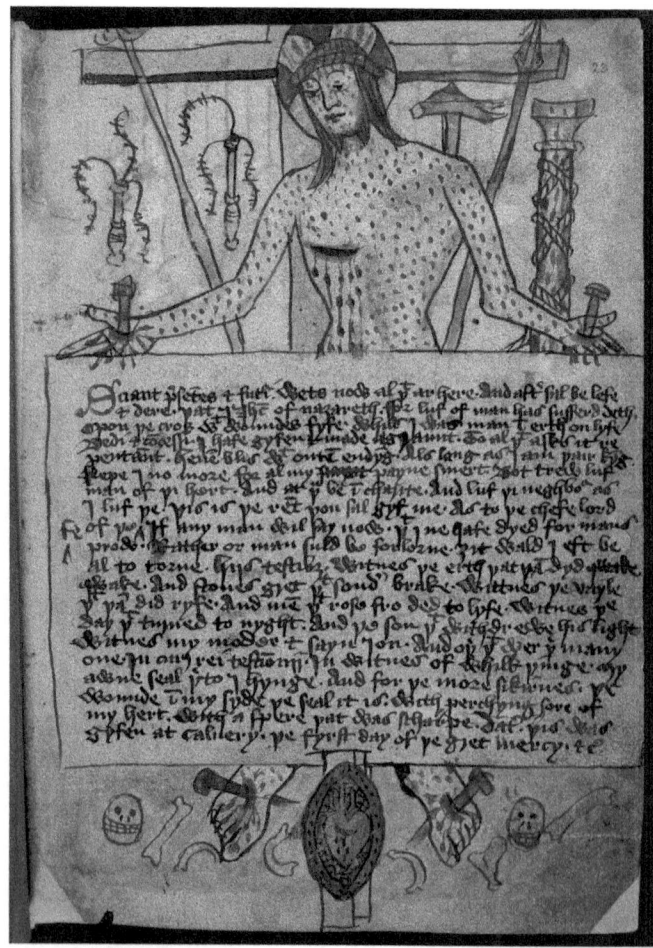

Fig. 7. The Charter of Human Redemption. London, British Library MS. Add. 37049, fol. 23r. © The British Library Board. By permission.

and perforation. The reader becomes Matthew Paris's Socrates with instruments in hand. Salvation is a perforated postcard, as Christ proclaims: "ȝit wald I eft be al to-torne" ("yet would I again be all torn apart").[18] For Bataille, Christ on the cross is the point that would "radiate arms, cry out, set itself ablaze."[19] And Norman, in his description of the stages of *lingchi* execution, also evokes the rhetoric of the Passion, for "[t]he criminal is fastened to a rough cross."[20] The same posture is seen in Bataille's photographs of the young Chinese victim of *lingchi* and in Matthew Paris's illustration of Mongol cannibals. In Matthew's rendering, the naked victim, forever waiting to be dismembered and consumed, is tied to a tree with his hair standing up and is confronted with a horse's visible prick (fig. 4). No one stands behind him.

The perforation on Norman's page is a concatenation of pricks. In it, we see Christ's wounds, Matthew Paris's cannibals and philosophers, Bataille's *punctum,* and Derrida's serial replication and displacement. The photograph is imminently detachable, addressable, post-able. An image of death by *lingchi,* it may yet remain "living enough" to engender desire or rapture, albeit only through mutilation.

It is waiting to become a postcard.

---

18 Line 20, "The Short Charter of Christ." London, British Library MS. Add. 37049, fol. 23r.
19 Bataille, *Inner Experience,* 118.
20 Norman, *Peoples and Politics of the Far East,* 225.

Eszter Timár

Ateleia/Autoimmunity

I would like to highlight an important connection between Derrida's use of the term "autoimmunity" in his later work and the postal principle of *The Post Card*. Specifically, I want to point out that the notion of the stamp (stretching from "stamp" to "timbre" and the "post card" itself in "Envois"), which resonates in the associations of sending at the heart of the postal principle itself, connects to the logic of the *immunis* which generates "autoimmunity." The connection is articulated in the historical construction of the name of stamp collection, or love of the stamp as "philately," which is constructed with the help of the Greek *ateleia*. Both terms, *ateleia* and *immunis*, refer to tax exemption.

This is an important connection because in the recent secondary literature autoimmunity has gained the status as not just the last of Derrida's terms for deconstruction, but also as in many ways especially apt for conveying the project of deconstruction, better perhaps even than "deconstruction" itself,[1] which, coupling "deconstruct" with the "-ion" suffix, attracts too easily a facile understanding of a negatively critical project of general myth-debunking. To highlight this connection between *ateleia* and autoimmunity serves a double purpose. First, to demonstrate an important mark of the consistency that Derrida

---

1   See Michael Naas, "'One Nation... Indivisible': Jacques Derrida on the Autoimmunity of Democracy and the Sovereignty of God," *Research in Phenomenology* 36 (2006): 15–44, at 18; Geoffrey Bennington, "Foundations," in *Not Half, No End: Militantly Melancholic Essays in Memory of Jacques Derrida* (Edinburgh: Edinburgh University Press, 2010), 27–28.

himself considered an important feature throughout his work, by showing the continuity between the conceptual framework of Derridean deconstruction in its so called early/mid phase (which is often seen as primarily occupied with allegedly apolitical philosophy) and the later so-called ethical phase (which is seen as more overtly political since it features key terms which are conventionally considered more explicitly political). The second purpose is to emphasize, with the help of this link, the Derridean significance of what he called "life in general," i.e., that the concept of life cannot be securely placed as originating in the "biological" or the "organic."

Importantly for the purposes of the present collection, Samir Haddad has traced Derridean autoimmunity in the *The Post Card* by connecting it to an anecdote with the motif of suicide in "Envois."[2] Autoimmunity as suicide kills not merely the self, but kills that which would guarantee the organism's oneness through its boundedness, and thereby it compromises the conventional meaning, and stakes, of suicide itself. Let me briefly quote from *Rogues*:

> For what I call the autoimmune consists not only in harming or ruining oneself, indeed in destroying one's own protections, and in doing so oneself, [...] but, more seriously still, [...] in threatening the I [*moi*] or the self [*soi*], the *ego* or the *autos*, ipseity itself, compromising the immunity of the *autos* itself [...]. Autoimmunity is more or less suicidal, but, more seriously still, it threatens always to rob suicide itself its meaning and supposed integrity.[3]

I would like to suggest that the reference to suicide is not the only connection between autoimmunity and "Envois." Let me demonstrate this connection by putting side by side the mean-

---

2 Samir Haddad, "Reading Derrida Reading Derrida: Deconstruction as Self-Inheritance," *International Journal of Philosophical Studies* 14, no. 4 (2006): 505–20. For the anecdote, see *PC*, 14–15.

3 Jacques Derrida, *Rogues: Two Essays on Reason*, trans. Pascale-Anne Brault and Michael Naas (Stanford: Stanford University Press, 2005), 45.

ing and associated notions of *ateleia* as provided by Derrida in "Envois," and the footnote in the later "Faith and Knowledge" which inaugurates his use of autoimmunity:

ateleia:

> *Ateleia* is franking, the exemption from taxes, whence the stamp. It is true that it maintains therefore a relation with one senses of *telos*: acquittal, exemption, payment, cost, expenditure, fee. From acquittal one could go to gift, offering, and even, in Sophocles, marriage ceremony! Phila-tely then is love *without,* with/without marriage and the collection of all the stamps, the love of the stamp with or without stamped love. (*PC,* 55)

autoimmunity:

> The "immune" (*immunis*) is freed or exempted from the charges, the service, the taxes, the obligations (*munus,* root of the common of community). This freedom of this exemption was subsequently transported into the domains of constitutional or international law (parliamentary or diplomatic immunity), but is also belongs to the history of the Christian Church and to canon law; the immunity of temples also involved the inviolability if the asylum that could be found there (Voltaire indignantly attacked this "immunity of temples" as a "revolting example" of "contempt for the laws" and of "ecclesiastical ambition"); Urban VIII created a congregation of ecclesiastical immunity: against police searches, etc. it is especially in the domain of biology that the lexical resources of immunity have developed their authority. The immunitary reaction protects the "indemnity" of the body proper in producing antibodies against foreign antigens. As for the process of auto-immunization, which interests us particularly here, it consists for a living organism, as is well known and in short, of protecting itself against its self-protection by destroying its own immune system. As the phenomenon of these an-

tibodies is extended to a broader zone of pathology and as one resorts increasingly to the positive virtues of immunodepressants destined to limit the mechanisms of rejection and to facilitate the tolerance of certain organ transplants, we feel ourselves authorized to speak of a sort of general logic of auto-immunization. It seems indispensable to us today for thinking the relations between faith and knowledge, religion and science, as well as the duplicity of sources in general.[4]

We can see that tax exemption is the shared feature of both *ateleia* and the *immunis*. *Ateleia,* whose significance in "Envois" exceeds the mere choice for naming philately in the nineteenth century by connecting exemption with laws, paralysis, and love, reminds us of the political link. We can think of this as the stamp, between the postal principle of sending and receiving, and the concept of the immune. Autoimmunity, in the footnote from "Faith and Knowledge," is first and foremost a body's protection against its own immune system. The immune system is understood here as the sum of the processes that "protect" the body from alien bodies understood as coming from the outside and always considered as potentially threatening. Autoimmunity, then, is an immunization against limiting the body to itself. It is a logic which acts to undermine the principle of *immunis*. Other such terms in "Faith and Knowledge," are "unscathed," "*heimlich*," and "*indemnis*": these terms all denote a lack of having suffered "damage or prejudice," or a lack of contamination, in other words, a state of being "safe and sound," unthreatened, clean or proper, and whole, all of these terms are marked by the principle of ipseity.[5] In later texts explicitly thematizing the immune, autoimmunity becomes such an important term due to the tension between the auto and the embedded *immunis*, a

---

4   Jacques Derrida, "Faith and Knowledge: The Two Sources of 'Religion' at the Limits of Reason Alone," in Jacques Derrida and Gil Anidjar, *Acts of Religion,* 40–102 (New York and London: Routledge, 2002), 80.

5   Ibid., 61.

tension destabilizing the privilege of ipseity within the concept of the immune.

Ann Smock has traced *ateleia* of "Envois" to the significance of the figure of the stamp foreshadowed in *Of Grammatology* by commenting on the quote above from "Envois":

> Philately has to do with *atéléia*, we read: acquittal of a charge. Whence the stamp (timbre): an official indication payment has been made. Unless the stamp exempts from paying. For to stamp, to frank — *affranchir* — is to free from a charge, dissolve an obligation. A stamp, in other words, is never just one; philately is stamp collection. And it is love (*philos*, friend) — it is love of the stamp with or without it. Love of the bond that also unbinds and by dismissing engages. It is love with or without love — stamped and validated conjugal love ("l'amour timbré") or "l'amour timbré," crazy love.[6]

Here the exemption and acquittal from the postal principle in *ateleia* is linked to bonds, binding and unbinding, terms which, for Derrida, all concern the notion of paralysis in *The Post Card*. In "Paralysis" he writes "*To borrow* is the law" (*PC*, 384). In "Envois," we read the following about paralysis:

> Paralyzed: paralysis does not mean that one can no longer move or walk, but, in Greek if you please, that there is no more tie, that every bind, every liaison has been unknotted (in other words, of course, analyzed) and that because of this, because one is "exempt," "acquitted" of everything, nothing goes anymore, nothing holds together any more, nothing advances any more. The bind and the knot are necessary in order to take a step. (*PC*, 127)

---

6 Ann Smock, "Estampe (OG 208-9, DG 296-7)," in *Reading Derrida's Of Grammatology*, eds. Sean Gaston and Ian MacLachlan, 136-37 (London and New York: Continuum, 2011), 137.

The idea of binding and ties, notions of constraint, are posited as the very condition of movement, of process. Mechanisms which (en)force movement, and here we can add the concept of law, are necessary for movement. Exemption from the law—which in "Paralysis" decrees debt—entails a standstill. Exemption and acquittal in the quote above are considered in the same light as the terms organized by the idea of immunity in the later texts; they institute a boundary of inviolability, which cuts off the bounded from the context within which it is found. In the case of both *ateleia* and the *immunis*, exemption means exemption from the flow of tax or debt.

However, the idea of exemption does not solely organize the way in which Derrida uses the term "stamp." Indeed, stamping also stands for the institution of the debt which produces tradition. For Derrida, the postal is a certain cultural logic characteristic of what we conventionally think of Europe (but not contained by our conventional concept of Europe); in "Envois" the stamp serves to shore up various ways of the operation of the postal logic of this culture. Besides postal stamps, stamping issues tradition itself in such microscopic and ubiquitous ways that we have no choice but be marked by and predisposed according to its tendencies. It is in this sense that the postcard which *The Post Card* features as its true protagonist also becomes a stamp, the stamp of the metaphysics of presence which is so easily associable with Platonism:

> Whatever I say, whatever I do, I must paste on myself a stamp with the effigy of this diabolical couple, these unforgettable comperes, these two patient impostors. A little engraving this royal, basilical couple, sterile but infinite in its ideal progeniture. Cynically, without a cent, they have issued a universal stamp. A postal and fiscal stamp, by making themselves appear to advance funds. And on the stamp both are to be seen in the course, the one in front of the other, in the course, *en train,* of drawing a stamp and of signing the original. And they plaster themselves on the walls. An immense poster. This is a stamp. [...] This is what tradition is, the heritage

that drives you crazy. People have not the slightest idea of this, they have no need to know that they are paying (automatic withdrawal) nor whom they are paying (the name or the thing) when they do anything whatsoever, make war or love, speculate on the energy crisis, construct socialism, write novels, open concentration camps for poets or homosexuals, buy bread or hijack a plane, have themselves elected by secret ballot, criticize the media without rhyme or reason, say absolutely anything about chador or the ayatollah, dream of a great safari, found reviews, teach, or piss against a tree. They can even never have heard the name of p. and of S. [...] And the less one pays, the more one pays, such is the trap of this speculation. You will not be able to account for this currency. Impossible to return it, you pay everything and you pay nothing with this Visa or Mastercharge card. It is neither true nor false. The issuing of the stamp is seriously immense, it imposes and is imposed everywhere, conditions every other type, *timbre,* or tympan in general; and yet, you can barely see it, it is minuscule, infinitely divisible, composes itself with billions of other obliterating positions, impositions, or superimpositions. And we, my angel, we love each other posted on this network, [...] crushed by taxes, in permanent insurrection against the "past," full of acknowledgements however, and virgin from debt, as at the first morning of the world. (*PC*, 100–101)

The post card and the stamp are both forms of sending that traverse any possible distinction between public and private: the post card is something very private, but becomes accessible to anyone who happens upon it[7]; the stamp is a public institution of collecting private fees in advance. Stamping here now denotes being always already marked, in advance of one's arrival, by a

---

7 On the public/private distinction and the post, Derrida says the following: "This opposition [between public and private] doesn't work, neither for psychoanalysis..., nor for the post..., nor even for the police...,—and the secret circulates, as secret you promise I swear, this is what I call the post card" (*PC*, 185).

heritage that is neither true nor false, because it appears to have already "advanced the funds," issued the terms of the values of "doing anything whatsoever." To stamp and being stamped refer both to taxing ("crushed by taxes"), as well as to exemption or acquittal ("virgin from debt"). This double nature of the stamp is like that of the *pharmakon* as writing. Indeed, stamping here is also writing of the most mechanical kind: type and tympan are both terms of printing.[8] Love and sexual difference are also linked up to the chain of stamping: while "[a]*teleia* is franking" (*PC*, 55) making honest, making virile, it is also a means of maintaining inviolability in terms of virginity. Stamping is both *ateleia*, achieving immunity, and being imprinted by the chain of indebtedness of heritage — the chain which necessarily undermines any acquittal, exemption any codes of guaranteed inviolability. In other words, the stamp is autoimmune in the sense that Derrida uses this term from "Faith and Knowledge" onwards, perhaps most clearly articulated in the quote I shared above from *Rogues*.

I don't want to suggest that the logic of autoimmunity within the Derridean oeuvre as a whole originates in *The Post Card* and thus, in some general, political vocabulary of life. Derrida himself connects autoimmunity to "Plato's Pharmacy," when he referred to the *pharmakon* as an "old name" for autoimmunitary logic.[9] Indeed in "Plato's Pharmacy" we find the current medical sense of this logic:

> The natural illness of the living is defined in its essence as an *allergy*, a reaction to the aggression of an alien element. And it is necessary that the natural life of the body should be

---

[8] For a discussion of the tympan and related terms in Derrida's work, see Christopher Norris, *Derrida* (Harvard University Press: Cambridge, 1987), 77–80.

[9] Jacques Derrida, "Autoimmunity: Real and Symbolic Suicides: A Dialogue with Jacques Derrida," in Giovanna Borradori, *Philosophy in a Time of Terror: Dialogues with Jurgen Habermas and Jacques Derrida*, trans. Pascale-Anne Brault and Michael Naas, 85–137 (Chicago: University of Chicago Press, 2004), 124.

allergy, from the moment the natural life of the body ought only to follow its own endogenous motions.[10]

And:

> The immortality and perfection of a living being would consist in its having no relation at all with any outside. That is the case with God [...]. God has no allergies.[11]

Although allergies are not autoimmune in the strict medical sense, they are, in the medical sense, exemplary for understanding the concept of the immune in general and therefore help us to better understand Derrida's term of autoimmunity as well. We refer to allergies as problems of immune reaction: they emerge when the immune system reacts to external elements that do not in fact threaten the organism, for example, pollen or certain nuts. An allergic reaction is an unnecessarily triggered reaction. It may be dangerous because the severity of the immune reaction can harm and even kill the organism it ought to protect. This happens in the case of disease brought on by pathogens as well, but it is in the case of allergic reaction the harmful potential of the immune reactions appears exceptionally clear. This is the reason that Derrida identifies allergy as the essence of the disease: the essence of disease is the immune reaction that threatens both the organism and the pathogen. In other words, the organism as well as whatever labeled "foreign" by immune processes has to endure the immune reaction for survival. When we come down with the flu, we need to survive the flu with the help of our immune system, but we also need to survive the immune activity (high fever, inflammation, etc.) itself. While external pathogens and their threatening intervention are most often part of disease, immune activity (either too little or too much) is always at the heart of disease. To the extent

---

10 Jacques Derrida. "Plato's Pharmacy," in *Dissemination*, trans. Barbara Johnson, 61–172 (London: Athlone Press, 1981), 101.
11 Ibid.

that immune activity is necessary for maintaining health, health always includes the risk of threat. What Derrida identifies in allergy corresponds to his term of autoimmunity in the sense of the threat brought on by the immune, the exempt, the *heilig,* the inviolable.

Accounts of the Derridean use of autoimmunity often refer to it as his choice to select a medical term. These accounts usually don't concern themselves with questions of biology or the question of the relationship between the concept of life and the terms conventionally considered as referring to biological phenomena. Our conventional sense of designating medicine as the origin of the term autoimmunity yields easily to a general implicit sense of positing the origin of the idea of life in what is now accepted as what Derrida calls the "domain of biology. However, it is crucial for a general understanding of Derrida's project (from deconstruction to autoimmunity) and for understanding the political significance of his reading of seemingly different lexicons (of biological and political) life to pay attention to his treatment of "life" or "life in general."

In a footnote to "Autoimmunity: Real and Symbolic Suicides," Derrida assesses the footnote on autoimmunity in "Faith and Knowledge" as an intervention "to extend to life in general the figure of autoimmunity whose meaning or origin first seemed to be limited to so-called natural life or to life pure and simple, to what is believed to be the purely 'zoological,' 'biological,' or 'genetic.'"[12]

We can sketch, then, the arch of the development of autoimmunity from the lexicon of biology from at least "Plato's Pharmacy" to "Faith and Knowledge" and "Autoimmunity." Linking *ateleia* onto this line illustrates Derrida's insistence in the footnote in "Autoimmunity" that the organic is not the source of life, an insistence that he expressed very clearly elsewhere as well, for instance in "Biodegradables": "[T]he organic is not the

---

12 Derrida, "Autoimmunity," 15.

living; natural life is not the whole of life."[13] "Life in general" is more than natural life, because there is constant traffic between the vocabulary of "nature" and other lexicons: the link between *ateleia* and immunity insists that we contest any claims or compulsions to posit the vocabulary of "nature" as the anchoring repository, the place of organic origin of the political vocabulary of life, death, health, and protection. The reason that immunity could be picked up by "the lexicon of biology" is that this sense of inviolability animates the different legal meanings of the word. But as the etymology of *immunis* suggests, inviolability does not concern only bodies conventionally considered organic. Inviolability is also always a political concept of privilege. As such, it is necessarily violent; marking privilege by inviolability necessitates violence even in contexts conventionally considered non-violent. No principle of inviolability can function without allowing, facilitating, and managing violence. If indeed autoimmunity is an especially apt term for deconstruction, it stresses that deconstruction concerns the cloud of terms around the notion of immunity and its political significance. The immune, the exempt, the *heilig,* the inviolable are all terms of ipseity. It is the critique of this inherent link between ipseity and violence that motivates deconstruction and which, in part, attracts Derrida to the image on the postcard depicting a the scandalous reversal of S. and p. making public the perverse implication that the younger one, the pupil, might insert his manifest virility between his master's thighs.

---

13 Jacques Derrida, "Biodegradables: Seven Diary Fragments," trans. Peggy Kamuf, *Critical Inquiry* 15, no. 4 (1989): 812–73, at 828.

Hannah Markley

Philately on the Telephone: Reading, Touching, Loving the "Envois"[1]

For D.A.

In this essay, I read a phone conversation that Jacques Derrida alludes to in the "Envois," but never directly transcribes. The content of the phone call remains secret. However, I want to retrace the significance of the conversation and its organizing figure, "*philately*," but even before I begin, I acknowledge that the aims of this essay are paradoxically at odds: I am both on the phone and in a text, writing about love, but always at a distance from explicit emotional content. The entanglements of telephone and post, of emotion and its suppression, necessarily entail some detours that also perform *philately* on the telephone with Jacques Derrida. What is essential, then, is not the content of the phone conversation between Derrida and his lover, or my conversation with Derrida's text. Rather, this essay foregrounds the relays of telephone, postcard, voice, and emotion in effort to think through love itself as an *envois*. That is, I foreground the ways that Derrida's text recasts love as always already in the post.

---

[1] This essay was revised and prepared with the support of the Bill and Carol Fox Center for Humanistic Inquiry at Emory University.

1. Hang Ups

In a letter from the "Envois" dated 4 September 1977 Derrida reveals that he "would really like to call this book *philately* in order to commemorate secretly our somewhat nutty phone call" (*PC*, 56). However, this book is not the book we are reading, *The Post Card*. The book, named in the phone conversation, perhaps even before the thought of publishing the "Envois" as part of *The Post Card*, is a book never yet written, a phantom text that is definitively not the "Envois." The desire to name the phantom book *philately* emerges at the end of a telephone conversation, and the letter begins with the phone conversation's end: "Hanging up just now" (*PC*, 55). Subsequently, the addressor recounts the moment of "hanging up" in a parenthetical volley: "(as always, 'hang up,' — "No, you hang up,' — 'No, you,' — 'Hang, up you,' — 'Hang up, you,' — 'I'm hanging up,' etc), I was in seventh heaven, I was laughing softly over the sage conversation concerning the word '*philately*'" (*PC*, 55). *Philately* emerges from the volley of hanging up, an event that only takes place insofar as it has been transcribed, recounted, and repeated in a letter. *Philately* on the telephone. Just as Derrida situates the "Envois" "as a preface to a book I have not written" (*PC*, 3), the phone prefaces *philately*, the phantom text that is never explicitly written. The phone conversation, like the phantom book that the "Envois" nonetheless commemorates, is lost or "incinerated" at the moment Derrida writes "Hanging up just now." All that remains is the letter that records the phone call at the moment it is always about to be hung up.

However, if "hanging up just now" begins the letter, to what moment does the "just now" refer? "4 September 1977" marks a singular date, locating us an apparently specific moment: "Just now." But, hang on — or rather let's not hang up just yet by assuming we have identified the moment that Derrida hangs up. There are four consecutive letters dated "4 September 1977," each of which traffics in its own language, performing Derrida's "Postal Principle": "the Postal Principle [works] as [a] differantial relay, that regularly prevents, delays, endispatches the depositing of the thesis, forbidding rest and ceaselessly causing to run, deposing or deporting the movement of speculation" (*PC*, 54). Even if the date promises singularity, it also "prevents, delays, endispatches" the "just now" it sets out to mark. These four letters, written on the same day "4 September 1977," mark the internal division of dates and the "just now" of "hanging up."

Derrida writes in "Shibboleth" that the date must "divide itself in repeating itself, and in the same stroke encipher or encrypt itself."[2] While "4 September 1977" marks the "just now" of Derrida having hung up, it also obscures the very moment it sets out to record. The date marks time without distinguishing the moments, repeating itself four times, not unlike the volley on the telephone. So, the "just now" that marks the end-beginning-repetition of the "nutty phone conversation" — the *philately* — is also an unrepeatable instant that divides itself. After all, what would this lost "nutty" and wayward phone call be, if not, unrepeatable? The phone call is always already incinerated and burned away, made the ghost of a text that seems to record it.

Indeed, the only transcriptions that Derrida provides of the phone conversation are the interminable seconds that lead to "hanging up." The first iteration — "hanging up just now" — occurs in the present, marking an on going process that is never quite arrested by the "just now" that punctuates it. The process of never quite hanging up asserts itself in the parenthetical reiterations: "(as always, 'hang up,' — no, you hang up — No, you — Hang up, you — Hang up, you — hanging up,' etc)." Hanging up never ends. Instead, it remains suspended by "etcetera" — and so forth, *ad infinitum,* as if we could never finish "hanging up." Indeed, hanging up "always" happens; it is inscribed in the exchange, dividing the singularity of the phone call insofar as its singularity is only in the letter recorded as a repetition of the ritual of always "hanging up." The *philately* of telephony is marked through the repetition of the hanging up

---

2   Jacques Derrida, "Shibboleth: For Paul Celan," in *Sovereignties in Question: The Poetics of Paul Celan,* eds. Thomas Dutoit and Outi Pasanen, 1–64 (New York: Fordham University Press, 2005), 15.

that encrypts and obscures the secret of the phone conversation. The nutty telephone conversation is not only nutty by virtue of the encryption that makes its idiom impossible to read, but also nutty because the conversation cannot be reproduced in the text.

However, the hanging up ritual also makes telephony legible in the text. Hanging up is written into the transcription, as the "no's," the "you's" and the "hang ups" shuffle back and forth, exchanging places, and leap-frogging one another. Each "no, you hang up" strikes the ear differently. This is not simply a phone call we have overheard-read or a counterfeit we have been following; this is the postal principle on the telephone.[3] That is, the hanging up ritual is "the differantial relay, that regularly prevents, delays, endispatches" the account of what transpired on the telephone. Derrida writes the telephonic principle *qua* postal principle through "hanging up" because it is also the phrase through which we recognize the duration of a telephone conversation. No question my thesis has been delayed by "hanging up," caught up in this relay and the impossibility of locating the moment of the "just now," the moment at which Derrida hung up the phone and began to write of *philately* on the telephone.

2. Love-Stamp

Philately, the love of stamps or the activity of collecting them, not only precipitates out of the phantom phone call but allows us to uncover the ways in which the text and the phone conversation are subject to the same postal principle. As the whispered subtitle to the phantom book and the phantom phone call, *philately* is a secret word that touches the lost moment of "just now." Derrida writes:

---

[3] In "Ulysses Gramophone," Derrida writes of a "telephonic interiority," relating telephonic effects to the effects of phonetic enunciation and the voice: "...before any appliance bearing the name 'telephone' in modern times, the telephonic *techne* is at work within the voice" ("Ulysses Gramophone: Hear Say Yes in Joyce," in *Acts of Literature*, ed. Derek Attridge, 253–309 [New York: Routledge, 1992], 273).

No, *philately* does not mean love of distance, of the term, of the telos or of the tele-, nor the love of letters, no, [...] it is a very recent word, it is only as old as stamps, [...] and it treats of *ateleia* [...]. *Ateleia* is franking, the exemption from taxes, whence the stamp. It is true that it maintains therefore a relation with one of the senses of *telos*: acquittal, exemption, payment, cost, expenditure, fee. From acquittal one could go to gift, offering, and even [...] marriage ceremony! Phila-tely then is love *without,* with/without marriage, and the collection of all stamps, the love of the stamp with or without stamped love. (*PC,* 55–56)

Philately, then, names a principle "without," love "without," which is "the love of the stamp with or without stamped love." Love of the stamp cannot be read as a commentary on postage stamps because Derrida's are not material stamps in the ways we might want to conceive of the materiality of the "post card" or the letter. Rather, the figure of the stamp suggests that there is a form of love that precedes and exceeds the profession of romantic love. Love in this sense does not necessarily emerge in language as much as it names the possibility of language and the *envois.*

While letters, postcards, dates, and telephones make paradoxical bedfellows, the love-stamp reveals the ways in which these modes of transmission, despite differences of technology and medium, exist by virtue of an amorous condition of possibility. In another *envois,* dated "31 August 1977," Derrida returns to the stamp: "No, the stamp is not metaphor, on the contrary, metaphor is a stamp: the tax, the duty to be paid on natural language and the voice. And so on the metaphoric catastrophe. No more is post a metaphor" (*PC,* 46). This letter, which, we might add, is the only one written on "31 August 1977," singular even as it divides itself in the program of dates and letters, returns us to the stamp, inverting the figurative line of thought we have been following. That is, the stamp is not simply a metaphor for the postal principle and it does not merely mark the disruption of any definitive arrival. The stamp names metaphor, or the ways that "metaphor is a stamp: the tax, the duty to be paid on natural language and the voice." Metaphor marks a debt that can never be paid even though one is always paying it. While "metaphor" might signify within traditional rhetorical parameters, here "metaphor" signals a more general problematic. Etymologically, "metaphor" is derived from the Greek *metapherein*, which literally means to transfer or carry over. *Meta* indicates spatial designations of "over" or "across," while *pherein* means "to carry or to bear."[4] "Metaphor" carries over or bears across, operating as the figure in general for the movement of the postal system. That is, metaphor makes possible, even as it parasitizes, transgresses, and delays the "natural language and the voice" and the messages transmitted by them.

In this sense, the "just now" of the "nutty telephone conversation" is stamped; it reiterates the impossibility, even as it attempts to mark, the immediacy of the telephone conversation and the voice. Indeed, Derrida writes that on the telephone, "often I stop paying attention to what you are saying, so that the timbre alone resonates, […] I understand nothing" (*PC*,19). The word "timbre" means the sound of a voice. However, the French *timbre* also may be read as "stamp." The timbre and resonance of a voice *without* anything having been understood, like metaphor operates as a love-stamp. *Timbre,* designates both sound and stamp simultaneously, carrying connotations of both written and spoken language, as if written words were always wrapped in a voice, baring (and bearing across) the trace of enunciated speech. In this sense, the grapheme and phoneme, by virtue of the *timbre* that holds them together, are ghosts of one another. Just so, the voice on the telephone is estranged and at a distance, only ever heard insofar as one might "read," in or-

---

4   In "Anthropomorphism and Trope in the Lyric," Paul de Man reads metaphor similarly remarking that in Francophone cities a "correspondence" refers to a Metro transfer and is linked to the "trans" in metaphor ("Anthropomorphism and Trope in the Lyric," in *The Rhetoric of Romanticism*, 239–62 [New York: Columbia University Press, 1984], 253).

der to hear, the distinctions between phonemes.[5] Uncannily, the distance on the telephone might be thought as a distance that necessitates reading.

This ghostly principle, in which the grapheme and phoneme always bear the trace of one another, collected in the thought of *timbre* as the sound and stamp, situates both written and spoken language as always already taxed. Thus, the love-stamp sanctions even as it taxes the "sending"; the stamp makes possible the message's destination only insofar as the message is never quite carried to its precise addressee, disrupted by the inevitability that we always might misread or mishear. Perhaps even, the love-stamp means that messages, whether spoken or written, are never entirely "understood." *Philately*: the love of adestination.

Moreover, the love-stamp makes reading possible even as it divides that reading, transforming all letters, all phone calls, all *envois*, all writing, into an "open letter," which has always been intercepted from the very moment of inscription: "of course I felt it, at the second that I was writing, that this letter, like all others, was intercepted even before any hands could be put on it" and for all our ciphers or encryptions "still in advance it is intercepted" (*PC*, 51). The stamp seduces, drawing the reader in by the terms used to communicate meaning. Even as Derrida describes how writing is always already "interception," we read and intercept his open letter. We read over his shoulder as interceptors of a conversation made legible only by virtue of the love-stamp, the tax Derrida has paid in advance, in order to write anything at all. "At the second that I was writing," Derrida suspects, we have already been reading his postcard. Or, at least, insofar as his writing became legible *in a second,* it became legible to anyone and "once intercepted — a second suffices — the message no longer has any chance of reaching any determinable

---

[5] I am indebted here to a lecture given by David Wills entitled "Positive Feedback: Listening Behind Hearing," in which he discussed the various mediations and "reading" practices at work when we listen. This lecture was delivered November 7, 2012, at Emory University.

person" (*PC*, 51). Once written the letter is not only intercepted and itinerant, it is stamped-love because it has no "chance of reaching any determinable person."

Writing and interception take place and fall in love "in a second," echoing the "just now." However, like the "just now" of the phone conversation, this second of writing, interception, and love might be read not as the primacy of a singular moment, but rather, as the very configuration of delay. The "seconds" of writing and interception "second" themselves because the delay of writing has never come first and is never fully present to authorial intention. Rather, interception is the necessary disruption through which writing materializes — inscription *is* interception and, as Derrida tells us, "the message" just now, at the "second" of interception, "no longer has any chance of reaching any determinable person." Put another way, "the letter, at the very instant when it takes place […], divides itself, puts itself into pieces, falls into a post card" (*PC*, 81). So no more letters, only postcards. This is the love-stamp, the tax paid in advance, that is the condition of sending any message and, simultaneously, the interminable impossibility of a message ever arriving. All communication, writing, telephony, and love are always going postal.

Indeed, the possibility of love emerges through the postal principle. Derrida, just after consigning every letter to the fate of the postcard "in pieces," affirms that if "this is our tragic lot, […] I begin to love you on the basis of this impossibility" (*PC*, 81). The "adestination" of the letter that "falls into a post card" is the predicate for love. Because, even if we "recognize that such a certainty [of the postal principle and adestination] is unbearable for anyone…and most energetically" denied by those "people charged with the carrying of the mail, guardians of the letter, archivists, the professors as well as the journalists… the philosophers…and the literature people," there remains some residual effect, some erotics of "adestination" that gets us closer to *philately* (*PC*, 51). For, even as Derrida suggests that the postal principle is "unbearable," it is this "unbearable" element that makes possible any "bearing across" or "carrying over." The unbearable bears. The "guardians of the letter," the writers who wish most vehemently to secure the arrival of a thesis are interminably engaged to the problem of "carrying the mail" and the taxes that must be paid. Moreover, "carrying the mail" like "hanging up," never finds its end—"forbidding rest and ceaselessly causing to run, deposing or deporting the movement of speculation" (*PC*, 54).

So, "philosophers," "literature people," writers in general are only ever "carrying the mail" in an effort to bear the unbearable thought of love's possibility. The vertiginous erotics of adestination, the "love of the stamp with or without stamped love," compels such a movement. Moreover, the movement of interpretation, the carrying of the mail, knows no end, producing an *eros* of interception in which, even as we read, we always have been delayed, deferred, or endispatched. In a manner, we always, at the moment of our readings, have not yet begun to read. The "unbearable" work of carrying the mail, of literary interpretation or theoretical inquiry, also entails an affirmation of love that invigorates our efforts.[6] A love of letters, can only ever be, in the first instance, a love letter. Criticism is written in an amorous rhetoric that, even in the moment of critique, luxuriates in the stamp, the *timbre,* and the resonance that affords the writer such an opportunity. Even this opportunity right now of writing about "love letters" and their "amorous rhetoric" is invigorated by the love-stamp that precedes each and every letter, each and every postcard.

3. Touching

Even as Derrida insists that the work of reading and interpretation necessarily entails a restless *philately* that regularly endispatches speculation, he elaborates on the erotic elements at

---

[6] Peggy Kamuf argues in "Deconstruction and Love," Derrida's "practice of deconstruction proceeds out of love rather than under the sway of a destructive impulse;" it cultivates "the force of *affirmation* to what otherwise appears destined to have only the negative force of [a] technical, dismantling operation" ("Deconstruction and Love," in *Deconstructions: A User's Guide*, ed. Nicholas Royle [London: Palgrave Macmillin, 2000], 153).

work in the love of letters. "We are monstrous angels," he writes, naming himself among the mail carriers and suggesting that carrying the post is perhaps a waste of time:

> all this bad economics, this expended energy, this time that we will have spent analyzing the tax that we pay in order to remain together, the price that it costs, [...] the secret debts, the charges on the suffering of the others within us, these step-by-step discussions, these interminable analyses, all our ratiocinations would have been ignoble, the opposite of love and the gift, if they had not been made in order to give us again the time to touch each other with words. What counts and is counted then, is what we do while speaking, what we do to each other, how we again touch each other by mixing our voices. (*PC*, 56)

Significantly, the "interminable analysis," "all our ratiocinations," our messages on their way to "adestination" *would have been* "the opposite of love and the gift" only "had they not been made in order to give us again the time to touch each other with words." Herein resides the corollary to the love-stamp — the chance that even if messages never arrive to a fully present person, at a fully present moment, words might allow us to *touch*. The movement of deposed and deported speculation paradoxically affords the opportunity "to touch each other with words," to "move" one another with language.

The end of speculation then would be no end at all, but an engagement in and through language. Significantly, touching must also be thought in terms of feeling, which is not necessarily tactile, but emotive, causing one another to feel with words and in language, even if the love letter never fully arrives. In *On Touching — Jean-Luc Nancy,* Derrida elaborates on touching as precisely this kind of telephonic, phantasmatic, and affective experience:

> Imagine: lovers separated for life. Wherever they may find themselves and each other. On the phone, through their

voices and their inflection, timbre, and accent, through elevations and interruptions in the breathing, across moments of silence, they foster all the differences necessary to arouse a sight, touch, and even smell — so many caresses, to reach the ecstatic climax from which they are forever weaned — but are never deprived.[7]

Touching is, like the "just now" of the phone conversation, repeating and dividing the moment of affecting another person. Love takes place in touching not as physical experience, but as a force of attraction that traverses the distances put in place by phone lines, voices, "elevations and interruptions of breath." Love emerges as the ecstatic climax of telephonic deprivation. However, these lovers' words never touch once, they only ever touch again. As voices intermix through words, touch must be reconceived as spectral qualia. Put another way, in the context of these postcards and the engagement that they imply, "touching" becomes the process by which the addressee and signatory appear and disappear to and for one another through the phantasmatic love-stamp of the letter. What "counts" is not that the love letter arrives because the message is always already intercepted and the interception is what makes it a love letter. Rather, "What counts is what we do while speaking, what we do to each other, how we again touch each other by mixing our voices. [...] What counts then is that it is still up to us to exhaust language, and reason swerves" (*PC*, 56). What "counts" for Derrida is that in "interminable analysis" and the necessary interception of all messages there is also a possibility "that again we touch each other," and transform one another with, through, and in language. The love-stamp on language becomes the principle and possibility of love suggesting that we, all of us, might touch each other with words. Touching names a medium through which two people (be)hold one another.

---

[7] Jacques Derrida, *On Touching—Jean-Luc Nancy*, trans. Christine Irizary (Stanford: Stanford University Press, 2005), 112.

4. Burn Everything

If the love-stamp that intercepts any message whatever is the condition of possibility for touching with words, what precisely are the effects of touching? That is, what effects do love and touch have for the "Envois"? Derrida asks,

> How could I ask you to burn, which is as much as to say not to read, what I was writing you? [...] [D]o not read me, this statement organizes its own transgression at the very instant when, by means of the single event of understood language, it assumes command. It compels the violation of its own law. (*PC*, 59)

"Incineration" and "burning" are the products of touching one another with words. The injunction to "burn everything" suspends legibility and illegibility, because it is a figure that demands to be read yet disrupts its own reading; burning appears only insofar as it haunts and recursively undoes "the single event of understood language." Derrida names the impossibility of legibility at the moment of any reading or touching with words: "But I will arrive, I will arrive at the point where you will no longer read me" (*PC*, 59). We might gloss the arrival as "I will touch you at the moment of my incineration." That is, Derrida arrives, becomes legible, only insofar as he resists any reading. He touches with the utterance "do not read me." Derrida does not literally suggest that we should stop reading, but rather, that we only ever read or touch insofar as we understand reading, interpretation, and touching as the possibility of always not reading, of missing one another entirely. Derrida loves the stamp, the *timbre* or resonance, even at the moment of transgressing its law and commanding his addressee, and by extension, all his reader-interceptors, to "burn everything." To burn is to love.

He writes of burning love: "you had understood my order [...]: 'burn everything,' understood it so well that you told me you copied over [...], in your writing, and in pencil, the words of that first letter" (*PC*, 59). In this moment, Derrida equates "understanding" to "transcription" or "another way of saying that you had reread it [sc. the letter], no?" (*PC,* 59). Even as Derrida acknowledges that his addressee has "understood" the injunction insofar as she repeats his words, disassociating them from their context by "citing" them in her own writing, she has incinerated any possibility that they might mark singularity—burned away from the very injunction that they would seem to record. The addressee transgresses whatever might be "understood" in the phrase "do not read me" by disrupting the singularity of the demand. The injunction "that violates its own law" is simultaneously violated and reasserted by its transcription; its not being understood performs the touch that Derrida formulates as "burn everything." The addressee has copied "in pencil," transcribed with another writing utensil, the supposed singularity of such an injunction. A pencil, after all, is a peculiar writing tool that, when stood on its head, unwrites what it "just now" records. The spectral pencil mark invigorates the thought of this injunction by producing a writing always haunted by the possibility of erasure. The appearing-disappearing mark of the pencil figures, even as it suspends, the possibility of transcription and touching.

I transcribe the transcription that Derrida has, in his fashion, transcribed for his reader-interceptor's benefit. Derrida tells us his addressee has copied his words, which he then copies in parentheses for the reader. Subsequently, I retype-recopy this reiteration *en abyme,* in an attempt to trace the moment of transcription, the act that understood and preformed the injunction "to burn everything" in a gesture of "rereading." Here, what might seem like an endless recirculation of misunderstandings, must however be understood not merely as repetition. Rather, "burn everything" gestures toward the matter at hand: insofar as transcription has been a process of "rereading" (or in the case of the telephone, recording to reread) it has modeled "what one *begins by doing* when one reads, even for the first time." Derrida short-circuits the singularity here of at least three "rereadings" or "transcriptions": his addressee's, his own written into the text of this letter *in parentheses,* and our own *cited* above. These transcriptions are neither unique nor singular, consigned as they are to "what one *begins by doing*" when we read anything at all, "even for the first time." Reading only ever occurs through the processes of "repetition, memory, etc." Graphemes are only ever understood, made to sound some never-present-voice, by virtue of their the repetition — inscribed as the principle of any letter, character, document or date — that makes possible our reading. And so forth or "etcetera," the never arrested processes of repetition and memory that allow us to carry the mail.

"I love you by heart," Derrida announces, "there, between *parentheses* or *quotation* marks, such is the origin of the post card" (*PC*, 60, my emphases). Notably, this declaration of love comes on the heels of the "repetition, memory, etc.," not as a departure from the thought of repetition, but rather as dilation. As I describe above, Derrida transcribes or "recites" *in parentheses* that which his addressee has transcribed, copied, or "cited" to send back to him. The proclamation "I love you by heart," points to a "there, between *parentheses* or *quotation marks*," referring to his doubly recited injunction: "('I am burning, stupid impression of being faithful, nevertheless kept several simulacra, etc.')." The profusion here of *parentheses* and *quotation signals* something about the nature of "love by heart." Love by heart, it would seem, occurs at moments of citationality in which the physics of an always already reiterating language allow us to touch, repeat, and rewrite one another's words, incinerating (even at the moment of our reading "for the first time") whatever might have been the intended meaning. The interminable "hanging up" of the telephone conversation occurs between *parentheses* and *quotation marks,* secreting even as it performs this "loving by heart," this *philately* on the telephone. "Such is the origin of the post card," but not just the postcard. The postcard, the *envoi*, the open letter, the always already intercepted, legible only in and through "memory and repetition," name the act of "loving by heart." "To reread before burning" is impossible because "to reread," to read even for the first time, is already to burn up in love. There is no "before" to "burning," but we burn in an effort "to incorporate the letter [...] and to take it in [...] by heart. Keep what you burn, such is the demand" (*PC*, 60).

Again, incineration, transcription, rewriting, or citationality are not only figured as the taxes that disable the arrival of the letter that Derrida names in his definition of *philately*; they are the very possibility of love, providing the chance of commingling *timbres* and touching with words. So Derrida offers the subtitle *philately* in order to figure love not only as a condition of possibility for language, but as an emotion that operates through interruption, itineration, and absence. Love, like the letter, never quite arrives. The love we have for carrying the mail is the action and possibility of love between people: interminable sending, missing, and burning, all for the chance of "touching one another with words."

4. *Myself, Under Your Skin*

If one aim of the "Envois" is to read romantic love through the postal principle along with writing, the voice, the letter, and the telephone, then Derrida also posits a bittersweet theory of emotion. To "love by heart" is to burn a letter such that I might incorporate otherwise the words that never fully arrive. At work in love then is a restless exchange between self and other where the differences between self and other, signatory and addressee blur. When Derrida quips "[I] distance myself *in order* to write to you," (*PC*, 28) he is not negating "himself"; rather, he marks the difficult operation whereby in order to send a letter, he deposits a trace that is always not "himself," but a remainder. In order to "mix voices," there is an immediate interception in which Derrida the signatory endispatches himself in language, sketching a "myself" which is in no way self-possessed. This self-dispossession may seem like an existential estrangement from any touch at all in language or without. However, the *envoi* of the self, distanced and dispatched from the self-same individual, is precisely the postal mechanism that makes love possible.

Derrida, on the heels of his injunction "to burn everything," to incinerate so as to know "by heart," elucidates the "self" that the *envoi* performs: "Mourn what I send to you, myself, in order to have me under your skin. No longer *before* you, […] but within you, speaking to you and kissing you without interruption even before you have the chance to breathe and to turn around" (*PC,* 60). Derrida emphasizes that all this burning and incineration — this "knowing by heart" or "touching" — is not vital or present, but only ever occurs as a process of mourning. The letter, which must be in principle operational in the radical absence or death of its author, predicts and performs the death of its author in the process.[8] This is not to say that the author is dead or that the author must be dead, but rather, that to read is to mourn the absence of the signatory and, in so doing, to take the signatory within the self. To mourn is the process of loving and knowing by heart; the other erupts, touching, appearing-disappearing "under your skin." Indeed, "touching with words" is a form of mourning in which the other is "no longer before you," but "uninterrupted" and "kissing you." As if mourning allowed you to touch the other, kiss the other, and tattoo the other on the inside of "myself," leaving the pronoun and the ipse riven, mad, and in love. Touching in this way is no longer a phenomenological experience, but bound up in the deconstruction of the self by the others that fissure it in mourning and ultimately in love.

Still, touching with words involves having "the other within oneself, right up close but stronger than oneself, and his tongue in your ear." So, as we read, we mourn the absence of the author in an effort to take in and revivify the language: to be touched by words and commingle our voices, drawing the other "up close" "stronger than" ourselves, displacing ourselves in order to be touched. Derrida's *langue* in our ear is both a tongue and language. We read in order to have a tongue in ear, kissing us not

---

8   Roland Barthes elaborates this principle in "The Death of the Author," substituting the reader or interpreter for the "author-God," as the locus of textual meaning ("The Death of the Author," in *The Norton Anthology of Theory and Criticism,* 2nd ed., ed. Vincent Leicht, 1325–28 [New York: Norton & Co., 2010], 1325–26). We differ from Barthes on the second point. By virtue of the postal principle, the reader would be equally engaged to the vicissitudes of adestination and the postcard.

necessarily as a physical sensation, but as the erotic principle of language that allows another's words to operate closer than whatever we might assume "ourselves" to be. Importantly, this "*langue* in our ears" is both the singular tongue of our signatory and, simultaneously, the entire differential relay that makes his *langue* legible and, ultimately, illegible. The process of mourning the signatory, of taking in the other "up close," can occur only by virtue of *langue* having always already been in our ears and entirely senseless.

While Derrida's *langue* is in our ears, touches us "before being able to say a word," simultaneously the readers are left "looking at [themselves] in the depths of the rearview mirror, in an automobile that passes [*double*] all the others" (*PC,* 60).[9] Reading, like love, recalls and requires a displacement of self, a mourning that makes the other stronger than the self, requiring a reconfiguration of everything one might mean when one designates a self. The reading self looks at [itself] "in the depths of the rearview mirror," which is to say that we can only ever configure ourselves as selves through a retro-specular relation. We do not see ourselves, but rather, are projected, rear-viewed, even as the movement of our "automobile," the continual movement, "running" or "dispatching" of the *autos,* keeps producing new rear-views. The automobile "passes all others," which would be the passing of all others in more than one sense; the automobile passes all "other" versions of its own autos and, in the same breath, passes all the "others" who have touched us with their words. The verb translated as "passes" is given in the French *double*. For the sake of metaphor, the translator perhaps chooses to gloss this as "passes." However, *double* might be more literally translated as "doubles all the others." As if the movement of this auto-mobile, this self always on the move, only ever constitutes

---

9   Derrida describes what Nicholas Royle refers to as a telepathy effect in which at the moment of reading we are already "being-two-to-speak" or "being-two-to-feel," perhaps even, being-two-to-touch ("The 'Telepathy Effect,'" in *The Uncanny: An Introduction* [Manchester: Manchester University Press, 2003], 267–68).

its "autos" in terms of a retrospective, rear-viewed doubling of each and every other: "Limited Inc"[10] in the rearview mirror.

Derrida sums up the chiasmic displacement of self and other as "the most mysterious thing, the most worthy of being thought, the least thinkable, my idea of you, the infinite anamnesis of that (which) I saw" (*PC*, 60, my emphasis). Significantly, Derrida's tries to imagine his "idea of you" through the metaphor of this "automobile" that figures the movement of a self to which he has no access. A challenge no doubt, thinking the "least thinkable." "My idea of you" is only ever an "infinite *anamnesis*," the infinite process of gathering together under the pronouns "my" and "you" all the memories, the retrospecular rear-views that necessarily pass and double (double as they pass) "all the others." "My idea of you" becomes an interminable analysis in and of itself, an interminable envoi in which the relations between self and other are not only always on the move (*autos*-mobile), but also are only ever constituted in and by the resounding displacement of self for other, the mixing of voices, *timbres,* and love-stamps.

What remains here in the final lines of *this envoi* is the event of such an encounter; the event of my reading-intercepting in which all along Derrida has had his *langue* in my ear without ever having intended it. A love from *without,* a *philately,* in which by virtue of the love-stamp, the tax he paid, the *timbre* which is simultaneously of his voice and not his voice, touches me — our voices intermixing and deporting whatever thesis I had intended to offer. The love of the stamp sanctions my reading, touching, burning and citing of the *envois* never meant for me. Yet I have never quite hung up, or will be always just hanging up, awaiting the sound of this *timbre* in my ear, "in a

---

10 In "Limited Inc a b c…," Derrida deploys the phrase "limited inc" not only to refer to the explicit influences that an author might name, but also the "entire more or less anonymous tradition of a code, a heritage, a reservoir of arguments" to which an author has recourse (*Limited Inc,* ed. Gerald Graff [Evanston: Northwestern University Press, 1988], 36). This "heritage" would be radicalized by this figure of the retrospective view, expanding the configuration of the self to a limited, but nonetheless uncountable, company of others.

language that is all the closer for being foreign, […] [in which] I understand nothing" (*PC,* 19), only ever resounding the amorous rhetoric of this adestined text, carrying the mail, speaking with and through Derrida on this telephone, this telephony, this *philately.* "Hanging up just now," etc.

Éamonn Dunne

Entre Nous

> *I repeat, my love: for you. I write for you and speak only to you [Je le répète, mon amour: pour toi. J'écris pour toi et ne parle qu'à toi].*[1]

> *Love. Has Derrida ever spoken of anything else but love?*[2]

Love is…

Love is the obvious word in the "Envois" to *The Post Card* and maybe the most difficult to say anything about. How can one speak intelligibly about it? One falls hopelessly into cliché when speaking of love, as Derrida does in the Kirby Dick and Amy Ziering Kofman's film. "I have an empty head on love in general," says Derrida. "And as for the reason philosophy has often spoken of love, I either have nothing to say, or I'd just be reciting clichés."[3] And yet, love is certainly the guiding principle, beyond pleasure, behind and before Derrida's corpus, behind and before everything he says about adestination, destinerrancy, arrival, the gift, the messianic, the secret, others, and also the promise; behind and in front of which is a double affirmation, a

---

1 *PC*, 73/81.
2 See also John Protevi's penetrating essay, "Love," in *Between Deleuze and Derrida*, eds. Paul Patton and John Protevi, 183–94 (New York: Continuum, 2003).
3 Jacques Derrida, *Screenplay and Essays on the Film Derrida*, eds. Kirby Dick and Amy Ziering Kofman (Manchester: Manchester University Press, 2005), 81.

yes, yes to an unknown future, a oui oui that haunts language as the memory of an ad-venture, an other *a-venir,* each time a new beginning. Each time beginning; anew. Every time I open my mouth I am promising something, even when I am lying I am promising, opening myself up to a possible future, to a future anterior about which I can truthfully know nothing for certain.[4] Speaking opens me up to the world, to the love of the world, to the promise of an other world. Who could deny that?

How then to trace all those moments of reference to "you," "my love"? How to trace all those addresses to the beloved, the one that remains secret, a-b-s-o-l-u-t-e-l-y secret, in the "Envois"? Undoubtedly an interminable task. That "my love" remains at the secret heart of everything Derrida says, the wound of the text, opening itself to the future, to the to-come of the other, exposed to it, naked, *entre nous,* nude. Indeed, my love, my love is exposed to the impossible. Derrida, "having never loved anything but the impossible," is engaged in *The Post Card* to the promise of love, to the reader to come who will fall in love again with the letter of the text.[5] Even the bad reader, says Derrida, solicits his love (*PC,* 4).

Without precaution or predilection I will take two entries from the same day (3 June 1977) to illustrate why these "Envois" are Derrida's most sustained and important contribution to the discourse of love. First entry:

3 June 1977

and when I call you my love, my love, is it you I am calling or my love? You, my love, is it you I thereby name, is it to you that I address myself? I don't know if the question is well put, it frightens me. But I am sure that the answer, if it gets to me

---

4 Jacques Derrida, *Monolingualism of the Other; or, The Prosthesis of Origin,* trans. Patrick Mensah (Stanford: Stanford University Press, 1998), 67.

5 Jacques Derrida, "Circumfession," in Geoffrey Bennington, *Jacques Derrida* (Chicago: University of Chicago Press, 1993), 3.

one day, will have come to me from you. You alone, my love, you alone will have known it.
we have asked each other the impossible, as the impossible, both of us.   *"Ein jeder Engel ist schrecklich,"* beloved.   when I call you my love, is it that I am calling you, yourself, or is it that I am telling my love? and when I tell you my love is it that I am declaring my love to you or indeed that I am telling you, yourself, my love, and that you are my love. I want so much to tell you (*PC*, 8).

What exactly is frightening about this question? And why does Derrida ask if the question is well put? How could the question be put otherwise? And if so, how does the phrasing of the question effect the response? Why the repetition of the phrase "my love"? not only here but throughout the "Envois," over and over again, until the locution becomes intrinsic to the rhythmic fabric of the text: "et quand je t'appelle mon amour, mon amour, est-ce toi que j'appelle ou mon amour?" (*PC*, 8/12).

One answer lies in the discrepancies between use and mention Derrida traces so tenaciously in *Limited Inc* and elsewhere, the ungroundable chasm forged by the great J.L. Austin between performative and constative utterances, which are always leaking uncontrollably into one another, never quite sustainable, saturable or definable. When I say "my love" am I stating or instigating, declaring a matter of fact or making something happen? Calling you to me, I call you out, create you, my love. Calling you my love, my love, I am inventing the impossible, inventing the event of love; I am promising my love. To you. One can never know for sure that love does not appear in the naming, that the locution "I love you" doesn't create what it names, even if I'm joking or acting on a stage; and by creating what it names, it is susceptible to being confused with a declaration postcarded to who(m)ever gets in its way.[6] Sending it out, I can

---

6   See J.L. Austin, *How to Do Things with Words*, 2nd ed., eds. J.O. Urmson and Marina Sbisà (Oxford: Oxford University Press, 1980), 22: "a performative

never be sure of its destination, its active sonar, its "tranche-mission," seeking out the monstrous contours of some wholly, unknowable, beloved other. The performative is therefore always already a perverformance, provoking the serious and the non-serious simultaneously, again, anew each and every time. "Perhaps," says Derrida, "they are going to find this writing too adroit, virtuosic in the art of turning away [*l'art de détourner*], perhaps perverse in that it can be approached from everywhere and nowhere, certainly abandoned to the other, but given over to itself. Why, they ask themselves, incessantly let the destination divide itself? You too, perhaps, my love, you too question yourself, but this perversion, first of all, I treat." (*PC*, 223/239).

To whom or to what does Derrida refer to with "my love," the hidden god of *The Post Card*? To what other is it abandoned? "Quid ergo amo, cum Deum meum amo? Can I do anything other than translate this question by SA into my language, into the same sentence, totally empty and huge at the same time, the change of meaning, or rather reference, defining the only difference of the 'meum': what do I love, whom do I love, that I love above all?"[7] What do I love when I love my God? Whom do I love? Who or what? "the history of love, the heart of love, is divided between the who and the what."[8] The question is terrifying. Love, riven from itself, bifurcated in the crucible of the idiomatic moment of its enunciation. In saying "I love you" I am repeating a cliché, I am bound to a context, to a tradition, to the moment of saying, to a language that is not my own; I have only one language and it is not my own.[9] My tongue is not my own tongue, but the other's tongue in my mouth. And yet I am saying something absolutely singular, absolutely new that marks an ineluctable alterity at the heart of iterability, the *itara*, which

---

utterance will, for example, be *in a peculiar way* hollow or void if said by an actor on the stage, or if introduced in a poem, or spoken in a soliloquy" (emphasis in the original).

7 Derrida, "Circumfession," 122.
8 Derrida, *Screenplay and Essays on the Film Derrida*, 81.
9 Derrida, *Monolingualism of the Other*, 1.

calls to the other in Sanskrit.[10] No amount of repetition can ever exhaust the novelty of what comes by way of that locution: "I love you."

But Seriously

The Post Card is indeed a text that makes writing about it a peculiar task: "Was there ever such a text as 'Envois' for making you say strange things? And for making you unable to say anything?"[11] Undoubtedly. But seriously, can it be taken seriously? Quite a lot hangs on how you interpret that question. That one can never know to whom it is addressed lends to it a fictive status, a secrecy all its own: "no one will ever know from what secret I am writing and the fact that I say so changes nothing."[12] And yet, it *is* addressed. To you, my love. Derrida has said quite a lot about the phrase "Je t'aime" elsewhere, as J. Hillis Miller has pointed out in a chapter on Derrida in his *Speech Acts in Literature* (2001).[13] In 1992, Derrida presented two seminars on the phrase at the École des Hautes Études in Paris and then again in an English improvisation at the University of California at Irvine in 1993. One says in French "Je t'aime" in the second person singular, which is not something we can say in the English language, since "you" is never obstinately singular. One can only do this contextually by pointing or directing one's speech directly to a loved one, a loved one who is in some sense, and however negatively, "touched" by that speech act, a speech act which is not a constative but a felicitous performative event, doing what it is saying. Here is what Derrida says of the peculiarity of the

---

10 Jacques Derrida, *Limited Inc,* trans. Samuel Weber, ed. Gerald Graff (Evanston: Northwestern University Press, 1988), 7.
11 Sarah Wood, "Edit," *Mosaic: A Journal for the Interdisciplinary Study of Literature* 39, no. 3 (2006): 47–58, at 48.
12 Derrida, "Circumfession," 207.
13 See J. Hillis Miller's commentaries in *Literature as Conduct: Speech Acts in Henry James* (New York: Fordham, 2005), 204; *Black Holes* (Stanford: Stanford University Press, 1999), 279–311; *Speech Acts in Literature* (Stanford: Stanford University Press, 2001), 134–49; 159–60.

phrase as it is cited in Miller's translation of this as yet unpublished seminar:

> "Je t'aime" is not a description; it is the production of an event by means of which, claiming not to lie, claiming to speak the truth (the "Je t'aime" is always true, deemed to be true, immediately true, and [...] [it has an] extraordinary allure of indubitability [...]), I tend to affect the other, to touch the other, literally or not, to give the other or to promise the other the love that I speak to him or her [...]. This performative declaration creates an event in manifesting, in attesting to that of which it speaks, in bearing witness to it; and that to which it testifies is not elsewhere, but here and now, nearly merging [*se confondant*] with the act that consists in saying it, which has caused more than one to say [*ce qui a ou faire dire à plus d'un*], from Stendhal to Gide or to Proust (I can't remember), that one begins truly to love after or at the earliest from the moment when love is declared and not before that" [*qu'on commence veritablement à aimer après que après que ou au plus tôt au moment où l'amour est déclaré et non plus tôt*].[14]

Strange to think that love might not come about before it is expressed concisely and in the singular unanimity of those three small monosyllables; that I may not be truly in love until I express it in some way. Only after I say "I love you" am I really in love: "when I tell you my love is it that I am declaring my love to you or indeed that I am telling *you,* yourself, my love, and that you are my love" ("quand je te dis mon amour est-ce que je te déclare mon amour ou bien est-ce que je te dis, toi, mon amour, et que tu es mon amour") (*PC,* 8/13). Saying "I love you" almost merges with the time of its being said in the here and now, *but not quite.* For when does one know that one is in love, or at what moment precisely does one *fall* in love? It is surely the case that one is either already in love or not in love and that the moment

---

14 Quoted in Miller, *Speech Acts in Literature,* 138.

of its enunciation is deferred, altered, perverted in some sense in the crucible of the first fall, a fall that is always already falling. One is therefore thrown into love; *Dasein*-like we find ourselves in love, inventing love, and in loving being already in love, within it. At what moment(s), to put this another way, does one decide, in all the madness of a decision that is not purely a reasoned calculation, that one loves?

"I love you" is a promise that may or may not be kept, which is not to say that one was never in love at all, but that the condition of being in love is that the promise may not be fulfilled and I might say that I am no longer in love. I may have been joking either. I may have said "I love you" and not meant it, which doesn't prevent the other being touched by what I have said. I may have been writing a poem or, indeed, a novel called "Envois." But that does not prevent the power of what I have said from being taken as serious and in that regard as some way felicitous, and therefore from affecting or touching the other: "When I speak to you, I touch you, and you touch me when I hear you, from however far off it comes to me, and even if it is by telephone, the recollection of a voice's inflection on the phone, or by letter or e-mail too."[15] One may be aware that one is reading a fictitious account by Jacques Derrida, and that the speaker is one of many personae, both male and female, a polymorphous polyglot toying with conventions of literary-romantic-philosophical discourse, but that oddly also brings the text out of itself, breathes life into it and challenges the reader to uncover its secrets. Those secrets we are never finished with, those secrets which incite us from their place of hiding to account for the unaccountable, to say outrageous things to the other, about the other.[16] Those secrets that leave us naked — nude before the other, nude together.

---

15 Jacques Derrida, *On Touching—Jean-Luc Nancy,* trans. Christine Irizarry (Stanford: Stanford University Press, 2005), 291.
16 See also Jacques Derrida, *A Taste for the Secret,* trans. Giacomo Donis, eds. Giacomo Donis and David Webb (Cambridge: Polity Press, 2001), 58: "Fundamentally, everything I attempt to do, think, teach and write has its raison d'être, spur, calling and appeal in this secret, which interminably disqualifies any effort one can make to determine it. As I have attempted to show in

Passion

"Without a certain love of the text," says Derrida elsewhere, "no reading would be possible. In every reading there is a *corps-à-corps* between reader and text, an incorporation of the reader's desire into the desire of the text."[17] Derrida's desire is projected onto the postcard he picks up in the Bodleian library, just as the desire of his readers is projected into his texts, just as my desire is projected, yet again, into the strange body of his writing. "Philosophy," as Jean-Luc Nancy puts it, "never arrives at this thinking — that thinking is love."[18] Love never arrives. Full stop. If it did it would mean death, death to the promise of a future to come and a kind of thinking in process, in the process of desire and love. In short — to get to the point — "the destination is death" (*PC,* 33).

It is the secret that impassions, impossibly. It keeps us locked into a contest with the doorkeeper that says thou shalt not, who stands before the law in Kafka's parable, never arriving, prolonging, protracting, and unwinding in an endless *différance.* "The text guards itself, maintains itself — like the law, speaking only of itself, that is to say, of its non-identity with itself. It neither arrives nor lets anyone arrive. It is the law, makes the law and leaves the reader before the law."[19] Each of those doors is only for us. It stands before us in the singular light of an unheard of promise. But it is the love of literature, of its absolute secrecy, if it can be called that, which keeps us coming back. There is something "about" literature, neither wholly intrinsic nor wholly extrinsic; there is something, that is, that is not reducible to the aesthetic,

---

Given Time and in Passions, we never finish with this secret, we are never finished, there is no end."

17 Jacques Derrida, "Deconstruction and the Other," in *Debates in Continental Philosophy: Conversations with Contemporary Thinkers,* ed. Richard Kearney (New York: Fordham University Press, 2004), 156.

18 Jean-Luc Nancy, *The Inoperative Community* (London and Minneapolis: University of Minnesota Press, 1991), 86.

19 Jacques Derrida, "Before the Law," in *Acts of Literature,* ed. Derek Attridge, 181–220 (London: Routledge, 1992), 211.

something surrounding it, something which cannot, will not, be divulged or brought to light which keeps open the possibility of saying more *about* it, something which gives itself to us. The love of the text, of the good reading, is each time unique; one way or another it keeps us going, searching, beyond hope that some other might surprise us. Love of the text is the expectation of surprise. Derrida speaks of his beloved in this way too: "the uniquely each time that I love: beyond everything that is, you are the one — and therefore the other" ("l'uniquement chaque fois que j'aime: au-delà de tout ce qui est, tu es l'un — et donc l'autre") (*PC*, 143/155).

Rilke's words from the *Duino Elegies,* "Ein jeder Engel ist schrecklich," are also fascinating because they too are impassioned responses to the arrival of a letter and its unexpected results. There is a beautiful story surrounding Rilke's writing of these poems.[20] After finishing his much renowned novel *The Notebooks of Nolte Laurids Brigge* in 1910, Rilke experienced a profound spiritual malaise, writing little for a period of two years. An invitation from his wealthy friend, Princess Marie von Thurn und Taxi-Hohenlohe, to spend some months at her castle at Duino on the Adriatic Sea offered Rilke some respite from a nomadic lifestyle taken up after 1910: Rilke had also contemplated giving up poetry at this time and entering the medical profession. Upon receiving a business letter that he had to attend to immediately, Rilke walked out onto the castle's bastions in howling winds, along a narrow path separating cliffs that dropped off some two hundred feet into the sea. At that moment, out of the blue and on the wind, so to speak, came the following words: "Wer, wenn ich schriee, hörte mich denn aus der Engel/ Ordnungen?" ("Who, if I cried out, would hear me among the angels' hierarchies?"). In the same day Rilke completes the following lines:

---

20 The following story is recounted in Stephen Mitchell's preface to Rainer Maria Rilke, *Duino Elegies & The Sonnets to Orpheus,* trans. Stephen Mitchell (New York: Vintage, 2009), xiii–xv.

> Who, if I cried out, would hear me among the angels'
> hierarchies?
> and even if one of them pressed me suddenly against his
> heart:
> I would be consumed in that overwhelming existence.
> For beauty is nothing but the beginning of terror [*Denn das
> Schöne ist nichts als des Schrecklichen Anfang*], which we are
> still just able to endure,
> and we are so awed because it serenely disdains to
> annihilate us.
> Every angel is terrifying [*Ein jeder Engel ist schrecklich*].[21]

The German word "schrecklich" can be multifariously rendered as critics of Rilke's *Duino Elegies* have testified over the years, noting each time just how difficult it is to translate that word into English. Locked within it are some of the following meanings: awful, heinous, terrible, appalling, awesome, monstrous, dreadful, sublime. It is also nightmarish, ghostly and spectral, as in the word "Schreckgespenst." The word makes translation tremble at the crux of a vicious paradox. Rilke's angel is at once both absolutely beautiful and absolutely dreadful. Every other angel is unique and arresting, overwhelmingly terrible and beautiful. Like Yeats's, Rilke's terrible beauty remains secret and exposed; it is an oxymoron veiled and unveiled, translatable and untranslatable; and it is this secrecy that impassions us to say more about it. And when Rilke repeats Derrida's phrase again at the beginning of the "Second Elegy" one is surely no nearer to an explication of what that secret is that so impassions. This is perhaps the "it" that frightens Derrida when he poses the question, is it you I am addressing? It somehow remains impossible to say anything about it and yet its call is for an infinite reading, a unique reading that begins again to read it as if it were

---

21 Ibid., 3.

never read before. "And that's the impossible, that's the poematic experience."[22]

Translating, my love

I said there were two entries from the same day that I wanted to speak of in this brief accounting for "I love you". Here is the second entry, again from the same day — 3 June 1977:

> and you, tell me   I love all my appellations for you and then we would have but one lip, one alone to say everything   from the Hebrew he translates "tongue" [*langue*], if you can call it translating, as lip [*lèvre*]. They wanted to elevate themselves sublimely, in order to impose their lip, the unique lip, on the universe. Babel, the father, giving his name of confusion, multiplied the lips, and this is why we are separated and that right now I am dying, dying to kiss you with our lip [*de t'embrasser de notre lèvre*] the only one I want to hear (*PC*, 9/13).

"Babel" itself names the myth of the origin of translation. Derrida has spoken at length of this in his essay "Des tours de Babel," and again in "No Apocalypse, Not Now," "Ulysses Gramophone," and later on again in *The Post Card* (*PC*, 165/240). In Genesis the people of Shem, sons of Noah, descend on a plain in the land of Shinar after the great flood; all of the earth speaking a single language. In order to "make a name for themselves" they build a tower and a city surrounding the tower. This is the fabled city and tower of Babel designed to reach up to Heaven. God descends from the heavens to scatter the people and their language, to sever their tongues and impose translation on them and forbid it simultaneously. The word "Babel" is translated as a proper name and a common noun, an event, and a

---

22 Jacques Derrida, *Points… Interviews, 1974–1994*, trans. Peggy Kamuf et al., ed. Elisabeth Weber (Stanford: Stanford University Press, 1995), 295.

confusion of tongues; it is a place and a happening, the name of God as confusion and impossible translation. The story of Babel is a story then about the (im)possibility of translation and the proper name, a name which is the name of God and the name of the confusion wrought on the people of Shem by that name, the name of their city and their failure to impose their name and language on the universe. Various translations of this story render the Hebrew word for language, through a metonymic shift, as "tongue," whereas others (André Chouraqui) translate it as "lip." Hence the slippage between tongue and lip in the extract cited above.

But what Derrida means by the various multiplications in this extract is not all that easy to grasp. To have one lip means in this context to have one tongue or language, to speak the same language. If, like the people of Shem, Derrida and his love share one universal language — "one alone to say everything" — it would mean the end of translation. There would be no need to interpret what the other said. There is therefore an interesting play in this section between the "I," "you," "me," and "we" which begins right from the beginning with the double syntax of the following phrases: "and you, tell me [*et toi, dis moi*] [...] I love all my appellations for you." Who speaks in this? Who is telling? Is the beloved speaking or one of Derrida's personae? The closer you look at the strange phrasing in this segment the stranger and more complicated it becomes, until we hit upon the marvelous concluding line, "that right now I am dying, dying to kiss you with our lip the only one I want to hear."

In the *Derrida* film mentioned above Derrida responds to Amy Ziering Kofman's question about love firstly by saying: "Why have philosophers always spoken of love? That's how philosophy started —" And then breaks off.

Philosophy started with a kiss. At least this is how it started according to Novalis, who in the final pages of *On Touching — Jean-Luc Nancy* Derrida treats in the following manner: "this may be where 'thinking' begins — when a mouth comes in contact with another mouth and when lips, and sometimes tongue and teeth, get mixed up in it."[23] The mixing and the multiplication of lips is important because it speaks of a certain translation of the you *into* the I, of the multiplication of selves that are always breaking into one another, shattering love, shattering the distinction between bodies and thinking, between mind and body.

Can one kiss another in language? Can one caress the other in the words, touching oneself touching another in the idiom of love? Does speaking in some way kiss the other on the lip? If language is by metonymic transfer a lip, it would follow that our lips could touch in the language of love. In saying "I love you" I kiss you on the lip with my lip. And I want more than anything else to hear you say "I love you" and for you to kiss me on my lip, with your lip, in your tongue. Yes, "I love you" is, in a manner of speaking, a way of kissing the other's lips. Difficult then not to think of *The Post Card* as a work of love, as a first kiss, first and last.

For
when I call you my love, is it that I am calling you, yourself, or is it that I am telling my love?

---

23 Derrida, On Touching, 306. See also J. Hillis Miller's discussion of the kiss in Derrida and Henry James in *Literature as Conduct*, 30–83.

Zach Rivers

Derrida in *Correspondances*:
A Telephonic Umbilicus

For Raminta

*The chthonic ones are not confined to a vanished past.
They are a buzzing, stinging, sucking swarm now, and human beings are not in a separate compost pile.*
— Donna Haraway[1]

*At bottom I am only interested in what cannot be
sent off, cannot be dispatched in any case.*
— Jacques Derrida[2]

*Which side are we on, life or death, reason or madness, in or
out? The question of my life. What if reason were mad?*
— Hélène Cixous[3]

"6 October 1978.   I am writing you
in a taxi. I avoid the subway, here too, precisely because I like it

---

1   Donna Haraway, "Tentacular Thinking: Anthropocene, Capitalocene, Chthulucene," *e-flux journal* 75 (2016), http://www.e-flux.com/journal/75/67125/tentacular-thinking-anthropocene-capitalocene-chthulucene/
2   *PC*, 14–15/19.
3   Hélène Cixous, *Manhattan: Letters from Prehistory*, trans. Beverley Bie Brahic (New York: Fordham University Press, 2007), 32; *Manhattan: Lettres de la préhistoire* (Paris: Éditions Galilée, 2002), 48–49; Emphasis in original.

[*parce que je l'aime*]. And because I get lost [*je m'égare*] in the *correspondances,* although the system is much simpler than in Paris" (*PC,* 166/179). This passage from Jacques Derrida's "Envois" in *The Post Card: From Socrates to Freud and Beyond* in which he writes from a New York City taxi seems relatively mundane. Perhaps it is. Yet, I'd like to linger within this unexceptionable scene for the paths it might already be leading us down. Derrida's avoidance of the subway precisely because he loves it (*parce que je l'aime*) betrays a logic of pleasure deferral as well as something of the postal principle: "relays, delay, anticipation, destination, telecommunicating network, and therefore the fatal necessity of going astray, etc." (*PC,* 66/74). The taxi allows Derrida to minimize the spatio-temporal[4] catastrophe of destinerrance programmed by the postal principles that might lead him astray in the sprawling subway correspondances. There is something else, too, that draws me to this passage: something to do with dancing underground beneath the city, with sexual difference in politics (and the politics of sexual difference), with telephones, umbilical cords, and navels. Here it is pirouetting off the page: due to an astonishing line break in the English translation, *correspondances* becomes *correspon-dances*.[5] I follow (*je*

---

4   For a detailed discussion of *destinerrance* within Derrida's corpus see J. Hillis Miller, "Derrida's Destinerrance," *Modern Language Notes* 121, no. 4 (2006): 893–910. There, Miller characterizes *destinerrance* as that "fatal possibility of erring by not reaching a predefined temporal goal in terms of wandering away from a predefined spatial goal" (894). Moreover, this paper embraces the stylistic *destinerrance* that performatively manifests in Derrida's writing of which Miller writes that, no matter how "hard he tries to stick to the point, he is destined to wander" (900).

5   *Correspondances* denotes transportation transfer points in French, close proximity or connection in English, and various forms of communication in both languages such as the similitude of correspondence(s) and the distance(s) spanned through correspondence. I read the hyphen in *correspond-dances* as a ciphered telephone line that se-reparates *correspon-dances* in between French and English that textually perform its spatial and temporal dis-connective function (spatial: between French and English, between here, there, and beyond; temporal: between Ancient Greece and the contemporary, and its detours). For a discussion on sé-*réparation* as the interval between separation and reparation, separation as reparation,

suis...) these *correspon-dances* that Derrida lovingly avoids in dancing a movement through flickering subterranean passageways hidden from the light of day.⁶

I'd like to suggest that Derrida's attempt to avoid this pleasurable and fatal destinerrance in the underground subway *correspondances* hooks up with an interred feminine presence emanating from the "Greek World" that threatens to derail or explode everything, including patriarchy, from within the polis's most intimate and foundational of spaces.⁷ Following Derrida's Greek preoccupation in "Envois" fomented by Socrates and

---

and sexual difference see Jacques Derrida, "Ants," trans. Eric Prenowitz, *The Oxford Literary Review* 24, no. 1 (2002): 17–42. I thank Michael O'Rourke opening this path of thought for me, and for his countless generosities.

6 It is important to highlight here two scenes of dancing in Derrida's corpus. Scene one: Early in "Envois," Derrida narrates an exchange on an Oxford college lawn that occurred after giving a seminar. A student, "très beau" and "seductive," asks Derrida why he doesn't kill himself since, in the student's eyes, this would be the gesture par excellence of deconstruction given the thought of death that imbues its movements. Derrida responds with a "pirouette" of deconstruction that demonstrates the interlocutor's being-seduced by death at the time of questioning as well asserting that Derrida perhaps has committed suicide, otherwise, multiple times (*PC*, 15/19). Scene two: found in Jacques Derrida and Christie V. McDonald, "Choreographies," *Diacritics* 12, no. 2 (1982): 66–76. Beginning with a discussion of Emma Goldman's statement, "If I can't dance I don't want to be part of your revolution," Derrida reflects on the need to displace questions of woman from a topological matrix that so often assigns place. Rather, Derrida calls for a questioning of this place, which would be urge the questioning of the "(entire history of the West and of its metaphysics) and that it dance otherwise" (69). Learning to dance otherwise helps to guide the aims of this paper that seeks to "invent incalculable choreographies" and "unheard of and incalculable sexual differences" through demystifying the surreptitious operations of phallogocentrism (68, 76).

7 Derrida's *Of Hospitality* inspires this paper as much as *The Post Card* in its interrogation of the inheritances bequeathed to us by the "Greek World" that insists on the necessity to "to multiply the two-way journeys, a to-and-fro between the matters of urgency that assail us at the end-of-millennium, and the tradition from which we receive the concepts [*la tradition dont nous recevons les concepts*], the vocabulary, the axioms that are elementary and presumed natural or untouchable" (Jacques Derrida, *Of Hospitality: Anne Dufourmantelle invites Jacques Derrida to Respond,* trans. Rachel Bowlby [(Stanford: Stanford University Press, 2000], 45; *De l;'hospitalité: Anne Du-*

Plato's postal library apocalypse that launches his discussions of destiny (*Geschick*) and destination, sending (*schicken*), history (*Geschichte*), identity, filiation, the secret, address(ees), temporality, reproduction, substitution, reversibility, dissemination, cinders, and writing, I'd like to pursue a similar line of ancient Greek thought that will eventually bring us to two scenes of an effaced feminine presence in Aeschylus's *Eumenides,* that triumphant tragedy that depicts Athens' juridico-political foundation and the ascension of the Olympian gods through the absorptive abjuration of more ancient feminine spaces and deities.[8] Cards on the table: I view the subway *correspondances* that Derrida loves yet avoids as ciphered feminine spaces under a phallic metropolis (*mētēr*-polis, mother-city) weaving hidden, vital communicatory lines in which the Erinyes, Gaia, and the Python offer their interference.[9] As an effect of relay and delay, this paper makes a dancing gesture — perhaps a clumsy leap at first glance — attended by Derrida's pirouetting along and away from the *correspondances'* subterranean shores that bear, from afar, an intimacy with an effaced maternal space of the all too quickly named "'Greek World' (to presuppose provisionally its unity or self-identity)" (*H*, 45/45).

What ancient investments that continue to compound interest can be discerned in listening to the ciphered calls of these *correspond-dances, khōraspondances,*[10] *cœurespondances* cease-

---

    fourmantelle invite Jacques Derrida à répondre [Paris: Calmann-Lévy, 1997], 45. Henceforth, *H*).

8 Aeschylus, "Eumenides," in *Aeschylus: Oresteia — Agamemnon, Libation-Bearers, Eumenides*, trans. Alan H. Sommerstein, 353–485. (Cambridge: Harvard University Press, 2008).

9 In order to connect these lines that are often covered over, deadened, and disavowed, I take the call from Derrida's *Monolingualism of the Other* that marks the necessity to hyperbolize, exaggerate — "everything that proceeds under the name of 'deconstruction' arises from it [hyperbolism]." (Jacques Derrida, *Monolingualism of the Other; or, The Prosthesis of Origin*, trans. Patrick Menash [Stanford: Stanford University Press, 1998], 49; *Le monolingualisme de l'autre, ou la prothèse d'origine* [Paris: Galilée, 1996], 82 Henceforth, *M*).

10 Texts from Derrida's whole oeuvre address *khōra*, a figure appearing in Plato's *Timaeus* that exists outside of the Platonic intelligible/sensible dyad

lessly traveling beneath Derrida's taxicab? What connections and separations can be discerned in these dark *correspon-dances* that Derrida loves but avoids? Crucially, what can be gleaned about the anxious motivations of masculine fantasy in its unceasing, almost obsessive production of accounts that denigrate the feminine? How do such denigrating assumptions surreptitiously persist in contemporary language, labor, and geopolitics? Specifically in the context of Derrida's reading of Plato in *The Post Card*, what inheritances, locations, and temporalities converge, diverge, and unfold before us in these *correspondances* where Derrida gets lost?

In order to traverse this admittedly dis-connected jump regarding the gendered link between the New York City subway and Ancient Tragedy, we'll navigate through a multitude of disconnective subterranean *correspondances* that seemingly transport us in different directions. This chapter emphasizes the contemporaneity of Ancient Greek attitudes toward the intertwined various embodiments of (and structural positions assigned according to) sexual difference, race, class, ethnicity, ability, and citizenship. Moreover, studying the banished and threatening

---

yet within the sexual dyad of male/female, which allows Plato to famously name *khōra* as receptacle of all becoming [*geneseōs hupodokhēn*], wetnurse [*tithēnēn*], and mother [*mētri*]. *Khōra* gives rise to and receives the entirety of the perceptible world: "[it] receives all things [*pandekhes*] and shares in a most perplexing way in what is intelligible [*metalambanon de aporōtata pē tou noētou*]" (51b). *Khōra* thus "exists," Derrida claims in "Faith and Knowledge," "Before and after the logos which was in the beginning," thus requiring us to think its abstraction without any temporal or ousiological assurance. Moreover, as Derrida argues in "*Khōra*," we can only ever know its structure through *mise en abyme* that will always have preceded and exceed a philosophical, logocentric search for origins. Plato's feminizing and maternalizing assignations of *khōra* whisper everywhere throughout this paper's discussion of the postal principle. See Plato, *Timaeus*, in *Complete Works*, ed. John M. Cooper, 1225–91 (Indianapolis: Hackett, 1997); Jacques Derrida, "Faith and Knowledge: The Two Sources of "Religion" At the Limits of Reason Alone," in *Acts of Religion*, ed. Gil Anidjar, trans. Samuel Weber, 40–101 (New York: Routledge, 2002), 60; Jacques Derrida, "*Khōra*," in *On the Name*, trans. Ian McLeod, 89–127 (Stanford: Stanford University Press, 1995), 104.

feminine elements of the polis necessarily discusses the operations of masculinity (fragile and threatened, thus all the more violent) that sanctions and unceasingly inflicts gendered, sexualized, and racialized violence. I hope to make a small step toward transforming these long-standing arrangements. First, we'll look to the interweaving of the postal principle with a telephonic principle and its relation to a masculine mastery of the household in *Of Hospitality*. Next, we'll observe the masculine State's ear held up to the telephone receiver in *The Ear of the Other* and *Monolingualism of the Other*, which both figure the telephone as a maddened umbilical cord mediating between life and death. Finally, we'll channel effaced maternal spaces in Aeschylus's *Eumenides* to argue that the palimpsestic layering of masculine over feminine spaces via continued usurpation and burial instills an anxiety of the mutinous possibility of the banished femininity that lurks under the polis's political and religious spaces. Eventually we will come to the telephonic umbilical cord of a disavowed and effaced maternal current flowing throughout these umbilical telephonic network *correspondances* of the underground. We are never far from Derrida's becoming lost in the *correspondances,* of an originary errancy of these underground labyrinths that Derrida's work performs and traverses. He cannot get over it. He must follow it is as it haunts him.

In each step, this paper traces a specific operation through which the masculine nourishes itself through incorporating the feminine — and the anxious desire that propels this process — to only then immediately cover its tracks to deny such intermingling. For all attempts are made to make this appear like business as usual, as if it was always already this way. If, according to Nicole Loraux, Ancient Greek masculinity erects itself through "incorporation and encirclement [of the feminine] — in short, they pertain to logics of inclusion," then the feminine is made to work in the service of the masculine and threatens the masculine due to its blurry proximity.[11] In a similar register, Ann

---

11 Nicole Loraux, *The Experiences of Tiresias: The Feminine and the Greek Man*, trans. Paula Wissing (Princeton: Princeton University Press, 1995), 9; *Les*

Bergren claims that the "appropriation by the male of what he attributes to the female persists throughout Greek literature," which, as displayed by the various instances of masculine appropriations of the feminine discussed in this essay, suggests an inheritance that persists in the contemporary language, philosophy, and human relationality.[12] Damningly, this very process of incorporation programs a haunting remainder and anxiety for the masculine that possess these repudiated feminine elements. I follow Loraux's counsel to not impose a clear binary between the feminine and masculine, in Ancient Greece or otherwise, but rather to tarry with thick complexities and avoid merely recapitulating "a table of antithetical categories again and again."[13] Things are not so simple as (Greek) men vs. (Greek) women or masculinity vs. femininity, but rather, any relation between the sexes implies a certain imbrication and exchange. Still among the many others by which the man defines himself, this paper wagers that it is the feminine operator *par excellence* who constitutes the otherness by which masculine identity can erect itself.[14] Emanuela Bianchi describes the feminine in the Ancient Greek imaginary as "always [signifying] the scene of a certain adulteration," thus implying an impurity evading its assigned proper place in a system obsessed by the white purity of the masculine logos.[15] In the course of this chapter, we'll come to see that there is no pure masculine, no pure *andreia*, left untouched by the always-already impure feminine that the masculine must incorporate in order to be itself. But the Greek male does not know this feminine, *kalon kakon* (beautiful evil), that consist-

---

    Expériences de Tirésias: Le féminin et l'homme grec (Paris: Éditions Gallimard, 1989), 15.

12 Ann Bergren, *Weaving Truth: Essays on Language and the Female in Greek Thought* (Cambridge: Harvard University Press, 2008), 15.

13 Nicole Loraux, *The Children of Athena: Athenian Ideas about Citizenship and the Division Between the Sexes*, trans. Caroline Levine (Princeton: Princeton University Press, 1993), 4; *Les enfants d'Athéna: Idées athéniennes sur la citoyenneté et la division des sexes* (Paris: François Maspero, 1981), 8.

14 Loraux, *The Experiences of Tiresias*, 4/8.

15 Emanuela Bianchi, *The Feminine Symptom: Aleatory Matter in the Aristotelian Cosmos* (New York: Fordham University Press, 2014), 11.

ently evades logos all while occupying the disavowed other at its core.[16] And this is the maddening threat that never ceases.

It is important to be clear that I do not wish to assign an ontology, essence, or identity through employing the term "feminine" or "masculine" in the following discussion that pursues an effaced feminine presence. Ever aware of essentialism's odious deeds, my discussions of "feminine" and "masculine" rupture with "female" and "male" in order to highlight how such heterosexist understandings of embodiment and experience have limited and continue to limit our understanding of what a body is, what it can do, what it can feel, and how we talk about them. Thus, I employ the term "feminine" catachrestically.[17] In this sense, the feminine does not have any proper referent within phallogocentrism, but rather names something that exceeds, interrupts, and jams the logocentric discourse that attempts to define it. This understanding emerges from thinkers like Hélène Cixous and Luce Irigaray who each, differently, affirm difference between sexes, genders, races, nationalities, and class in order to displace the overdetermined social, cultural, and political field usurped by a "neutral" (i.e., white, western European or North American, heterosexist, patriarchal, masculine) subject that has historically murdered, exploited, excluded, and/or assimilated alterity. Importantly, sexual difference is not reducible or limited to one's embodiment, which in normative accounts comes down to having- or not-having-a-penis: "sexual difference is

---

16 Hesiod, *Theogony*, 585.
17 My thought here is grateful to Gabriela Basterra who, in discussing ethical subjectivity as unending substitution for the other, defines catachresis as something that, "substitutes itself for an absence it names [...] something that eludes representation." Moreover, Judith Butler describes Irigaray's understanding of the feminine as a "[figure] that function[s] improperly [...] the use of a proper name to describe that which does not properly belong to it, and that return to haunt and coopt the very language from which the feminine is excluded" (Gabriela Basterra, *The Subject of Freedom: Kant, Levinas* [New York: Fordham University Press, 2015], 121; Judith Butler, *Bodies the Matter: On the Discursive Limits of "Sex"* [New York: Routledge, 1993], 37).

not determined simply by the fantasized relation to anatomy."[18] Through my readings of Irigaray and Cixous, I argue that feminisms of sexual difference work to enact a world that will no longer rely on violent polarization and valorization of the selfsame/one but rather generate endless proliferation of embodied differences beyond any binarism.[19]

Finally, I do not wish to scrawl yet another text in the long history of men writing about women. These typing hands — connected with the assemblages of matter, experiences, and environments — that I look at with mistrust for their histories of violence and privilege quiver with desire to enact otherwise histories and futures of experience that can finally ring through when, in the words of Hélène Cixous, the "living structures" bound to "historicocultural limits" are displaced from an enforced masculine primacy.[20] As a person who expresses myself as a male and who lives a much more wandering gender identity, this paper acts as an affirmation of the constitutive feminine voices that too weave the multiple contradictions that are "me."

Tele-postal Hospitality: The Home, the State, and the Penetrable Masculine

The Post Card interweaves the postal principle with a telephonic principle through their shared "differantial relay [*relais différantiel*]" that immediately pluralizes any being or foundation all while structurally necessitating the possibility of going astray, becoming lost, and of never arriving (*PC*, 54/61). Derrida playfully grants to the post an originary principle, or rather, "a non-

---

18 Hélène Cixous, "Sorties: Out and Out: Attacks/Ways Out/Forays," in *The Newly Born Woman,* trans. Betsy Wing, 63–132 (Minneapolis: University of Minnesota Press, 1986), 82; "Sorties," in *La jeune née,* 114–246 (Paris: Union Générale D'éditions, 1975), 151.

19 Irigaray too affirms that both the feminine and masculine are "unfinished and open," which allows for future significations and embodiments that would be otherwise than their present conceptions (Luce Irigaray, *An Ethics of Sexual Difference,* trans. Catherine Porter and Gillian C. Gill [Ithaca: Cornell University Press, 1993], 112).

20 Cixous, "Sorties," 83/152.

origin which is originary"[21] that displaces the possibility of any teleology or *arkhē*:

> In the beginning [*Au commencement*], in principle, was the post, and I will never get over it [*je ne m'en conselerai jamais*]. But in the end I know it, I become aware of it as our death sentence [*notre arrêt de mort*]: it was composed, according to all the possible codes and genres and languages, as a declaration of love. In the beginning the post, John will say, or Shaun or Tristan, and it begins with a destination without address, the direction cannot be situated in the end… The condition for it to arrive is that it ends up and even that it begins by not arriving. (*PC*, 29/34)

This formulaic characterization substitutes the Biblical *logos* of John 1:1, "In the beginning [*en arkhēi*] was the Word [*logos*], and the Word [*logos*] was with God [*theon*], and the Word [*logos*] was God [*theos*]," with *la poste* that is always already a télé-post presupposing a relation with distance, non-presence, and alterity. Later in "Envois," Derrida writes that this reformulation is merely "for laughs" in that the postal principal *precedes, exceeds, constitutes,* and provides the medium for the very possibility of logos, and therefore the possibility of chronology (*PC*, 66/73). The inscribed signs and the postcard itself that materially supports the postal principle "must bear within itself a force and a structure" that enforces the impossibility for it to arrive at its destination in that even its very scene of arrival is one of evasion, arriving in multiple registers "elsewhere, several times," to the multitudes within the addressee, composed of the traces, spaces, and play of the letters on the card (*PC*, 123/135). It is this force and structure, Derrida explains, that enables the very possibility not only of language, but being itself: "as soon as there is, there is *différance* [*dès qu'il y a, il y a différance*] (and this does not await language, especially human language, and the

---

[21] Jacques Derrida, "Freud and the Scene of Writing," in *Writing and Difference*, trans. Alan Bass, 246–91. (London: Routledge, 2005), 255.

language of Being, only the mark and the divisible trait)" (*PC*, 66/74). For any "foundation" of being or origin is constituted by *différance*, that is postal delay, relay, spacing, parasites, and the structural possibility of going astray.

Telephonic logic of differantial spacing flourishes in the Derrida's works that consistently demonstrates how the self is continually initiated and coming from the elsewheres of others.[22] In other writings, Derrida playfully grafts a telephonic principle to this "originary" postal principle that confounds the possibility of origin — or rather institutes multiple origins forever existing spatio-temporally elsewhere. In *H.C. for Life, That Is to Say...* Derrida echoes the above scene of logocentrism's birth: "In the beginning, there will have been the invention of the telephone [...], the unique infinity of a telephone line."[23] Similarly, "Ulysses Gramophone" asserts that, "Before the act or the word, the telephone. In the beginning was the telephone. We can hear the telephone constantly ringing, this *coup de téléphone* [...]. In the beginning, yes, at the beginning of the telephone call, in the beginning, some telephone call [*au commencement du coup de téléphone*]."[24] The differences here between *was* and *there will have been* multiplies the telephonic links of past to future in a destinerrant scene thrown askew by such *correspondances* that link the post to the telephone. This postal principle of *The Post Card*, likened to getting lost in the indeterminate spaces of the *correspondances'* transfer and movement, informs a télé-logic that pluralizes, spaces, and interweaves alterity with all language and being.[25]

---

22 I follow Avital Ronell's description from *The Telephone Book* that "telephonic logic means here, as everywhere, that contact with the Other has been disrupted; but it also means that the break is never absolute." (Avital Ronell, *The Telephone Book: Psychoanalysis, Schizophrenia, Electric Speech* [Lincoln: University of Nebraska Press, 1989], 20).

23 Jacques Derrida, *H.C. for Life, That Is to Say...*, trans. Laurent Milesi and Stefan Herbrechter (Stanford: Stanford University Press, 2006), 17.

24 Jacques Derrida, "Ulysses Gramophone: Hear Say Yes In Joyce," in *Acts of Literature*, ed. Derek Attridge, 253–309 (Routledge: New York, 1991), 270.

25 In *Of Hospitality*, Derrida designates language as the most "mobile of telephones" that we bear [*tragen*] with us as "the absolute ground of all dis-

These ciphered textual *correspondances* simultaneously bear the promise of connection and threat of abyssal severance as it bespeaks distance and heterogeneity. Regarding this primary role the other plays for the self, Avital Ronell claims that, "Telephonics imposes the recognition of a certain irreducible precedence of the Other with respect to self. […] [T]his is what makes it uncanny, the inside calling from an internal outside."[26] The telephonic could be spoken of as the literalization of our intimacy with distance and alterity via a telephonic mourning in which we become receiver for the voice and words of the animating other(s) within us. In "Envois," Derrida coins the term *teleorgasmization* [*télé-orgasmisation*] — the self-shattering, ecstatic, non-boundary dancing between pain and pleasure borne by the veils of the "technoteleothingamajig [*technotéléomachinchouette*]" through which Derrida sends off his language from a place of no return (*PC,* 108, 155/119, 168). This telephonics bespeaks language's, subjectivity's, and Being's abyssal, originary trauma of destinerrance that fractures logos's dream of autofoundation.

Drawing on the télé-postal principle, we must follow another detour that has unfurled beneath us to some of Derrida's writing on the masculinity of hospitality. *Of Hospitality* parses a telephonic connection that transports the Greek world into our most private spaces through inheriting its words, concepts, assumptions, and truisms presumed to be "natural or untouchable" such as hospitality, the foreigner, the home, and the private/public distinction (*H,* 91/85). Such haunting inheritances of the Ancient world too concern *The Post Card* as Derrida chides Socrates and Plato: "They are dead, those two dogs, and yet they step up to the cashier, they reinvest, they extend their empire with an arrogance they will never be pardoned for. […] [T]heir phantom comes back [*leur fantôme revient*] at night to do the accounts, in their name" (*PC,* 98/108). Of these capital

---

placements" on which we travel our palintropic path in search for an origin that only results in finding a prosthesis" (*H,* 91/85).
26 Ronell, *The Telephone Book,* 82.

returns still circulating between the present and past, in *Of Hospitality* Derrida discusses Sophocles' *Antigone*, which depicts that the bounded patriarchal household forms the paradoxical ground to offer hospitality. Bringing this ancient scene to the present, Derrida leads us to question how the state interrupts the phantasmatic distinctions between *polis* and *oikos*, public and private, and *xenos* and citizen that subtend the master's ipsocratic household propriety, which provide the paradoxical ground from which to offer hospitality. Is there a gendering at work — circuitously relayed between past to present — in the state's telephonic incursion into the *oikos*? (Many pages should be devoted to this topic in relation to the current refugee crisis and the various state and ideological actors that simultaneously foment and ignore this massive humanitarian catastrophe.)

The image of the home provides Derrida the means to explicate the other's — more specifically, the foreign other — centrality for subjectivity: "We thus enter from the inside: the master of the house [...] comes to enter his home through the guest — who comes from outside" (*H*, 125/111).[27] Telephony links subjectivity to (household) mastery through its structure that requires an other to call up and create the master's phantasmatic position of self-sufficient propriety. Yet the master's *chez-soi* and domestic propriety is instituted and deconstituted by the structuring telephonic principle that transports the other's (non)presence to the very core of subjectivity.

Of Hospitality specifically turns toward the collusion between the state, the home, and juridical hospitality (all to be understood as *masculine*) to discuss how the sovereign, home-possessing subject can only be *himself* (for the master is always a he) after he picks up the call of the other through his living room telephone that the State might be listening in on:

---

[27] Moreover, in *Monolingualism of the Other*, Derrida recalls this strain of thought: "We only ever speak one language, [...] it exists asymmetrically, always for the other [...]. Coming from the other, remaining with the other, and returning to the other [*Venue de l'autre, restée à l'autre, à l'autre revenue*]" (*M*, 40/70).

> Now if my "home," in principle inviolable, is also constituted, and in a more and more essential, interior way, by my phone line, but also by my e-mail, but also by my fax, but also by my access to the internet, then the intervention of the State becomes a violation of the inviolable [*un viol de l'inviolable*], in the place where inviolable immunity remains the condition of hospitality. (*H*, 51/49–51)

Derrida's assignation of the telephone's centrality within the home also emphasizes that for the *master* to accept another, he must give up that mastery and lay bare that mastery has structurally always relied on the coming other. There is no ipseity, no sovereignty, no internal familial space, and thus no hospitality without a pervertability and impurity initiated by the guest who can always become parasitic host.

Rogues further highlights the entrenched masculinism subtending these claims to hospitality, autonomy, or the *propre* in that the "autonomy of the self, of the ipse, namely, of the one-self that gives itself its own law," always presupposes a "father, husband, son, or brother, the proprietory, owner, or seignior, indeed the sovereign" as a ground from which to welcome the other.[28] One must position oneself as a masculine proprietor — indissociable from claims of sovereignty — who lays claim to a space from which to offer hospitality to the coming other. Moreover, hospitality's masculine, paternal foundations are shaken by the threat of a (state) surveillance through the home-constituting telephone line by which the other *and* the surveilling state both enter. Here we hear echoes of the "Envois" and the possibility of one's letter to be intercepted and read by prying eyes (multiple addressees without anyone know it), the naked and exposed postcard being particularly vulnerable: "With the progress of the post the State police has always gained ground" (*PC*, 37/43).

Derrida — who is always on the phone — wishes to portray the impure presence of télé-postal parasites (*static* is one mean-

---

28 Jacques Derrida, *Rogues: Two Essays on Reason*, trans. Pascale-Anne Brault and Michael Naas (Stanford: Stanford University Press, 2005), 10–11, 12.

ing of *parasites* in French) within the foundation of any subjectivity or polity. Rather than being accidental or secondary, Derrida displays parasitism as constitutive for the self. Returning to the "filtered" purity of the telephone, Derrida writes that,

> it is a bit in this element that I imagine the return of revenants [*le retour des revenants*], by means of the effect or the grace of a subtle and sublime, essential, sorting — of parasites [*entre les parasites*], for there is nothing but parasites, as you well know [...]. Now, parasites, here it is, can love each other [*peuvent s'aimer*]. (*PC*, 10–11/15)

Similar to the openness of the postcard's reversible faces, Derrida demonstrates that a network of parasites always populates the two-way openness of the telephone line. The telephone line's violability becomes a pressing issue in that it imbues any self or home with a radical instability coming from the other. This death sentence writ by parasitism for the self-sufficient aspirations of subjectivity, propriety, and hospitality paradoxically provides the ground upon which they stand. Such télé-postal pervertability, which in other texts of Derrida might be called auto-immunity, arises from a structure that maintains "a threat within the promise itself," which structurally maintains an opening to alterity that thus harbors the risk of the self's destruction.[29] No ipseity without an open telephonic connection to alterity, no *chez-soi* without a telephone cord to the outside, no internal hearth to offer hospitality without an other to fill its space. No males without a repressed femininity.

Speaking of such contemporary parasitic hauntings and *revenants* that telephonically accrue interest from Ancient Greek accounts, we must make a stopover in the early nineteenth century, to tarry with Hegel, an interlocutor *Of Hospitality,* and his discussions of Ancient Greece's household incursions. For it is in Hegel's characterization that we slowly approach an interred feminine presence keeping threatening watch over both the *oikos*

---

29 Derrida, "Faith and Knowledge," 82.

and *polis*. Keeping in mind Derrida's writings on the masculine propriety that gives rise to a *chez-soi*, Hegel's *Phenomenology of Spirit* transmits a gendering at work in the State's relation to domestic space within the Greek World.[30] Hegel shapes Sophocles' *Antigone* into a paradigmatic example for his philosophical system in which Antigone (in her familial devotion) embodies the Universal while Creon (in his devotion to the *polis*) embodies the Particular.[31] Hegel identifies this feminine, familial, and divine law with the lower world or underground [*unterirdisches Recht*] and a masculine, statist, and human law with the upper world [*oberes Recht*]: "divine and human law, or the law of the nether and of the upper world — the one the Family, the other the State power, the first being the feminine and the second the masculine character."[32] This feminine character forms the inner feeling [*innerliches Gefühl*] confined to the household, "which is not exposed to the daylight of consciousness," while the masculine is drawn outwards into the polity's bright actuality.[33]

---

30 G.W.F. Hegel, *Phenomenology of Spirit*, trans. A.V. Miller (Oxford: Oxford University Press, 1977); G.W.F. Hegel, *Phänomenologie des Geistes* (Frankfurt am Main: Suhrkamp, 1970).
31 This distinction is well document by many critics, including many included in this paper: see Cixous "Sorties"; Irigaray "Eternal Irony." Tina Chanter cautions that such works "even in their attempts to distance themselves from [Hegel's] legacy, are still beholden to a framework that privileges Hegel" (*Whose Antigone? The Tragic Modernization of Slavery* [Albany: State University of New York Press, 2011], xii). While sympathetic to such work, Chanter looks at the colonial aspects of *Antigone* to reveal the colonial configuration of Antigone's claim for her brother. Chanter argues that Anitgone's royal position founded upon a slave economy drives many of her claims in that her defense of Polynices is largely propelled so as to differentiate Polynice's body from a slave's body as mediated through burial rites.
32 Hegel, *Phenomenology of Spirit*, 445/536.
33 Ibid., 274/336–37. Perhaps in reference to the above passage, Cixous writes, "she is in the shadow [*elle est dans l'ombre*]. In the shadow he throws on her; the shadow she is." *L'ombre* is close to being polyphonous with *l'homme*, thus mimicking the incorporating gesture Cixous identifies of the masculine's relation to the feminine. She is in the man/*ombre* which also highlights the inversion of human generation that gives the power of creating life to the male so rampant in the history of philosophy ("Sorties," 67/123).

Hegel's words portray what Hélène Cixous delineates as the empire of the Selfsame [*L'Empire du Propre*], which describes a masculine economy that values return, unity, self-possession, and a desire to assimilate (foreign and threatening) otherness at the sake of the feminine.[34] The empire of the Selfsame in Hegel's schematization of a masculine worldview systematically suppresses the feminine within the household and elevates the masculine out of the household in a movement that goes "out into the other *in* order *to come back to itself*" through the appropriation of alterity.[35] Luce Irigaray similarly describes the gendered relations espoused by Hegel's logic: "The male one copulates the other so as to draw new strength from her, a new form, whereas the other sinks further and further into a ground that harbors a substance which expends itself without the mark of any individuation."[36] Cixous and Irigaray's contributions signal the movements of appropriation, suppression, and burial that will preoccupy this paper's final pages.

Hegel writes that the feminine is bound (*geknüpft*, implying to be tied or knotted) to the household divinities through which she receives only partial intuition — or, more perjoratively, *intimation* — of her universal and individual existence. This intuition of individual existence, that is self-consciousness, will never arrive but will remain hidden in shadows. Moreover, woman's desire (as for Hegel it performs an individuating effect) must never leave the walls of the home or even become recognizable to itself: the relation that binds woman to the household does not confer individuality as this is not its "is not the natural [relation] of desire [*natürliche Beziehung der Lust*]."[37] Rather, woman, through her "relations of mother and wife," intuits individuality by merely "seeing it disappear [*das nur sein Verschwinden darin erblickt*]."[38] For woman, individuality is on the horizon, never to see the light of reason's dawning. This statement and sentiment

---

34 Cixous, "Sorties," 78–83, passim/144–53, passim.
35 Ibid., 78/144. Emphasis in original.
36 Irigaray, "Eternal Irony," 223.
37 Hegel, *Phenomenology of Spirit*, 274/337.
38 Ibid., 274/337 (translation modified).

is discussed when Cixous replays the timeless, mythic, and current situation that dictates to women: "There is no place for your desire in our affairs of State."[39]

Finally, we come to a famous scene that forms a *correspondance* between Ancient Greece, *The Phenomenology of Spirit*, and *Of Hospitality*. Here, Hegel nervously discusses — in his heterosexist framework — the feminine enemy to the polity [Gemeinwesens] paradoxically cultivated by the ipsocratic State's intervention into the home:

> Since the community only gets an existence through its interference with the happiness of the Family, and by dissolving [individual] self-consciousness into the universal, it creates for itself in what it suppresses [*unterdrückt*] and what is at the same time essential to it an internal enemy-womankind in general [*Weiblichkeit überhaupt seinen innern Feind*]. Womankind-the everlasting irony [in the life] of the community [*die ewige Ironie des Gemeinwesens*].[40]

Interestingly, the polity creates this eternal enemy itself in that, "it suppresses [*unterdrückt*, closely related to *unterdrückung*, meaning repression] [...] [that] which is at the same time essential to it" in a scene marking the feminine as the mere matter that gives rise to the masculine form that enters the polity: "for she is never anything but the undifferentiated opaqueness of sensible matter, the store (of) substance for the sublation [*Aufhebung*] of self."[41] Regarding Hegel's description of the tenuous space upon which the masculine order maintains itself, Cixous writes, "No matter how submissive and docile she may be in relation to the masculine order, she still remains the threatening possibility of savagery, the unknown quantity in the household whole."[42] The feminine can easily become the excess that can never be

---

39 Cixous, "Sorties," 67/122.
40 Hegel, *Phenomenology of Spirit*, 288/352.
41 Irigaray, "Eternal Irony," 224.
42 Cixous, "Sorties," 91/169.

repressed enough as it is infinitely displaced downward beneath the *polis*. Our task has become more complicated: In addition to the pervertability of the self-constituting phone line linking the home and alterity, the masculine State's intervention into the home at once suppresses the feminine enemy that it also creates. The *unterdrückt* feminine, literally pressed downward, stifled, and withheld in a place of fixity thus forms the necessary and reviled oppositional threat folded within the polity's structure.

Unbearable and Unburiable Madness: The (Living) Feminine, the (Dead) Masculine

In a telephoned interview with Nicholas Royle, Hélène Cixous describes the telephone as a life-line: "for me, it's life itself. It's never death. On the contrary. It's non-death… And it's true — It interrupts death… It's like a huge thread of life."[43] Discussing her daily telephone calls with Derrida, Cixous explains that she could "hear before even the first word was completely uttered, I could captivate, I could catch his mood. His state of mind or soul."[44] The telephone allows their exchanges to become immediately intimate and deep through the *tympanizing* — as Michael O'Rourke terms it in "Telephantasy" — work of the ear, through a "linguistics of breath" and oto-attunement (*oto-* meaning "of the ear").[45] O'Rourke's reparative and innovative line of inquiry reveals Cixous and Derrida's woven telephonic tongues as a collective and dispossessing loss of self that affirms life through an unconditional hospitality, "yes, yes," over their shared telephone lines. We glimpse the telephone's ability to transgress death in that, as O'Rourke claims, "one gets the sense that the telephone allows Derrida and Cixous to cross a line, to talk infinitely, without borders, before and beyond death."[46] Perhaps this telephonic

---

[43] Hélène Cixous and Nicholas Royle, "Hélène Cixous on the Telephone," Interview, 1 hour and 18 minutes, 2011, http://www.sussex.ac.uk/video/schools/english/HeleneCixousOnTheTelephone.mp3, 5:40.
[44] Cixous and Royle, "On the Telephone," 26:00.
[45] Michael O'Rourke, "Telephantasy," unpublished manuscript, 20, 16.
[46] Ibid., 2–3.

interrelation realizes Derrida's dream in *The Post Card* of a ringless telephone call in which, "There would be a warning light or one could even carry it on oneself, near the heart or in the pocket" (*PC*, 87/96).

Derrida and Cixous' life-affirming telephonic coeuresponddances disrupt what Derrida names as their différend in *H.C. for life, That Is to Say...*: "This is why I...who always feel turned towards death, I am not on her side, while she would like to turn everything and make it come round to the side of life."[47] Elsewhere, Cixous playfully upbraids Derrida's claim that, "I am not 'against life,' but neither am I 'for life' like [you, Cixous]," by stating, "You are against death and fiercely for life. But otherwise. Dis/quietedly."[48] To discern the echoes of telephonically mediated feminine life and masculine death, Derrida's "Otobiographies" further brings out the gendering of such telephony through issues of the umbilical cord, the mother tongue, and the ear's role for both.[49]

"Otobiographies" brings us to issues of sexual difference in its parsing of *Ecce Homo*'s first chapter in which Nietzsche identifies with both aspects of his "dual origin": "I am [...] already dead as my father, while as my mother, I am still living and becoming old" (*O*, 15/62). Derrida reads this claim through a sentence from *Ecce Homo*'s preface: "Hear me! For I am such and such [*ich bin der und der*]. Above all, do not mistake me for someone else!" so that *ich bin der und der* affirms that he is both his (dead) father and (living) mother, "the dead (man) the living (feminine) [*le mort la vivante*]" (*O*, 10,17/50,65). Echoing Cixous, Derrida, and O'Rourke's characterization of the telephone

---

47 Derrida, *H.C. for Life*, 36.
48 Hélène Cixous and Jacques Derrida, "From the Word to Life: A Dialogue Between Jacques Derrida and Hélène Cixous," *New Literary History* 37, no. 1 (2005): 1–13, at 7.
49 Jacques Derrida, "Otobiographies: The Teaching of Nietzsche and the Politics of the Proper Name," trans. Avital Ronell, in *The Ear of the Other*, 1–38 (Lincoln: The University of Nebraska Press, 1988); *Otobiographies : L'enseignement de Nietzsche et la politique du nom propre* (Paris: Editions Galilée, 1984). Henceforth, *O*.

line, le mort la vivante, the dead father and the living mother, carries Nietzsche "one foot beyond [*au-delà*] life" to surpass any duality of life and death, feminine and masculine (*O*, 19/69). Importantly, this discussion of the masculine and feminine develops through issues of the paternal state telephoning through a maternal umbilical cord.

Following this discussion of *le mort la vivante*, Derrida turns to "On the Future of our Academic Institutions," Nietzsche's abandoned and auto-redacted early lecture series, in which he calls for a renewed German education system that privileges the mother tongue beyond statist thinking that nevertheless was later used to corroborate and buttress Nazism. Indeed, central to Nietzsche's concern in "On the Future..." is the German language's disfiguration by contemporary pedagogic institutions that treat the mother tongue as dead with no future ahead of it. Thus, this treatment of the German language as dead operates in the name of the (dead) father. In order to reanimate this mother tongue and thus *Bildung*, Nietzsche affirms, according to Derrida, some pact of, "the language of the living feminine [*la langue de la vivante*] against death, against the dead [*contre la mort, contre le mort*]" language through which the law is stated (*O*, 21/78). A maternal signature thus directs the always-masculine teacher to respect and protect the feminine language through which the stultifying state must speak.[50] Importantly, Nietzsche elevates the importance of the German language's vivacity *and* radically separates it from any notion of the state, which he calls the "coldest of all the cold monsters" where "the slow suicide of all [*se donnent eux-mêmes la mort*] is called 'life'" (*O*, 34/105–6). The State, for Nietzsche, is on the side of death, to which the living mother tongue can never be absolutely usurped by.

---

50 Towards the end of "Otobiographies," Derrida remarks on the profound absence of woman in the educational institution both envisioned by Nietzsche and the contemporary academic institution: "Yet, even if we were all to give in to the temptation of recognizing ourselves, and even if we could pursue the demonstration as far as possible, it would still be, a century later, all of us men—not all of us women—whom we recognize [*nous tous que nous reconnaîtrions. Je n'ai pas dit toutes*]" (*O*, 38/117–18).

Derrida's explication suggests the pervertable doubleness of Nietzsche's text — as well as all language and meaning — that admonishes the state while also being amenable to a political project beholden to the most violent of nationalisms, Nazism. Derrida takes seriously the fact that the only "teaching institution that ever succeeded in taking as its model the teachings of Nietzsche on teaching will have been a Nazi one" (*O*, 24/84). Following Derrida's observation that both Nietzsche's insistence on the *life* of the mother tongue and Nazism's deforming of this language for the purpose of death, "draw their points of origin and their resources" from something resembling a maternal tongue, I heed the fascistic dangers that maternal idealization can produce (*O*, 29/95). Indeed the nineteenth- and twentieth-century German preoccupation with Ancient Greece is well documented, and the Athenian ideology of autochthony must be read in Nazi Germany's ideology of *Blut und Boden*, blood and soil. This is the maddening pervertability and/of substitution inscribed in Nietzsche's text: language's infinite parasitic pervertability perhaps arises from its errant destination and source whose assurances have become buried in interred *correspondances*.

In Derrida's reading of Nietzsche, the dead, paternal state "wants to pass itself off for the mother — that is, for life [*la mère, autrement dit la vie*], the people, the womb of things themselves" (*O*, 34/106). This stultifying simulation performed by the professor connects the student's ear with the dead state through appropriating the living maternal tongue. This pervertability of the mother tongue brings us back to the uncanny ear. Nietzsche describes the dead paternal state's transmission through the professor's words that travel through the student's ear to then be recorded in their notebooks, "very often the student writes as he listens; and it is only at these moments that he hangs by the umbilical cord of the university [*an der Nabelschnur der Universität hängt*, literally meaning hanging on the line]"; Derrida follows up: "Dream this umbilicus [*Rêvez cet ombilic*]: It has you by the ear" (*O*, 35/109). The paternal belly of the state appropriates a maternal role that speaks through a living umbilical cord hooked up to the student's uncanny ear. An oto-umbical cord strings all this along, yet this is an umbilicus that disavows any feminine presence as the masculine state usurps this huge thread of life, as Cixous might say, for death's purposes. Indeed, a woman "never appears at any point along the umbilical cord, either to study or teach" (*O*, 38/118).

In Nietzsche's figuration, the disembodied trace of the appropriated mother's umbilical cord that Derrida describes as *omphalos*—the Greek navel stone marking the center of the world that we will soon discuss at length—strings together the state, professor, and student. In the text's final paragraph, Derrida asserts this oto-umbilical cord operates only on through the effacement of the living feminine mother tongue:

> No woman or trace of woman [*pas de femme*], if I have read correctly—save the mother [*fors la mere, fors* both meaning "except for" as well as "deep inside"] [...]. She gives rise [*Elle donne lieu*] to all the figures by losing herself in the background of the scene like an anonymous persona. Everything comes back to her, beginning with life; everything addresses and destines itself to her [*tout s'addresse à elle et s'y destine*]. She survives on the condition of remaining at bottom [*au fond*]. (*O*, 38/118)

We must attempt to follow this usurped telephonic maternal umbilical cord that addresses and destines every *correspondance* from its subterranean realm from which the masculine law gathers its energy. We're trying here to no longer allow this maternal imprint to remain on bottom, in the subway's *correspondances* due to this paternal appropriation. And we're still on the call with the home, whose state law infiltrates this living life-line with its dead decrees.

Madness haunts this interminable telephonic relation that mediates the line between life and death. This connected-severance, this se-reparative break marked by the *omphalos*'s umbilical traces arrogated by the masculine calls forth Derrida's discussions in *Monolingualism of the Other, or, The Prosthesis of Origin* of the inseparability of the mother tongue — "something like the law or the origin of meaning" — with the always possible becoming-mad that lurks within it (*M*, 88/106). This mother tongue rests on an abyss that provides meaning with a spectral and non-localizable foundation, remaining always to come, postal, as an *arrivant*. Responding to Hannah Arendt's statement that it was Nazism and not the German language that went mad, Derrida asserts a founding madness saturating all language and *logos*: "the mother as the mother tongue, the very experience of absolute uniqueness that can only be replaced because it is irreplaceable, [...] *is madness*" (*M*, 89/107).[51] This madness of the maternal language marks a structure that always differs from itself in that it inscribes the possibility of madness — the "amnesic, aphasic, delirious" — due to its very *inappropriability* (*M*, 87/105).[52] Moreover, (one manifestation of the) madness imbuing and emanating from and of the mother tongue wreaks its havoc precisely when it becomes petrified and locked into meaning — that is the totalitarianism enacted by Nazism and warned of by Nietzsche.

Possibly hinting at the Classical Athenian obsession with paternity and legitimate children that assigned the strictest laws to "safeguard the virginity of unmarried woman and the fidelity of those who were married," Derrida assumes the masculine position that that mother's fidelity can never be certainly known, the moment of conception will never become present.[53] Moreover, in order to become legible, the absolute uniqueness of the mother as mother tongue must be susceptible to the maddening logic of iterability and substitution that divests its uniqueness. The mother as mother tongue at once engenders the spacing and difference necessary for legibility while also exceeding those very constructs. Via language's legibility and repeatability, in the as-

---

51 Emphasis in the original.
52 For further explication of this point on maternal madness see Jennifer Gafney, "Can a Language Go Mad? Arendt, Derrida, and the Political Significance of the Mother Tongue," *Philosophy Today* 59, no. 3 (2015): 523–39.
53 Eva Keuls, *The Reign of the Phallus: Sexual Politics in Ancient Athens* (Berkeley: University of California Press, 1985), 100.

signation of proper names, of producing the illusion of propriety in general, the mother tongue itself is not one: "monolingualism is not at one with itself [*ne fait pas un avec lui-même*]" (*M*, 65/123). The mother, whose absolutely unique language one tries to (and must) translate, veils and veils itself of any assured self-presence of meaning. This maddened law of the mother tongue is at the same time the law and the undoing of law. This mother as mother tongue generates the very bodies that later enter into language and is thus the experience and space that prefigures, bears, and exceeds any sign system. She is unique in that she engenders from a space at once representable and exterior to representation. The mother as the mother tongue arrives, works, and produces in excess of the masculine logos that attempts to speak through it.[54]

Like the telephonic logic that welcomes the other into the subject as the site of its very constitution, this law of language speaks through the dead paternal's belly as a ciphered maternal presence that threatens an always possible becoming-mad at the very core of masculine logos. The state speaks through a prosthetic umbilicus of its own origin — a usurped and incorporated maternal tongue that instills the menacing prospect that it might not comply. Madness haunts paternal logos, the madness of the living feminine mother who provides its matter but only on loan. No one can predict when she will rise again to collect her debt. Dream this umbilicus, it is calling into our ears.

---

54 I am tempted here to summon *khōra* that follows an analogous logic (although a "bastard logic" or a/logic). *Khōra* can only be thought of or approached asymptotically and does not carry the assurances of a paternalistic genealogy. Thus, it is immediately impure, illegitimate, does not carry a certain authorizing patronym to guarantee its logos. In "*Khōra*," Derrida asks, "how is one to think the necessity of that which, while *giving place* to that opposition [of *logos* and *mythos*] as to so many others, seems sometimes to be itself no longer subject to the law of the very thing which it *situates*? What of this *place*? It is nameable? And wouldn't it have some impossible relation to the possibility of naming?" (90–91).

Transmissions from the Omphalos

We have never left the subterranean *correspondances* whose transfers and relays have errantly led us through bugged telephone lines interrupting and constituting masculine mastery, an appropriated umbilical cord, a buried mother, and thus the always possible becoming mad of logos. We are torsionally traveling these *correspondances* of history, imagination, and anxiety to (never) arrive at a maddened and maddening interred place upon which ancient accounts circulate their influence through present day language, embodiment, economy, relationality, and geopolitics. And hardly discernible in the waning light of these abyssal *correspondances,* just before being immersed into subterranean darkness, we perceive the outline of a small stone.

The *correspondances* that we are following lead us to Aeschylus's *Eumenides*. In this play we find a double movement of 1) Apollo expropriating the Delphic temple — the navel, *omphalos,* of the world — founded by Gaia and successively watched over by her two daughters Themis and Phoebe, and 2) the chthonic Erinyes becoming interred under Athens by Apollo and Athena, those children of Zeus. Forgotten yet preserved, the eternal irony of the community are locked away and ciphered in the *omphalos* (the material vestige of the earth's umbilical cord), buried beneath the earth, and enshrouded in murky prehistory all in the blink of an eye.

Eumenides opens at the already Apollonian Delphic Temple where we find that Orestes has just arrived while being maddeningly pursued by the Erinyes for the matricide of Clytemnestra. The Erinyes, or Furies, are chthonic goddesses (ancient deities associated with the earth) of retribution who punish those who break natural law such as committing filial bloodshed. [55]

---

[55] The Chorus of Erinyes described their vocation as "For I have chosen for my own the overturning / of houses: When Violence / turns domestic and destroys a kinsman, / we chase him — oh! —" (ll. 354–57). Aeschylus identifies the Furies as daughters of Night — Who give mortals at birth good and evil to have, /And prosecute transgressions of mortals and gods. / These goddesses never let up their dread anger / Until the sinner has paid a severe

Through reading Aeschylus's description of the Erinyes, one can almost discern the characteristics of the Others so necessary yet excluded by Classical Athens: barbarian, black, earth-bound, elderly virgins, etc. The Erinyes are racially other: "black [*melanai*] and utterly nauseating"; they are non-reproductive and thus undesirable women: "abominable old maidens, these aged virgins [*kataptustoi korai, graiai palaiai paides*], with whom no god holds any intercourse, nor man nor beast either"; they are of subterranean darkness and hate the Olympian gods (thus constructing a temporal and spatial binary between chthonic and Olympian gods): "born for evil, for [*epei*, implying causality] they dwell in the evil darkness, in Tartarus beneath the earth [*chthontos*], and are hateful to men and to the Olympian gods"; they are likened to barbarians (a Greek word denoting otherness in general, Ancient Greek slaves were almost all of "barbarian" descent) through their "un-Greek" actions: "you belong where there are head-chopping, eye-gouging judgements and slaughters, where eunuchs are punished by the destruction of their children's seed."[56]

The history of the Temple at Delphi is one of maternal beginnings — Delphi bears a hazy etymology with the cognates *delphos* and *delphis,* respectively meaning womb and *dolphin* (the -*adelph*- of philadelphia means "of the same womb"). In *Eumenides'* opening lines, the Pythian priestess evokes these maternal currents: "First among gods, in this my prayer, I give pride of place to the first of prophets, Earth [Gaia, implying a prophet-mother]."[57] The prayer depicts a peaceful history of the successive gods that have occupied the Temple, moving from chthonic female lineage later taken over by Apollo, son of Zeus: Gaia, Themis, Phoebe, and finally Phoebus Apollo (also known as

---

penalty" (Aeschylus, *Eumenides*, ll. 219-222). Hesiod's *Theogony* describes the Furies as being born from Earth's generation with the blood from Ouranos' pruned genitals (lines 175-185). In this way, the Furies are spawned from a paternal castration. See Hesiod, *Theogony*, in *Works and Days, and Theogony*, trans. Stanley Lombardo, 61-90. (Indianapolis: Hackett, 1993).

56 Aeschylus, *Eumenides*, l. 51; ll. 67-70; ll. 71-73; ll. 186-88.
57 Ibid., ll. 1-2.

Loxias), who is the "spokesman of his father Zeus."[58] Nicole Loraux acerbically writes how this teleological story enacts an assimilation and displacement of these feminine deities by Apollo that relegate them to the primordial past: in "his magnanimity Apollo exalted the powers of ancient Gaia at the very instant he absorbed them. Without any violence. Utterly naturally."[59] However, the Homeric Hymn to Apollo sharply contrasts with Aeschylus's description of Apollo's felicitous genealogical ascension. According to this hymn, the area where Phoebus Apollo built his temple was guarded by the Python and her double Typhaon, elsewhere described by Hesiod as, "a plague to men."[60] The Hymn describes Apollo killing the Python with an arrow and boasting as the Python becomes one (again) with the nourishing Earth:

> "Now rot [*putheu*, imperative form] on the soil that feeds man [...]." Thus said Phoebus, exulting over her: and darkness covered her eyes. And the holy strength of Helios made her rot away there; wherefore the place is now called Pytho, and men call the lord Apollo by another name, Pythian; because on that spot the power of piercing Helios made the monster rot away.[61]

When we take into account the etymology for Python (*puthein* meaning to rot) and the belief that the Temple at Delphi houses the world's navel, then this rotting serpent begins to look very much like a feminine, chthonic umbilical chord shriveling in the masculine, light of heavenly Helios. The whole of *Eumenides* could be described as choreographing this gen(d)erational dispute between the chthonic and Olympian gods and the simultaneous assimilation and repudiation of the by which the

---

58 Ibid., l. 19.
59 Loraux, *The Experiences of Tiresias*, 185/221.
60 "Homeric Hymn to Apollo," in Hesiod, *Homeric Hymns, Epic Cycle, Homerica*, trans. Hugh Evelyn-White, 324–61 (Cambridge: Harvard University Press, 1914), l. 352.
61 "Homeric Hymn to Apollo," ll. 362–74.

Olympians silenced (or naturalized) of this violent overtaking of the chthonic. Or as the Erinyes explain the situation: Apollo is "a thief, a youth riding roughshod over ancient divinities."[62]

Following the play's opening prayer, the Pythian priestesses describes her entrance to the temple where she encounters sleeping Erinyes and the suppliant Orestes: "I am on my way to the inner shrine richly hung with wreaths, and there I see a man sitting at the navel stone [*omphalos*] [...], a man polluted in the eyes of the gods."[63] The *omphalos*, the navel of the earth, which once connected the earth to the womb of Chaos can be read as the traumatic split between earth and sky, mother and child, the forever lost plenitude of the One. Next, Orestes flees the temple towards Athens at Apollo's suggestion and the freshly woken Erinyes lament, "the navel of the earth has acquired for its own a horrible blood-pollution."[64] Irigaray alludes to this scene with, "the phallus becomes the very organizer of the world through the man-father at the very place where the umbilical cord, that primal link to the mother, once gave birth to man and woman."[65] Thus, we have a scene in which the cursed matricide Orestes asks for supplication at the *omphalos*, the Earth's navel, within Gaia's ancient temple named after the rotting umbilical-cord-like Python. Orestes thus continues his stain of maternal defilement by a perverse inversion of birth: The blood soaking the umbilical cord is no longer the blood spilled in childbirth from the once nourishing cord that connected Orestes to his mother, but the blood is that of the murdered mother dripping from the hands of her murderous offspring. Orestes dripping his mother's blood on the *omphalos* is a rehearsal and retelling of the feminine's violent usurpation within these maternal-laden spaces whose etymologies and histories mediate maternal connection, sustenance, and beginnings. Just as *le mort* state's decrees that

---

62 Aeschylus, *Eumenides*, ll. 149–50.
63 Ibid., ll. 40–41.
64 Ibid., ll. 166–67.
65 Luce Irigaray. "Body Against Body: In Relation to the Mother," in *Sexes and Genealogies*, trans. Gillian C. Gill, 9–20. (New York: Columbia University Press, 1993), 14.

speak through *la vivante* in Nietzsche, the once connective *omphalos* has been severed to rot in the sun of the masculine expropriation that eclipses a maternal lineage.

Following this scene at Delphi, Aeschylus brings us to Athens for a trial between Orestes (legally represented by Apollo on behalf of Zeus) and the Erinyes presided over by Athena and ten jurors. The tense courtroom proceedings again construct gen(d)erational oppositions that juxtapose the chthonic with the Olympian: "Orestes: O Phoebus Apollo, how will the verdict turn out? / Chorus: O black Mother [*melaina mēter*] Night, do you see this?"[66] After hearing Apollo's and the Erinyes' testimonies, the jury's votes result in a tie that will be resolved by Athena. Athena decides: "This man [Orestes] stands acquitted of the charge of bloodshed."[67] With two children of Zeus holding important courtroom roles, one might have been able to foresee this verdict. Anyways, Athena had already confided her affiliations: "There is no mother that gave birth to me, and I commend the male in all respects."[68] And in the words of Donna Haraway: "we expect no better from motherless mind children."[69]

Having lost the trial, the Erinyes threaten to "fill the land with miasmas fatal to humans" due to their "unbearable treatment at the hands of the citizens [*politais*]."[70] After thrice repeating their threat, Athena suddenly succeeds in appeasing the Erinyes (this begins their transformation to the Eumenides, meaning "Gracious Ones") by promising that they will hold an esteemed position for all Athenians to which they bashfully respond, "*You* will bring that about, so as to give *me* such great power?"[71] Athena's charming and flattering of the Eumenides portrays them in a feminine light of impressionability subject to adulation. Athena leads the newly-named Eumenides underground to, "show you your chambers [*thalamous,* inner room generally defined as

---

66 Aeschylus, *Eumenides*, ll. 744–45.
67 Ibid., l. 752.
68 Ibid., ll. 736–37.
69 Haraway, "Tentacular Thinking," n.p.
70 Aeschylus, *Eumenides*, ll. 787–90.
71 Ibid., l. 896.

women's quarters], [...] and when you have passed under the earth [*kata gēs*] [...], keep down below [*katekhein*] what would be ruinous to my country, and send up what will benefit my city and give it victory."[72] Eumenides' final lines speak of the ensuing peace that Zeus has brokered through the reconciliation between Athens' citizens and the new resident aliens [*metoikōn*]. Buried in the feminized and buttressing darkness underneath Athens, the chthonic Erinyes are sealed up, closed off, encircled. But there is a remainder.

We've traversed télé-postal *correspondances* of maternal presences usurped by ipsocratic masculine authority through a sampling of Derrida's texts back to Aeschylus's haunting scenes of buried feminine power. The Eumenides apparently rest appeased below Athens and Apollo presides over the Omphalos: "the original and secondary origins constitute two defeats (for the feminine in the form of Themis and Gaia), as opposed to two victories for the Olympian order (for Apollo and Zeus). The daughter is defeated, as is the mother, while the son's victory reinforces his father's power. Once again, everything is there."[73] Yet the compost of the rotting Python and the memory of the Eumenides' rage beneath Athens insist as an unsettling debt lurking in reason's shade. What *correspondances* do the Eumenides, now interred in their subterranean *thalamos* and who once pursued Orestes for matricide, maintain with the subway *correspondances* avoided by Derrida? In what ways does the *omphalos*, once presided over by Gaia and overtaken by Apollo, still call out to us? What gendered and sexed relations and economies might proliferate within a different history and language not subject to such masculine appropriation of the feminine?

In the beginning was the post. In the beginning was the invention of the telephone. Such originary traces, echoes, screen memories, substitutions, supplements, and parasites perhaps suggest an effaced maternal principle that informs both the telephonic and the postal as inscribed in, by, and through the navel

---

72 Ibid., ll. 1004–9.
73 Loraux. *The Experiences of Tiresias*, 186/222.

scar. Traveling this umbilical telephone line would read a telephonic structure of subjectivity and propriety through the navel scar through which a hospitality emerges beyond life and death. Herein lies the importance of disinterrance and destinerrance that injects breath, through the telephone's static, to these buried maternal traces which have been jammed to the bottom. Derrida performs an abyssal maternal language by compelling to "make something happen to this language [*faire arriver quelque chose, à cette langue*]," which erupts in a maternal madness that no longer remains on bottom (*M*, 51/83). Derrida welcomes the Eumenides' return all while recognizing their threat to become the Erinyes they really are, which the Olympian gods and the polity already know them to be. He keeps his space as he loses himself in innumerable textual and archival *correspondances* while apparently avoiding the subterranean *correspondances*. But I just don't believe him. He feels the mad choreography always lying in wait in the shadowy *correspondances* underfoot — it is calling in to his ear hooked up to his pen. And we can faintly discern the Erinyes' voices accompanied by dance in the hazy distance as they sing a song from a time before their courtroom defeat and subsequent interment, before the Olympian gods swooped down to assimilate and usurp their powers while locking away their bodies. Performed in a moment in which the future's infinite paths remain suspended and brimming, the Erinyes' song transports the living possibility of another history within the very foundations of our most familiar structures and stories. Feel their encircling song:

> Men's conceit of themselves, however proud while under the bright sky,
> dwindles and melts away into worthlessness when beneath the earth,
> thanks to our black-garbed assaults
> and the angry dancing of our feet.[74]

---

74 Aeschylus, *Eumenides*, ll. 368–71.

Kamillea Aghtan

Glossing Errors:
Notes on Reading the "Envois" Noisily[1]

> *This is why more and more I believe in the necessity of burning every-*
> *thing, of keeping nothing of what has passed (been given) between us:*
> *our only chance.   no longer spermit.*[2]

"No longer spermit," Derrida(-Bass) writes (*PC*, 195), violating grammar and spelling rules, abusing "language itself" as he promises on the back cover of *The Post Card*. This slip is one of many studded throughout the "Envois," rupturing the sense of sentences and recoding the delicate mechanisms of meaning embedded within linguistic coils. The strange new grammar within this section of *The Post Card* spreads like a trap to net the impatient reader, the analytical thinker, and the careful glossator all at once. This fine gauze of error invites complicity while refusing participation and twists us towards a reading of mixtures and of multiple, contrary truths.

Amongst the intimacies of Derrida's missives, silent and glossily impenetrable to a first reading, the pencil meanders and underscores aimlessly, deferring hidden currents of the text. A second, more concerted reading (specifically for this issue),

---

[1] The author would like to thank Michael O'Rourke for the invaluable discussion he has shared on this topic and Karin Sellberg for her sometimes coerced but always critical and attentive ear.

[2] *PC*, 195/210.

transforms each earlier palliative underline into an excruciating return. The pencil threatens to perform a biblioautopsy and turn the textual body's insides out (*invertus*); the previous scribbles are revisited by the kind of parser that Derrida indicts — the "*bad* reader," tortured rather than pleasured by "retracing one's steps" over the uneven terrain of previous readings (*PC,* 4).

In other terms: the words of the "Envois" *resist*. They intimate a multitude of perforations and non-closures — a landscape of gappages in sentence structure; lines of text deferred, promised but never given; and endless, interminable wanderings — while, frustratingly and simultaneously, they refuse entry for this glossator's markings. The text seems strangely pre-emptive: its intimacy stakes a high, albeit silent, value of possible meanings against less familiar bidders; it feels bought and owned before we have even entered into bargaining — and perhaps it was so even when the book was at in its infancy, or further back, at the limits of its very incipience.

Yet, perhaps strangely or maybe with utter reasonableness, it becomes apparent that what Derrida owns is *nothing*. His *envois* witness the beginning of empty space; they execute a quite masterful feint of reading and writing. This is a trick which reveals itself at the very first instance, upon the book's title and cover: *The Post Card*. There are, of course, no postcards in the *envois* (nor in any other part of this text), just text about postcards, explaining postcards, reproducing postcards. The postcard has always been the void around which Derrida spins a chrysalis of words. Is it this vacant space which beckons or necessitates the gloss?

Derrida is, of course, already glossing postcards, just as he glosses the Plato–Socrates relation and he glosses his own glosses by leading us into (that is, in his introduction, *intro-ducere*) his own *envoi*-gloss apparatuses through a strategy of what he characterizes as burning. The idiosyncratic smelting of these postcards denies their very penetrability: "As for the 'Envois' themselves," he writes, "I do not know if their reading is bearable" (*PC,* 3). If, as Jean-Luc Nancy supposes, reading is always a "melee," a skirmish of reader and text meeting each other with undeniable, potentially violent traction,[3] Derrida's cauterized *envois* have offered no openings in which to engage in this fight.

"Save [*fors*] a chance" (*PC*, 3). (Is there ever a text which is not always-already permeated by chances either to enter, as he speaks of here, or to abandon, as he notes later on page 195?) An abrupt grammatical fracture, a spelling foible — "no longer spermit" — snags this glossator's eye, even as it skids without discrimination over other passages of text. The very possibility of mistake *permits* the gloss; it opens the page to an almost involuntary multitude of preliminary questions of intentionality (a pun, wordplay, a displaced *s* before a *p*?) and authority (Derrida, Bass, the mark of a silent, overlooked typographer?). Circled, interrogated, speculated upon, this gloss's entry point into *The Post Card* begins with the possibility of *error*.

Reading is here ensnared in the folds of language not by the exigencies of content, not by words or meanings, but by faults: typographical hiccups and apparent slips within the printed page appear like chinks within a previously impenetrable defense. In such places intervenes the gloss, which slides explanatory addenda within the white spaces of leaves, seeking to rescue aspects of textual and linguistic obscurity from "between the lines or in the margins" (*OED*, "gloss, *n.*¹"). Simultaneously, it calls attention to fractures of meaning in the narrative landscape and levels them out; it veils the text with explanation (*OED*, "gloss, *n.*¹"). The gloss bestows an un-parsable (and unpassable) protective coating, converting fragments of text into the unitary page and laying words under a paper sheen; and like glossy varnish, as Steven Connor notes, "it magnifies every dot and dimple in the surface to which it has been applied; but it also repels, remaining impermeable."[4] Thus the addition of glosses allows us exactly *not to stop*, filling in gaps with black ink piles towards the

---

3 Jean-Luc Nancy, *On the Commerce of Thinking: Of Books and Bookstores*, trans. David Wills (New York: Fordham University Press, 2009).

4 Steven Connor, "Intact," talk delivered for the John E. Sawyer Seminar Series at the Institute for Advanced Studies in the Humanities (IASH), University of Edinburgh, May 20, 2011.

smooth reading of unimpeded comprehension. It gifts us with a contrary, impenetrable glaze of understanding.[5]

So the slip of "no longer spermit" *permits* a certain entry into the "Envois," one which allows the insertion of a secondary text that seeks to negate the very slip that it parasites. It legitimizes this labor of the gloss for extending our reading efficiency within an economy of understanding. Indeed, a thorough glossator may note that while the slip permits the gloss, the *envoi*'s "spermit" also *permits* the slip. The text of *La carte postale* reads, "*ne plus s'permettre*" (*PC*, 195/210) — *no longer s'permit* — and furnishes proof of Derrida's intention. An undated forewarning in a previous missive, "almost all my slips are calculated" (*PC*, 135), anticipates this as a willing work of a playful linguist. It is another feint — that of the mistake which is not one.

Reconstructing this scene of accident, we have evidence enough to establish a single narrative of origin, of intent and of a causal chain of events through which this error has been fabricated. Like a confession of violence, his statement to the reader on the back jacket contains an admission of guilt: "I [...] abuse dates, signatures, titles or references, language itself," signed, "J.D." We know who is responsible. The slip of spermit, transmogrified now into *s'permit*, no longer permits its own spreading. Already these three words have been glazed, embalmed by the activity of the gloss — we can see this inanimate textual corpus there complete, but we cannot touch or interact with it. Now, however, its new signification denies even the variegation of possible readings and the dissemination of meaning in multiple; rather than being unpicked, this tapestry of potential multiplicity is burned to cinders, with "nothing out of the

---

5 And, of course, a gathering of glosses forms the back or front matter of so many books as a "Glossary," as it has between pages xii and xxx of *The Post Card*. The compiled Glossary allows readers to refer to its explanatory notes without "losing place" (or pace) in their reading. Indeed, the glossary is most appropriately labelled a *reference tool* as, like the plasterer's toolbox, it enables the reader to carry back (*referre*) explanations to fill in the holes in understanding. It is the distinct labor of the glossary to make reading smooth.

reach of what I like to call the tongue of fire, not even the cinders if cinders there are" (*PC*, 3). Thus this sentence is left with only one recognisable account of the past. "No longer s'permit": s[ocrates] slips in before p[lato] and the order of history is reassured. After the funeral, cremation.

As criminal mastermind, Derrida pre-empts the glossator's maneuver of glazing by entering his own name as instigator of this arson — "I believe in the necessity of burning everything," he professes (*PC*, 195). Yet cast to the tribunal, he is equally quick at rejecting culpability as he is at presenting himself: "I have forgotten the rule as well as the elements" (*PC*, 5); "It doesn't touch me, doesn't concern me myself" (*PC*, 76); "I am not involved" (*PC*, 178), he denies, all the while carefully and meticulously shredding to pieces the wads of historico-philosophical currency that has amassed in the account of Plato-*cum*-Socrates, stuffing the valueless fragments under the robes, the hats, and the impotent inkpot of this other perverse plato and this turned-around Socrates. Derrida's arson effaces his presence from the crime; it turns even him to cinders, that which "erases itself totally, radically, while presenting itself."[6]

We sacrifice these "other" texts of Derrida in order to reconstitute him as author of this sentence and this crime of grammatical abuse, by excising this passage from the other *envois*. Skilled at incorporation rather than dissection, the glossator is a poor surgeon; perhaps a bad reader is a better murderer (and arsonist) for the sake of history. The "spermit" invites commentary to enter it but once inside, this new text turns violent against its host. *Hostes hospites*, Michel Serres writes — the guest–enemy creates the originary moment of this slip by surviving off its donor's death, as a flame eating the matter it lives on until it is reduced to ash.[7] The glossator's complicity carries us to the

---

6 Jacques Derrida, "On Reading Heidegger: An Outline of Remarks to the Essex Colloquium," *Research in Phenomenology* 17, no. 1 (1987): 171–85, at 177.
7 Michel Serres, *Rome: The Book of Foundations* (Stanford: Stanford University Press, 1991), 148, 155.

contradiction of this error's origin: to impose it, the text which it identifies must be destroyed.

We take Derrida as the excluded third in this game of relations — *envoi,* glossator, and author. He is our corpse upon which the corpus can be founded. Analytical addenda are accumulated as if organically, branching arboreally from a solid trunk of text, yet all the while we must ignore that as parasite, as fire-starter, as dissector, we desiccate the text upon which we build. "Criticism," Serres writes, "is indeed a science of limits. It is the science of death."[8] *The Post Card*'s contradictions shrivel and disappear on this inscrutable stage of murder. "This will kill that, the book will kill the edifice, the poem requires that Moscow burn"[9]: socrates writing at a desk in Matthew Paris's manuscript irrumates and asphyxiates the bodiless, scriptless Socrates; Derrida's *The Post Card* cremates the postcard artifact upon which his *envois* are written. This gloss right now varnishes the word spermit until it too is rigid and lifeless behind the sheen. The process is done in three concurrent steps: we must kill Derrida, the founder of the text; we must present his seamless body in a glass coffin over which the eye can swiftly skim without obstacle; and we must burn the ligaments of all his other possible meanings until nothing is left. The (textual) body is killed; it is shown to the crowd; it is disposed of.

How does one gloss a text without participating in its murder? These *envois* retrace one another, tracking again and again over earlier assessments. This is a killing field for the frontispiece to Paris's *Prognostica Socratis basilei* and for the two depicted upon it, even for plato who "did not want to die" (*PC,* 109). Derrida enacts so many murders — plato and Socrates in this postcard, at once laughable mistake, then Socrates turns his back, and plato is jealous, is caught *in flagrante delicto* in the moment of frottage, is tyrannically ordering Socrates to bend over the desk, telling him to write. Yet, somehow, each progres-

---

8   Michel Serres, "Exact and Human." trans. Winnie Woodhull and John Mowitt, *SubStance* 6/7, no. 21 (1978–79): 9–19, at 18.

9   Ibid., 12.

sive death, palimpsestically interweaving with the others, seems here quite contrarily to bring a little un-death: a little fusion instead of inertness; some movement rather than cold dissection.

Perhaps the trick is not to follow a principle of growth but of *spread,* like vermin or parasites that will happily hollow out a tree from the ground, circumventing the hierarchical order of its limbs in growth. Mixture presides over the process of spreading—by *multiplying* meaning, instead of cruel distribution, Derrida's Socrates, his plato and his spermit insist upon invagination.

Contrary texts thus also map this word "spermit." The gloss enters the text, cued by the gappage opened by the mistake. It settles there, seeking (and failing) to smooth over a part of the void at the center of the "Envois"—this place where the actual postcard has never really resided—by suggesting the slip was intentional. But it flounders, attempts to gloss over the text again and again (a pun on dissemination, a historical reversion of Socrates before Plato, a devious trick to turn us into authorial killers), and gradually losing its purpose, it strays to other texts, to accusations and to murders. These narratives amass like layers on letters (*s*'s on *p*'s); finally we have submerged the solitary voice of the *envois*; one becomes many talking *around* one another. Derrida wants to burn, but he will have to settle on drowning instead.

The undifferentiated noise of these glosses sinks the concrete confession that had been given to us in the past—the French *ne plus s'permettre* that recalls Derrida back to his mistake and transforms the misplaced "s" into a sign of intentionality. These alternative, glossy investments of "s" and "p" simultaneously *di-*vest the error of its singularity of meaning and deny the possibility of origination. In failing to identify an origin, the gloss loses the ability to make reading smooth. The explanatory order of the gloss breaks down. The "s" that has crept onto page 195 and undermined the meaning of "permit" in grammar has also changed the licence of my supplement. In these conditions, the permit of meaning converts to the open access principles of *deregulated* invagination and dissemination. The "s" abolishes the "permit" to which it has so tentatively latched.

Is it possible to write a gloss that is no longer legitimated by textual permittance? No, the gloss sustains itself via parasitic association: it cannot live on its own; it requires the relation of another. We must bring Derrida, once the excluded third party, to this dependent glossing, included back again into this patchwork coat of narratives. Of course, this is not hard. Already, we have called him mastermind and feinter, but in truth he is a comedian, equipped with gags and puns. Following this master of paronomasia, we have obsessively tracked the entendre of his "s" and "p" as a single, then a double and a triple, getting drunk with laughter off the fumes of his possibility. He parasites glosses such as this one — and indeed, even his own — to play his jokes; he becomes the third-*included* in this game of meanings.

As mastermind, we have seen him deny culpability, but as a joker he has already readied his text for a facetious paradox by assuming "without detour the responsibility for these *envois,* for what remains, or no longer remains, of them." This in his very first *envoi,* the prefatory *envoi* (what belongs at the end placed at the beginning, already a contradiction), of which he writes: "I am signing them here in my proper name" (*PC,* 6). He marks the text with the legitimacy and ceremony of his *full* proper name (not merely his initials) just this once in the text, "Jacques Derrida," followed by the date "7 September 1979" like an authorial fixative — indeed, like its baptism. The pages of the "Envois" are claimed with the writer's appellation, as the intimate remains of a mysterious lover's friendship and correspondences with the caress of diary entries. How is it ever possible for him to deny part in the production of his slips and puns?

Of course, as soon as Derrida should appear on paper, he evaporates, trailed by laughter at the ridiculousness of the event. His mirth takes the form of a dagger-like "7," his own supplementary gloss cutting through the meaning of the name. We would expect the addition of a footnote, even his own, in some small way to cause his own death. Yet instead of arson and the clean dissection of analytical murder, his joker's knife dehisces. In this footnote to his name, he writes: "doubtless we are several, and I am not alone as I sometimes say I am" (*PC*, 6). His remark (this re-marking of his mark) reverberates against the singularity of his proper name and cuts down his very identifiability — but from the wound explodes a clowning circus of Derridas. Refusing to close the valences of meanings, it has instead rendered him indiscernible. The once-inscrutable stage thus lightens to reveal a tragi-comic scene of murder and revivification — Derrida has been killed and yet is here again quite literally in multiple, inundating us his glossators with his different guises, inhabiting the "Envois," cramming into the gaps of his spelling error.

This is his second (or third, or fourth, or fifth?) punch line: Derrida (singular, recognizable) disappeared from the text long ago; we think we kill him, imprison him, cremate him as we gloss, but he always escapes us. His laughter is one of distortions, drowning the certitude of meaning which resides within the inscription. It is only ever joke. Similarly, laughter dogs the slip of "no longer spermit", chasing the "s" which precedes the "p": it becomes all meanings and none, diffusing the destructiveness of this gloss. In fact, the text parasitically perverts this gloss itself — it has escaped me; I no longer know where it goes, where it has gone, what it has taken into it. These deviations force a relinquishment of control. I thought that this gloss had made me complicit in a murder through the slip of "s" before "p." In fact, the murder I participated in was my own; I have glossed myself. Exhausted and tracked over again and again by a straying pen, I find finally that the joke is well and truly upon me.

Cave lapsum: "no longer spermit."

Peggy Kamuf

Coming Unglued

> "It may be that no work has ever been better fore-
> armed against commentary than Derrida's Envois."
> — David Wills

A commentary? On "Envois"? No, really, you're joking, right? Or else you just want to see what might result from the collision: commentary + "Envois." In which case, you no doubt already expect there will be accidents at the scene. I won't say you programmed it, since it will indeed have to have been an accident and therefore unforeseen, if not altogether unforeseeable. You don't know what to expect, exactly; perhaps you harbor a small hope of seeing commentary derailed, ruined in advance in its very possibility.

In advance: commentary supposes, at a minimum, an advance order, an order of the pre-position of the text to be commented *on*. It, the proposed preposed work, is already there, in advance and in front of the commentary, before it. But "Envois" demonstrates, and this is also its performance, that things in this regard are never really certain and thus a matter of certain knowledge. Rather, there is only belief to go on once it can be admitted — but can it? must it? — that what we call knowledge, the knowledge of some truth, is a phantasm and it is inherited, indeed, it is the phantasm *of* inheritance. The tradition of commentary is shaped by the supposed truth of inheritance: that the heir — the commentator? — *comes after* that which or that from which it inherits or claims to inherit.

I suppose you saw the catastrophe awaiting all these suppositions across the pages of "Envois." But perhaps you also saw the chance there for acts of displacement, or even destruction of this "thing" — concept, act, experience, practice, law, institution, discipline, what you will — that is called inheritance. "Envois" takes up the question of inheritance at the end of the postal epoch. It marks the end of the epoch of destinality by invoking the condition of possibility that is also a condition of impossibility (forgive me, I know you know all of this), which it calls, then, adestinality. Adestinality is something like the infinite suspension of the support of the whole postal era and system. It oversees the logic according to which it is correct to say: because a letter can never arrive at destination, it never simply arrives; or else, the addresser comes only after an addressee's act of reception, who thereby cannot have been the addressee intended ("receive everything you give, *there is* only that, you just have to receive" [*PC*, 231]). These are some of the seemingly perverse effects of "Envois" as argument, performance, novel, demonstration, autobiography, epistolary fiction, but above all as acts of sending without address, without destination readable by the technologies of the postal era.

By address, however, "Envois" wants to hear (*entendre*) the singular timbre that calls: come, you, *you over there*. This is an impossible address to comprehend without already repeating it and beginning to destine it to oneself. The timbre of a voice is stamped from the outset in this repeatability, the repeatability of a name, for example. Nevertheless, the writer of "Envois" wants to discern between name and address so as to write these letters into their gapping difference as gestures of pure address or pure apostrophe. Address without address, a-destined, carried only on the force of some reception or other, mine or yours, hers, his, theirs, ours: all the possibilities are open.

Before there can be commentary, then, there will have been reception at (of) one's own address. The writer of "Envois" formulates the rule as follows: "Moreover, the expert can be objective only to the degree (what degree) his [or her — PK] place is designated, assigned on the card-map, in the picture and not facing it" (*PC*, 187). The remark is prompted upon reading the report of the art historical expert solicited to comment on the Matthew Paris image of Socrates and Plato (or plato and Socrates). The writer of "Envois" receives the expert testimony reluctantly, for it puts an end to "history, our history," and to "my delirium around S and p," that is, around the post card image that the art historian has no trouble deciphering ("Your question can be answered quite simply," he replies [*PC*, 172]). For eighteen months or so, the writer has indeed made delirious associations on the subjects of the image as depicted. This *délire* — a madness of reading — has fit countless stories into its frame, often setting it up as a mirror for the couple(s) he forms with one or more women and to whom, according to the fiction, he is writing. So, into this scene of now desperate, now hilarious narcissistic phantasmatic projection comes the expert commentator, who has to fail to see himself "in the picture" in order to take up the objective position facing an image that bears no trace of him or of his desire. He *has to* do this, if we follow the writer of "Envois," by order of "a moment of the desire for objectivity, a stirring of the epistēmē the origin of which is looking at you here in two persons" (*PC*, 173). Objectivity: who cannot desire it? And desire to know how to look, objectively, at the origin of knowledge itself, even if it must be divided, parceled out, distanced from itself by the more-than-one of every possible copula (S is p)?

***

I think we should start over, at another allure, another pace. Or, better yet, at another distance. But precisely the question is at what distance to receive these "Envois." Consider how this corpus can address itself to any and all readers:

> this is my body, at work, love me, analyze the corpus that I tender, that I stretch out on this bed of paper, sort out the quotation marks from the body hairs, from head to toe, and if you love me enough, you'll tell me about it. Then you'll

bury me in order to sleep peacefully. You'll forget me, me and my name. (*PC,* 99)

The body, the corpus is this language seeming to address a most compelling imperative: "love me." It is the "materiality" (where? there) of a corpus stretched out on a bed, a bed that may also be a lap cradling the book's body on its knees so as to read it.¹ The corpus thus includes the reader in its bed, or rather calls her into the bed where it is stretched out head to toe (or from toe to head, *de pied en cap*, if one is speaking the writer's first language). It invites analysis (commentary?) of its finest traits, the closest examination of its intimate parts, its body hairs.² "Analyze me," it says. These imperatives — love me, analyze me, sort me — are all addressed in the plural second-person: *vous*. This is not polite address in the singular, but a plural, disseminating one, which opens up the space for one to hear her-/him-/themselves addressed: you, any of you. You respond one way or another, from a distance that you cannot fully calculate. In this way, you are like the writer of the "Envois" who imagines how people will respond to the book once published: "Certain people will take it into their mouths, in order to recognize the taste, occasionally in order to reject it immediately with a grimace, or in order to bite, or to swallow, in order to conceive, even, I mean a child" (*PC,* 177). Taste and distaste set the distance, or rather try to abolish it by either ingestion or rejection, *fort/da*. Meanwhile, the corpus *will have been* tendered toward you from the moment you respond to it.

This is my body, *au travail,* Derrida writes. The syntax here bears an irreducibly double sense at least. It depends on whether or not you hear the phrase "au travail" as an elliptical impera-

---

1   See the letter dated 10 June 1977: "I am writing (to) you between Oxford and London, near Reading. I am holding you stretched out on my knees" (*PC,* 32).
2   I follow here David Wills who modifies the translation of "poils" to read "body hairs" and not just "hairs" in his very fine reading of "Envois," in *Matchbook* (Stanford: Stanford University Press, 2005), 59; for this passage in French, see *La carte postale,* 109.

tive address: "allez au travail," "get to work," which is how Alan Bass translates it. Yet, it is syntactically and grammatically just as possible to read the phrase as predicating "my body": this is my body at work "au travail," which is then not at all imperative in force, but predicative, descriptive. The two-word phrase thus makes sense vacillate between, on the one hand, a constative description, a kind of caption for an invisible photograph (this is my body at work), and, on the other hand, a performative speech act, a command or order given (you, get to work). On this split surface of sense, two bodies of and at work are placed one before the other, that is, one after the other, one in front of and/or behind the other, etc., etc. Relation is posed at an undecidable distance, in an unfigurable difference. In a split second, one work begins to provoke or evoke or convoke another that, bending over the finest hairs of the corpus, learns to sort out from among them all the quotation marks that only resemble hairy extensions of the corpus itself. There is thus a division or a distance marked between the work of the one and of the other, which is the distance *from out of which* to respond to the vocative address. Take your time to take your distance, it says, before switching from the imperative mode to the future indicative so as to predict: "you'll tell me about it." In French, "vous m'enverrez des nouvelles," "you'll send me news." Something new, a figuration for the work that is yet to come, perhaps, "if you love me enough."

Let's pursue this "commentary" to the end of the quotation. Two more sentences, still in the future: "if you love me enough, you'll tell me about it, you'll send me news. Then you'll bury me in order to sleep peacefully. You'll forget me, me and my name." As marked by "Then," this sequence is also a consequence: for having sent me news — your work of analysis, in whatever form, for example and why not, "nouvelles" or short stories (the short story as commentary?) — you will (be able to) bury me and sleep peacefully. You're in bed once again, but the corpus is no longer beside you. Sending the response of an adestined work (of analysis or poetry) buries the ghostly phantasm of whatever, whoever it is to which, to whom one has responded. Or rather it *will* bury it, *you will* bury it. And then you will forget me and my name.

You try to imagine that future. Foreseeing it, you begin working to avoid it and prevent the forgetting. Meanwhile, there is the ghostly remains of a disseminal, adestinal address that must be buried, "laid to rest," within you. The promise of peaceful sleep is for the both of you: yes, yes, it says, forget me and my name, keep only what was received at the secret address.

***

— Where is that? I forget.

— Really?

— Unless it is jotted down somewhere in the margins of *La carte postale,* in the copy of it I first read in 1980. You can see that it's been opened many times, indeed too many times judging by the state of its binding. The book is barely a book any longer; now it is a thing unbound, untied, and unglued from its spine and cover. There remain just so many loose folded sections of sixteen recto and verso pages, spilling their slippery leaves and sheets out on the table. By the looks of it, there will have been some untying of ties, loosening of links, breaking down into elements. Some analysis, in other words.

— 5800 State Road, Hamilton, Ohio. Sound familiar?

— Yes, in 1980 it was the most familiar address, where I first read "Envois." I need no reminder for that.

— Perhaps, but there is one thing you regularly forget about the "Envois" delivered to that address. You only remember it once you fold back the now detached front cover and see again, on the very first leaf, a name (not yours, and not the author's, another's)...

— It's true, yes. A name is inscribed there — autograph or signature. It seals the signatory's act of claiming and proclaiming that this book belongs to him, the one who names and signs himself here (think of those printed plates you can still find in old books, pasted on the inside front cover: "From the library of _____," with a name written in the blank). Here the one-time owner's name is still very visible, readable: large and in bright red marker. Each time I uncover it, it's as if I am discovered to be guilty of a theft. This is true even though I have no memory of the circumstances whereby the book or what remains of it ended up in my hands. Did I steal it or was it given to me? Did I ask the self-proclaimed original owner to give it to me and did he consent? Or did I take it anyway, despite his prior claim? Or maybe it was this claim itself that was the theft, which was canceled once the book returned to me? It doesn't matter and, moreover, I will always prefer forgetting the details of whatever happened, if anything at all. But the fact remains that each time I have entered into some analysis of or with *La carte postale* — dare I say my *carte postale*? — the possibility of a diverted, intercepted, or stolen address hangs over or trembles beneath everything I read there. At every second.

— But notice how those singular circumstances — which are no doubt best forgotten — cannot finally be discerned from the general condition under which anyone may read and try to analyze the same text, another copy of the same text. Well, "the same," so to speak, except that no one will ever be able to prove that we — you and I, for example — respond to the same text. For if there is only response and if address is always divisible once it has to repeat, then we…

— …are a wager, a guess, a leap, a belief, an act of faith. Of course we are and we do all that in order to say "we." The limit of commentary is traced there.

James E. Burt

Running with Derrida

> *(but when I say that I run, I'm not talking about jogging, although… but even though they cannot bear that I run, or that I write, they infinitely prefer that I practise jogging or writing for publication: it never goes very far, it comes back in a closed circuit, like a child in its playpen. What they cannot bear is what you know: that jogging and writing for publication are for me only a training with you in mind, in order to seduce you, to have some wind, for some is necessary, the strength to live what I risk with you).*[1]

The exact difference between running and jogging is not established in the Oxford English Dictionary, which merely defines jogging as "to run at a gentle pace (esp. as part of a 'keep-fit' schedule)." When someone is referred to as a jogger the response will often be to correct this, to assert that they are, in fact, a runner, the activities treated as distinct despite one being a form of the other. The narrator of the "Envois" is aware of this distinction, saying that they "cannot bear that I run," preferring him to jog. Running is privileged over jogging.

It's not speed that separates running from jogging. There is something awkward about the motion of a jogger, expressed through its homonymic associations, jogging someone's pen for example. Jogging is more restrained than running, often part of a schedule, something programmed and therefore predictable. Certain people prefer the narrator to jog because it "never goes

---

1   *PC*, 247/264.

very far" — a runner's reach is greater than a jogger's. Indeed, jogging is "only a training," not an activity in itself, preparation to provide some wind, "the strength to live what I risk with you."

According to J. Hillis Miller, Derrida "briefly took up running at Yale in the campus cemetery [...] under the tutelage of James Hulbert," with Hulbert stopping Derrida every few hundred yards to check his pulse which, Miller writes, "must have been a funny scene."[2] Hulbert was a graduate student in comparative literature, one of the team that translated *Le facteur de la vérité* for Yale French Studies. Hulbert ran with Derrida in the Grove Street Cemetery and, according to Hulbert, Derrida took to the activity "like a duck to water," although some were concerned that he not be allowed to over-exert himself.[3] These runs are described by the narrator in the "Envois," who exercises in the same cemetery and writes of how "from time to time I stop, panting, next to a tomb" (*PC*, 157).

According to Derrida "*La Carte Postale* is haunted by Joyce, whose funerary statue stands at the centre of the Envois,"[4] and of whom the addresser asks, at one point, "what made him run [ce qui l'a fait courir]" (*PC*, 240/257). Murray McArthur has written about the interplay between Derrida and Joyce and how this works through pairings such as the two cemetery scenes, one in Zurich, where the narrator visits Joyce's memorial, the other when he runs in Yale.

Derrida has written about how the "Envois" have "a whole family of James, Jacques, Giacomo,"[5] and McArthur places "Jim" ("who sounds awfully like this Jim or James or Jacques"[6]) in the role of Joyce, the reverse of the Joyce portrayed by the statue,

---

2 J. Hillis Miller, *The Medium is the Maker: Browning, Freud, Derrida, and the New Telepathic Ecotechnologies* (Eastbourne: Sussex Academic Press, 2009), 50.

3 Personal communication.

4 Jacques Derrida, "Two Words for Joyce." in *Post-structuralist Joyce: Essays from the French*, eds. Derek Attridge and Daniel Ferrer, 145–59 (Cambridge University Press, 1984), 150.

5 Ibid., 151.

6 Murray McArthur, "The Example of Joyce: Derrida Reading Joyce," *James Joyce Quarterly* 32 (Winter): 227–41, at 235.

"the languid European with his sedentary position, his aerobically unsound cigarette, his cane."[7] The shifting of the relationship between the figures of Joyce and the narrator provide further examples of the strange baton passings that fill the Envois. For McArthur, the scene of Hillis and the narrator in the Swiss cemetery contrasts with the one in Yale: "the master in this cemetery who knows everything is Jim, a metaleptic troping of the European scenes, this running of jogging buddies running side by side."[8]

According to the narrator of the "Envois," Jim was "crazy with his jogging [*il est un peu fou avec son jogging*]" (*PC*, 157/170). This mention of jogging rather than running seems significant, particularly when Derrida is obviously alert to the difference between the terms. Indeed, as a runner, Hulbert asserts that he was not a jogger, stating that "I was perhaps more crazy 'about running' than 'with jogging.'"[9] Other than these brief mentions in the "Envois," jogging disappears from Derrida's work, as if running were a fad that he took up briefly in the 1970s.

I took up running and my study of Derrida at the same time, in my early thirties. In both activities, being a late starter does not devalue my participation — knowing that I will never win a race doesn't limit my enjoyment of such events. One can run with other people while still racing against oneself. Indeed, it is good to have someone to keep pace with, to force you to strive a little harder — to prove that one is running, not jogging.

Derrida's writing paces me. I enjoy his work because he is not simply "writing for publication," but seems driven by something more important. His prose sometimes feels like hard work, the epic sentences that are hard to read aloud, the breathless hitch of the ellipsis in the passage above ("I'm not talking about jogging, although... but even though"). A work like the "Envois" is exhausting, pursuing the proliferation of pronouns: I, they, you; a paranoid chase of correspondence that leaves me panting.

---

7   Ibid., 236.
8   Ibid.
9   Personal communication.

And then there is the confusion — can the narrator be directly identified as Derrida, am I chasing him or a literary phantom? While Miller is prepared to "testify under oath, moreover, that what the speaker says happened the three or four times I am mentioned by name in "Envois" really did happen as 'historical events,'" the "Envois" always disturb my footing and I am not sure whose trail I'm following. Does the narrator describe the runs Derrida took with Hulbert or not? Every word of Derrida's seem limitless, language coming alive. His work defies simple programs and schedules. Even a concept as peripheral as running explodes with puns and plays: the couriers and relays of the "Envois," the confused baton-handover between Plato and Socrates, the step in pas-sages, the jambes of the chimney in Poe's *Purloined Letter*. McArthur points out the "perpetual movement that the addresser engages in, an Odyssean voyaging, but also the theme of legacy or legs, the walking, running, pedalling, limping that the accident-prone addresser does throughout."[10]

Derrida claimed in 1982 that "I haven't even begun to read Joyce"[11] and I have the same feeling when I read Derrida. But from my experience of running I know that it is not what one achieves that is important but the feeling of striving, to be able to say that I am a runner, not a jogger. Even if I never "master" Derrida's work, the experience of reading it is still a positive one. It is about more than training. This experience of reading Derrida recalls something Haruki Murakami wrote in his book about writing and running:

> Most runners run not because they want to live longer, but because they want to live life to the fullest. If you're going to while away the years, it's far better to live them with clear goals and fully alive than in a fog, and I believe running helps you do that. Exerting yourself to the fullest within your indi-

---

10 McArthur, "The Example of Joyce," 236.
11 Derrida, "Two Words for Joyce," 148.

vidual limits: that's the essence of running, and a metaphor for life — and for me, for writing as well.[12]

This brief response can only be a prelude to a work that I will never have enough breath to write. I could never exhaust all meaning in Derrida's work, never reach a finish line. I will always be run ragged by the "Envois," its couriers always ahead of me, but when I run, my life feels fuller.

---

[12] Haruki Murakami, *What I Talk About When I Talk About Running* (London: Random House, 2008), 82–83.

Julian Wolfreys

Perception-Framing-Love

I

It's always about the name. Everything comes down to this.

> Everything is due to the difficulty of properly *naming* the thing itself. Actually this difficulty is an impossibility, a difficulty whose limits can only be indefinitely pushed back. (*PC*, 382)

Leave this, the limits being "indefinitely" pushed at, moved backwards, further and further, to recede, the harder one tries. This involves a question of perception.

Perceive: apperceive.

Always there: perception.

On the one hand: perception of another.

On the other hand: an other perception; perception of the other.

There is always another perception in perception: there remains, in secret, hidden away, just below the surface, underneath the tongue, sublingually, as if the two were entwined, one tongue insinuating itself with the other's tongue; or, say this the other way around so as to gain perspective if not to perceive correctly, the other's tongue always already having insinuated itself under, in the mouth of the one. So it is with the action of perception. So it is with perception of apperception, and what it means to perceive. Traveling across tongues, leaving, as it were, can you perceive this, the trace of another's perception in your own, Latin to French to English. To perceive: *seize, understand, take entirely.* The other's tongue, in its being carried over into my mouth, knows me. I believe I take it on, make it conform to my will, to the power of my language — as if there were such a thing — when, and here is the other perception, perception that will never be mine, in imagining the other's perception, perception of the other, I perceive indirectly, I apperceive, that there, there is the other perception, perception of, on perception. In taking the other, seizing its tongue, making it conform, I take on a perception that perceives without being perceived necessarily, and which, in so doing, apprehends me. I am taken entirely by the other.

A question of the trans-, of the *Über*, this matter of perception, of perception's perception, as if, imagine it, from some other place. One is taken unawares. I am *translated*. In "To Speculate — on 'Freud,'" the very title of which insinuates perception in its play on what is given to be seen, Derrida engages in a sustained reflection, meditation perhaps, on perception. Without stating it though, his passage, his discourse on the discourse situated by Freud "at the very heart of perception" (*PC*, 383) opens for the reader to perceive the questions of the narrator and framing (*PC*, 114–15) and also those perceptions that plague the post cards on memory, love, the self and other, which, for now, I will limit to one small exchange (*PC*, 432–33).

Where though, in this small weave I wish to ravel, might we begin? Pulling a thread, I find myself moving backwards. With perception, someone might say to you, seeing things from another side as it were, "[e]verything is due to the difficulty of properly *naming* the thing itself." But then, this is hardly new; for, "[a]ctually this difficulty is an impossibility, a difficulty whose limits can only be indefinitely pushed back" (*PC*, 382). "At this point," so to speak, I already have the sense that one perception entails within it the possibility of another, and another; from this perception, perception of the perception of perception (of perception *ad infinitum,* the scene of perception being one *en abyme*), we perceive, do we not, that there is that which "distances us from intuition, and legitimately provokes distrust" (*PC,* 382). Such distancing, such an opening that takes place from within the more or less reflective, and, it has to be said, belated, perception on perception's perception of perception's perception... (I could go on), the realization dawns that this is not simply a matter of seeing, of how one sees and so understands, seizes, takes hold of, takes entirely.

Do you see what I mean? Can you see? Is the meaning available to perception?

No, it is not simply, if ever, a matter of sight as apprehension. In the moment of seeing, in the naked experience of the other that touches me, from over there, from where, I realize, the other perceives me, I pass, too quickly doubtless, in the blink of an eye, to intuition. I have this feeling of being apprehended, of being taken. As if possessed, as if in a photograph. I am taken by the other, I perceive before perceiving, I intuit my being taken. Placed under arrest by, under the arrest of the other's perception, I come to realize *at this point.* That is to say, I realize *at this point,* or to put this differently, from the point where my perception takes place belatedly, that there is, there takes place the displacement, the translation — from experience, to intuition, to perception (and ultimately from there to memory, re-presentation, the difference of perception's perception) — ; or, following Derrida once more, the transposition, in fact "[a]ll the movements in '*trans-*,' the ones that involve repetitions, displacements, and *speculations* [...] [which] inhabit this origin [sc. the origin of perception, and therefore perception of the origin of perception] on its very threshold" (*PC,* 383; second emphasis mine). It is, to repeat, *at this point,* that the realization occurs that what takes place on the threshold, inhabiting the origin, is, in being what distances us from intuition, "the figurative nature of language and the necessity of borrowing these figures," borrowing, in Freud's case, (which is not our immediate concern here), according to Derrida from "already constituted sciences, [...] psychology, and more precisely the psychology said to be of the depths" (*PC,* 382). Where there is language, there is perception, separating me through the hinge it effects, which it causes to operate and which it is itself, on the very threshold of the origin of perception, by which "I" is distanced, I am constituted in my perception as always already at a remove, at a loss. The "I" is constituted, is given to oneself through the gift of perception, perception of the other, the other's perception, by this archeoriginary loss. I am therefore I am at a loss for words, wherever perception takes place, and everywhere it takes place.

"I" comes into being in this originary perception of originary loss, perception as loss, and precisely through transference, translation, transposition, all that which hinges on *trans-*. Being, becoming in the perception of Being as being-at-a-loss, if I can put it like this, takes place as perception of the self through the "metaphoric transposition within language [...], [through, in turn, that of which] the word transference reminds [us, its] metaphoric network, which is precisely metaphor and transference (*Übertragung*), a network of correspondences, connections, switch points, and a semantic, postal railway sorting without which no transferential destination would be possible" (*PC,* 383). Hence, from "the first intuition [as if there ever were a first, as if one could perceive such a possibility, imagine it if you will], from its threshold"; or to shift within language, transposing one metaphor for another, slipping from one tongue to another, in another register, on the tongue of the other, giving ground to another perception, from a "first step," all motion, all displacement is always already in play "as the very condition of what is called a perception or a description at the edge of perception" (*PC,* 383).

Therefore, if *I comes into being in this originary perception* (of perception's originary transposition, transference, etc.) it does so not as guarantor of presence, identity, Being's fixed point, its constant, pole star... (choose your own metaphor, whichever best suits your perception of a stable ontology); rather it *comes into being,* if I can put it like this, as the condition of perception's endless disorientation and reorientation. If, in reading this, you find yourself at a loss, disoriented, so to speak, this has to do with the challenge that recognizing, or speculating on the perception of perception as the perception of the other, of *différance* at, on the one hand, the heart, and on the other hand, the threshold, entails. For "[a]ll these trajectories — transitional, transcriptive, transpositional and transgressive, transferential trajectories — open the very field of speculation. It is there that speculation finds its possibility and its interest. There that is, in the trans" (*PC,* 382). Everything comes down to being opened to another perception, another way of seeing, of speculating on another perception, perception as always other, as always already an alterity informed and transposed in its speculation by *différance,* the singular manifestation of *différance* that is called, simply, perception.

But, "on the other hand" (*PC,* 383)… There is always another perception, we are back with this dislocating opening of the transgressive, transferential trajectory (open your eyes!). Transference (*Übertragung*) opens, causing the opening onto perception, but is too the condition of perception's possibility, the possibility of the "on the other hand." On the other hand, to look at this differently, it is not just, never merely a matter of what one is given to see. In understanding, in perceiving that the figure of sight is not simply the name for vision but also part of the metaphorical transference that names indirectly understanding — you see what I mean — there is always the apprehension that it is "discourse at the very heart of perception, from its first step as its condition" (*PC,* 383). Thus, as that which mobilizes perception discourse — that which has always already disrupted the one — erases, this is Derrida's word, the "oppositional limit between perception and its other" (*PC,* 383). In that visual "refraction" by which perception is understood to operate, *as if from a first place,* there in that return misunderstood as the inaugural opening of a perception, wherein there is traced the 'speculative transference orients, *destines,* calculates the most original and most passive "first step" on the very threshold of perception. And this perception, the desire for it or its concept, belongs to the destiny of this calculation. As does every discourse on this subject' (*PC,* 384). Within perception, at its heart, unseen, invisible, *there* is discourse, opening and destining. Transference has always already taken place, at least this is the speculation, in the act of perceiving, and I perceive this as the possibility of that perception. In the arrival of that "first" perception, before I am given the opportunity to reflect, to speculate, to look back on what in the "first" look has caused it to take place, the other has given the place, the threshold of perception, discoursing on, and, perhaps, framing, constructing the frame of perception in the deconstruction of the undifferentiated metaphor of the origin, the first, the one.

II

> "But that is the fiction. There is an invisible, but structurally irreducible, frame around the narration. Where does it begin?" (*PC,* 431)

Framing: if I am narrating here, in this reflective speculation on the speculative transference, then, it has to be admitted that standing in the position of a narrator, I find the figure of the narrator — and of course there is no "narrator" as such; mere "metaphor" there is only that insistent play of *différance,* the becoming-space of time and the becoming-time of space, deferral and differentiation, transferential trajectory, within the mobile network of trope and perceptual shift, elision, erasure, and reinscription — to be double, doubled, reiterated, and divided, in the act, any act of narration: "[t]he narrator (himself doubled into a narrating narrator and a narrated narrator, not limiting himself to reporting the two dialogues)" (*PC,* 431). It will, it should, be noticed that, at this introduction of the narration on the doubled, doubling narrator, there is a framing of the double. Parentheses frame. Arriving — but from where? — they enframe that division, an iteration potentially endless. Who gives the frame? Who frames? The narrating narrator? Or the narrated narrator? Neither, there is a performative at work here inasmuch as, without presence, without voice, writing enacts the opening we name framing, the opening onto, as a reinscription of, the *mise en abyme*. In this, the erasure or that oppositional limit between perception and its other, is implied, even as, in this gesture, the doubling doubles itself, marking as it erases, and leaving behind merely the ghostly, voiceless *trait* of framing-opening, the doubling play of narrators — narrated and narrating — in the narration of their division. Hence, the "invisible, but structurally irreducible frame" of which only the question of the beginning can be asked, without solution. Just one more — one in an endless sequence — speculative transference. Perception perceives; perception, of the other. Perception, *of* the other: on the one hand I perceive — the other. But then, the other perceives me, even, especially, when I am not aware; when, for example, I write. There is the other's perception all the time. Perception of perception then, more than one, and no one perception; despite the best efforts of narration to frame, and so control, to elide perception within the guiding frame of a reality presented as perspective, the phenomenological confused by, occluded by, the empirical.

I is a frame by which I name myself, believing in a unity that cannot, does not hold. A mere fiction, convenience itself, by which, believing, entertaining the narrative of an autonomous and unitary, stable self, always present to itself, I frame and am framed. *I,* frame of the other, this perception I mistakenly call, and believe to be, mine. Thus, the frame is never single, there is always a doubling of the frame, and the impossibility is in knowing what the proper perspective might be. Impossible to tell one frame from another, where one ends or the other begins, whether one is on the inside or the outside of the other, and so on, *ad infinitum*. While the image of the frame brings with it the notion of closure, and, with that, that which is framed, therefore closed off *and* opened onto, as a portal, giving access, and, therefore, to remind ourselves, place a threshold for the staging or reflection on perception — as if we were looking *into* the abyss; having a perspective on the abyss, from the safety of this "position" beyond the frame, outside it; to pursue the counterintuitive thought, the abyss is not simply that onto which we look as I would look at a stage, a photograph, an image, still or moving on a screen (computer, television, cinema), whilst remaining comfortable in and assured of my perspectival position and perception. No, mine is not the central location, the point to which the vision returns, the abyss presented, or from which the gaze emanates.

Mine is merely a locus, one perception, and perspective, amongst others, within others. I, in being framed, am not outside, above the abyss. Rather *I* is a moving point in an abyss that is "all around"; though of course this phrase is inadequate, inasmuch as it still suggests an implied or representable spatial dimension, with limits, ends — in short, its own frame. *I* is a small point, cursor if you will, for the convenience of reflection, within the abyssal, available to each and every other perception. "Not to take into account this complication," to move from Derrida's starting point, that of the embedded framing devices that function in relation to the idea of the (narrating and narrated) narrator in *The Purloined Letter*), is a failure of comprehending — a case of not gaining access to the nature of perception itself — of that which is always "twice-framed" in being "framed" in any "represented content" (*PC*, 433).

I realize of course that I am extrapolating, perhaps a little too hastily, from a specific example and narrative scenario, moving from the ontology of the literary, or the problematic of defining that through the limits of any analysis that does not take into account fully and comprehensively the nature of that which framing is, or what takes place through the gesture of "the frame, the signature, and the *parergon*" (*PC*, 432). In this move, opening onto, or reflecting on the possibility of a phenomenological apprehension of the self, irreducible to a subject, as provisional, informed not by any plenitude or auto-completion (a self-framing) but instead by the other's perception, I am seeking to show how, as soon as one shifts one's perception on the self, one has already entered into a mode of analysis that requires the beginnings at least of an acknowledgement of the extent to which I names itself only at the cost of loss.

Every time I say *I*, I reinscribe violently a limit, which will not hold for very long, and which, therefore, is untenable, for it admits or confesses to a limit that is exclusive and provisional. I am *this* rather than *that*. But at the same time, in saying *I*, which is always, also, I *am* (ontology is the framing limit of articulation, which by its discursive as well as epistemological nature must operate according to some framing or limiting gesture), I place myself at the threshold of an opening, in which the *I* loses its force in the moment of its utterance. Framing through narrative, producing the perspective, offering phenomenal perception as empirical detail, fact or "reality," I put myself forward "as a very singular character within the narrated narration, within the enframed," thereby constituting an "agency, a 'position'" (*PC*, 433). That there is agency at all indicates both how play, motion, is intrinsic to the assumption of the self; that this is a position at all indicates that, far from being free, absolute, sovereign, the self, the *I*, is only ever given, a "giving" given en-framed, framed, and framing, subject to the perception of another or perception of, on the part of the other.

III

> "As you come to me from the only place in which I do not feel myself loved, I also have the feeling that you are alone in loving me, alone in being able not to love me." (*PC*, 115)

Love comes, if it comes at all, as the singular expression, of the other; this is my perception, in the perception of the other: that love is given. Not a thing, irreducible to any ontology and therefore unavailable to deconstruction, it is the giving of perception to that place I name as myself, wherein I perceive myself loved or not loved in what is given, not given, or withdrawn, as the touching experience of the other. In this I apprehend analogically, indirectly, apophatically, the perception of the other; the other's regard, for me, of me. In this realization, I am seized, I understand myself to be taken, entirely, taken, captured, as in a photograph. This being-seized, being-taken, it marks not only a space, but also a time, however slight. There is a gap, a lag. This is doubled in my perception of being perceived. If this reflection illustrates or illuminates anything, it illustrates how love is never mine to give; it is not a gift in any conventional sense; I find myself having given love, giving love, without my consciousness taking part in that decision. I can of course decide that I believe I am withdrawing my love, but that is simply to frame my perception of the other in a particular manner, so as to save face, to turn my face away. But the truth of love is far from this; and, it might be, I come to realize that the love given was never mine to give all along.

Thus, without love being given, without the giving of love, there is no being in the perception of the other, for the other, "the one to the other" (*PC*, 114). I 'have to hang on to you […]. For I do write you […] even if I don't send everything" (*PC*, 114). No perception, no one without the other, the other always sending, giving, without acknowledgement of receipt, this is the hypothesis. I am taken in love, apprehended; framed, even as I ask, I demand that you "tell me, my love, give me the truth," a truth which — possibility of the impossible — would arrive only on condition that I could "erase all the traits of language, coming back to the most simple […] in order to send you 'words' that are 'true' enough for me not to recognize them" (*PC*, 114). So, here then, in this the perception of the frame having been riven arrives in the desire for that erasure of all the traits of language, save for the apprehension that "when I say '*je suis*,' with you, […] I am (following) you the way one follows a raise, and taking a step, betting on your faith (*PC*, 117). At least here is what I suspect, believe, perceive in the most indirect manner. I am with you, I am you, but I am never on time, I am always in your wake, following you, in the wake of the other, from when love seems to give itself most indirectly, invisibly. And all I can hope for is that other perception, the one that breaks through the frame in which I seem to see myself as myself, alone. Only "[y]ou who know, [can] tell me the truth, tell me your secret" (*PC*, 117). You remain though, you are "untranslatable" even when "you are there to haunt me" (*PC*, 113); especially then, for though I apprehend in the touching instant of the *as if,* in the analogical apprehension, the apperception of the other (conjuring all the doubleness that phrase can muster without at all framing the other in the phrase), then, there, in what I believe to have been given, what I am calling, naming impossibly love, without at all giving to that which is given a frame by which love comes to be represented, encapsulated, defined, perceived directly once and for ever; in this, you haunt me, you remain to haunt me as I am (found) (following) you, at a loss, because "you never sign" (*PC*, 163). Love never signs, the other never signs at the bottom of the card as if authorizing the frame of perception for the self. So, "I await you, there where we are not yet, neither the one, nor the other" (*PC*, 163). There is a difficulty here, clearly. I have to break off. Actually, as someone said, scribbled across the back of a postcard, this difficulty is an impossibility, a difficulty whose limits can only be indefinitely pushed back. Thus framed, and framing the reply, the response, we find ourselves opened, and opening, to one another, abyssally. *Mise en scène* transformed from within, translated by what remains, becoming what it always already is, a *mise en demeure*, which opens in the moments of its framing, its presentation, representation, and re-presentation, as the *mise en abyme*.

Dragan Kujundžić

En*voiles*: Post It

That the relationship between J. Hillis Miller and Jacques Derrida occupies a unique place in the landscape of contemporary criticism is no secret. They have played as well a significant role in my intellectual building, having encountered them some thirty years ago. I have written about that in my "Journey With J on the Jour J," an introduction to Derrida's essay "Justices" on J. Hillis Miller, and Miller's "Isabelle's Kiss" published in *Critical Inquiry* in 2005. There, I have likened these two essays to letters on the way "to further destinations of as yet uncharted parts. Like letters, sealed with a kiss."[1] Derrida's essay "'Justices'" includes a description of the scene in which he receives a letter from Miller ("Hillis" when referring to the film character, "J. Hillis Miller" or "Miller" when referring to Miller as author in further text), regarding the real name behind the "J" which has received extensive treatment in my film *The First Sail: J. Hillis Miller*.[2]

In *The First Sail*, the first thing Hillis comments upon when discussing the scene at the lecture when Derrida shows the letter, is Derrida's death, already presaged by his not looking too healthy to Hillis's eye in the filmed footage screened by Hillis in the film. This the first *bout de souffle*, breath turn, the pneu-

---

[1] Dragan Kujundžić, "Journey With J on the Jour J," *Critical Inquiry* 31, no. 3 (2005): 684–88, at 688.
[2] Dragan Kujundžić (dir.), *The First Sail: J. Hillis Miller,* DVD, all regions, 81 min. (Deer Isle Productions, USA, 2011).

matic turn of the soul, that fills the sails (*voiles*) of the film and the book and sends it on to its destinerrance, thus the en*voiles*. The counter-time of mourning Derrida is inscribed in my own desire to film J. Hillis Miller. Derrida's specter haunts me and it haunts the film, as much as it haunts J. Hillis Miller. But not necessarily in ways that are visible or re-presentable. The ways the spectral divides the frame of the cinematic representation, what I call the effects of division and devision (a *destinerrance* of the cinematic image, in fact), pose interesting and urgent questions about the modes and ethics (prost*ethics*) of representation. They go from the phenomenological to the political in a heartbeat. Thus, the question of the frame or the letter (be it a single letter, the initial of the first name, "J."), the letter which does or does not arrive, to the cinematic which does or does nor "represent" the Other, imposes itself as the burning issue pertaining to the very core of what is a tradition, history, and what our response and responsibility to it are or should be. Who writes what and who writes whom, how or whether we allow the Other to leave an imprint, what or who arrives: those are the issues which haunt the text below, from the film on J. Hillis Miller, Derrida's "Justices" episode reproduced in the film, to the burning political turbulences that have left their imprint on the body of Europe, Bosnia, and now, most recently, Greece. Joyce's *Ulysses* and Theo Angelopoulos's (1935–2012) *Ulysses' Gaze* serve at the end as exemplary sites calling for a destinerrant Europe, the Other Europe and the Other of Europe to be invented, in the face of a looming catastrophe.

The reflections below are also marked, truly haunted, by a telepathic encounter with the Other, marked in this text in italics. Someone else, Julian Wolfreys, dictated these italicized interventions to me on May 19, 2012. Having come to me after I almost finished writing, they have, I realize, from an infinitely distant telepathic proximity, taught me, unbeknownst to me, how to write my own essay even before it had been written, as well as taught me how to watch my film. What is really uncanny, is that at the same time I initially proposed to the editors to write on the scene from the film where Jacques Derrida discusses the letters he mis-addressed, in relation to *The Post Card*, Julian Wolfreys wrote about the same scene in *The First Sail*, starting with the description of his visit, on the day of his lecture, to the Bodleian library at Oxford University, in search for, as he says, "that" postcard which is on the cover of *The Post Card* (Plato teaches Socrates how to write, shown initially to Jacques Derrida by Cynthia Chase and Jonathan Culler). And thus Wolfreys relating the whole analysis of the letters sent to Miller with an erroneous appellation (John for Joseph), and Miller's response that Derrida quotes in the film, to the analysis of *destinerrance* in *The Post Card*. This was the same thing that I proposed! But the uncanny ghosts haunting these essays proliferate, with Julian Wolfreys's conclusion of his conference presentation (delivered at Oxford University on April 13, 2012 as one of the keynotes at the conference on "Giving up the Ghost: the Haunting of Modern Culture") with a reference and analysis of *Ulysses' Gaze* by Angelopoulos, which is exactly the ending of the essay which I had already initially proposed to relate to sailing in all senses of the term in *Ulysses* and *Ulysses' Gaze*, the destinerrant sailing of the tradition itself. In advance, I have followed Wolfreys's text blow by blow, my writing from the very start already sealed by this distant proximity and affinity that taught me how to write, in a scene of writing where I can no longer tell who or what came first. On occasion, our analyses reverberate with a gentle dissonance, like a contrapunctual musical motif, thus all the more underscoring the mutual affinity. I quote them here in indented italics with an infinite gratitude and without further explanation. "It is impossible not to believe that each of us has an internal television screen by means of which we have visions of what distant friends and relations are thinking, or not to believe that whatever we think is broadcast to the internal television screen of others," says Miller in *The Medium Is the Maker*.[3] This essay is exactly a product of such televised encounter with

---

3 J. Hillis Miller, *The Medium Is the Maker: Browning, Freud, Derrida and the New Telepathic Ecotechnologies* (Eastborne: Sussex Academic Press, 2009), 15.

Julian Wolfreys (whom I never met in person, except online, even though we overlapped for a while in the same University of Florida where we had arranged but missed encounters, tormented, like letters, with an "internal drifting").

> *Having arrived earlier this morning, and thinking about ghosts, the ghosts of Oxford, and, in particular, one shade, whose disturbing motions here I like to call to mind, I took a walk to the Bodleian, its gift shop at least. I was in search of a post card. I was less interested in what it represented or who was represented than the memory of another who had, in purchasing an untold number of these cards, had made it visible to the academic world in a rather provocative way.*

Derrida's death has also entailed the darkening of register of some of Miller's recent writing, the dark Derrida, a darkening in Miller of a wound that does not heal. I tried to exemplify this relationship in the scene where Hillis watches Derrida read a letter he had received from Miller. Relating the scene in the film about the destinerrance of the postal regarding J. Hillis Miller and Derrida with Joyce is justified on many levels, not least of all because of the entry in *The Post Card* on "20 June 1978. I had not come back to Zurich since spring 1972. You accompany: CHECK me everywhere. Hillis, who was waiting for me at the airport (the De Mans arrive only this afternoon,) drove me to the cemetery, near to Joyce's tomb, I should say funerary monument" (*PC*, 148). In his *The Medium Is the Maker* Miller (just after his description of how he took Derrida sailing on his boat, *The Frippery*, featured extensively in *The First Sail*, on a day when there was a "small craft warnings" and "look what happened to Shelley when he went sailing on a day when there was too much wind!"[4]), claims that he has no memory of that ever happening, not "having a car in Zurich." However, "Derrida and I did go together, as the 'Envois' report, on another occasion, to visit Joyce's tomb in the Zurich cemetery near the zoo. The ani-

---

4   Ibid., 49–50.

mal cries from that zoo appear in *Finnegans Wake*. We did stand laughing before the tomb of Egon Zoller, '*Erfinder des Telephonographe*,' with its engraved ticker tape machine and its carved Alpha and Omega. Derrida, as we stood looking at the tomb, connected it to his then current project about telecommunication networks, that is, the 'Envois.'"[5] From this scene I'd just like to retain the inscription of *The Post Card* in the neighborhood of the telegraph, tele-technology, the uncanny repetitions of uncertain memories, the sailing on Miller's boat ("6 October 1978. [...] Tomorrow, return to Yale, day after tomorrow excursion in Hillis's sailboat" [*PC*, 166]) and Joyce, in the cemetery, thus the relation of the letter with death.

In *The First Sail*, Derrida describes in the episode how he had once (or many times in the past) written to J. Hillis Miller addressing him, erroneously, as "John Hillis Miller." To which Miller responded in a letter, and that is the film scene, "My name is 'Joseph,' not 'John.' Not that it matters in the least, since I've never used that name in any case."

> The First Sail: J. Hillis Miller. [CLIP] *What have we seen? Let me break this down a little schematically: (1) we see J. Hillis Miller, watching something, someone, we cannot see. The who and the what do not exclude one another, there is not a choice here. We hear a voice, a recording within a recording, first French, then translating itself to English, the idiom resistant to direct transport. To this Miller responds with laughter. (2) From this, there is a cross fade, from Miller to Derrida, Derrida "after" Miller, the image "after" the voice, apparently. Derrida "arrives" without arriving, appearing, much as Plato appears after Socrates in that Post Card.*

In the film, Hillis minimizes the video tape of Derrida, as not "really the return of Jacques Derrida," something that I sense is also at work in Hillis's description of Derrida's book on touching and J.L. Nancy as "a book I find wonderful but exceed-

---

5   Ibid., 50.

ingly difficult,"⁶ as he said in an interview to Eamonn Dunne in Dunne's *J. Hillis Miller and the Possibilities of Reading*, and I wonder if it also means difficult to touch, to behold?

This subtle tone of positioning vis-à-vis Derrida comes across, at least to me, as an attempt to ward off Derrida's return, precisely as the return of the ghost. If he came back as a ghost, it would mean that Derrida had died. That is, as J. Hillis Miller says in *The Medium Is the Maker*, he cannot listen to Derrida's lectures on tape, because that would mean that he is really dead. But Miller knows better! We always return as ghosts, even in real life. As soon as there is a return, there is a ghost, I learned that form *The Medium Is the Maker*. And from Miller's analysis of *On Touching*. And from his writing about "Absolute Mourning." And from all those other writings on zero, on the empty core of literature, on living on, etc.

> *Miller continues, after reference to the recordings of Glenn Gould playing Bach; he considers how the filmmaker can fast forward, rewind, slow down, pause, play over and over again. The spectro-tele-technological archive gives one the illusion of power over the living and the dead, although I have to say it does not appear to occur to Miller that even were he hearing Gould play live, Gould, or whichever pianist you prefer for your Bach, Schubert, or whoever, is, even in live performance, nevertheless acting as a medium, a conduit for the trace of the other.*

What I sense in these subtle strategies of evasion to see Derrida as a ghost is a certain tenderness for Derrida which Hillis is trying to protect from opening or precisely from bringing into present or presence, like a wound which refuses to heal and which cannot or should not be touched. But not just because Hillis is protecting himself from the exposure to the death of the other, which would be understandable, anxiety-ridden, an

---

6 Éamonn Dunne, *J. Hillis Miller and the Possibilities of Reading: Literature after Deconstruction* (New York: Continuum, 2010), 134.

anxiety quite human and easy to explain. In this way, I would claim, Hillis is protecting Derrida's passing away to be worked through, obliterated, diminished, "properly mourned," and thus done away with. Geoffrey Bennington recently wrote about this as "militant melancholia," which I think describes Hillis in the film scene:

> Who or what, in these still dark days of an ongoing melancholia I began by declaring "militant," militantly melancholic, something that wanted to affirm, with Jacques himself, a certain refusal of the "normal" work of mourning and its "normal" dealings with the death of the other—a proudly militant melancholia that soon however settled into something much less glorious, much less proud, much more melancholic, in fact—who or what, then, might come to open something again that might lay some claim, however modest, to the sometimes very minimal dignity of what often bears the probably misleading name of 'thought'?"[7]

The music in the film, composed and performed by Natalia Pschenichnikova, to whom I left complete discretion as to the placement of chords, punctuates this countertemporality of a loss splitting the scene but refusing representation, as explicitly avowed by Hillis, and so subtending the whole set of representational, framing divisions and devisions.

There is even an instant when the ghost of Alexander's father [in Bergman's Fanny and Alexander] *is seen sitting disconsolately at the piano, playing notes my memory wants to tell me are very close to those used in the documentary by Miller.*

Hillis is protecting, in a sense, the wound or the loss from healing, by not allowing it to be touched, exposed, revealed, talked

---

7 Geoffrey Bennington, "For Better or for Worse (There Again…)," *Discourse* 30, nos. 1–2, special issue *"Who or What"—Jacques Derrida*, ed. Dragan Kujundžić (2008): 191–207, at 191–92.

about, worked through, by not allowing Derrida to come back as a visible ghost in short…. To do that would probably be admitting to the visibility of appropriation, an apparatic appropriation of an apparition, which I sense Hillis wants to avoid or ward off. In a sense, this subtle refusal of the programmed mediatic return is precisely the work of mourning which does not appropriate, which refuses a "revealed" and visualized ghost tele-programmed by manipulation, controlled videographic and prosthetic repetition. And thus is more faithful to Derrida and his "return," predicated on the possibility of a missed encounter and a non-return, thus allowing a return not only of an Other, but of every other, wholly other as well.

> *I am, therefore I am haunted; to say "I am" is to confess to the experience, perception and recollection, re-presentation of the singularity of every instant of an authentic spectrality, authentic because, violently anachronistic, resistant to all historical or temporal containment, the gift of haunting remains other than, and resistant to any mode of conventional, certainly visual, or let me qualify this, directly visual, visibly direct representation or mode of mimesis.*

What does it mean to be "really dead," which listening to Derrida's tapes would reveal or bring?

> *Coming from what I call with too much ease a "past," my own past, an historical past, memory is what remains, it is the remains, so to speak, but wildly anachronistic, it also remains this unpredictable future revenant, remaining to come.*

Seeing the "real" visible return of Derrida in the video clip would be nothing but the possibility of such an appropriation, of a completely controlled and programmed prosthetic substitute. In order to keep Derrida alive as much as possible, alive in memory, at least, one must not touch the dead or let the dead return in the exact, programmed form. Thus allowing it in this scene to return them or him more vividly in invisible forms of displacements configuring the singular scaping and escaping ("the queer inscape,"[8] or where more generally, "[t]o be is to be queer"[9]), of the experience of being J. Hillis Miller/Hillis. In any case, that is what I tried to edit "into" this film and the sequence (often very much blind to its effects), but the sequence operates here the displaced a- and ana-chronistic temporality whereby what comes before or after is scrambled, non-linear, in-visible, and di-visible. In a word, the scene is constructed or deconstructed as a counter-time in which one waits for or comes in the wake (the trace, the mourning) of the death of the non-appropriated other. "Each is already in mourning for the other. [...] It takes place every time I love."[10]

> *We cannot be prepared for what can always come, always haunt us, or hit us with the force of a dead man's hand. That unprogrammable future, distinguished by Derrida as l'avenir, the to-come, as opposed to la future, the certain future of the sun's rising, the 14th of April following the 13th, is where we cannot be prepared to let-go. The ghost makes us let go.*

These scenes are strewn throughout Miller's recent responses about Derrida. In the film, Hillis also speaks about the "dark side" of Derrida, the nocturnal Derrida, with which Hillis wants to "maybe disagree" but which I cannot but interpret as the nocturnal Derrida in Hillis, a counter-time of mourning which Hillis preserves as he keeps it at a distance, "*The sun for sorrow will not show his head.*" The conclusion of his *For Derrida* which was quoted in the film as an intertitle states as much: "That is my last word, at least for now. [...] If these essays are works of mourning, they have not worked." A certain absent core seems to open in Miller's work of late (and it is a question of coming

---

8   Nicholas Royle, *In Memory of Jacques Derrida* (Edinburgh: Edinburgh University Press, 2009), 126.
9   Jacques Derrida, "'Justices,'" trans. Peggy Kamuf, *Critical Inquiry* 31, no. 3 (2005): 689–721, at 703. Henceforth, "J."
10 Jacques Derrida, "Aphorism Countertime," trans. Nicholas Royle, in *Acts of Literature,* ed. Derek Attridge, 414–35 (New York: Routledge, 1992), 422.

too late, as we shall see), or seems to be the work of his writing itself, something like a touch that cannot be touched, a vacant center opened by Derrida's demise.

> *So, returning to the video of Miller and Derrida, to conclude with the video clip, even if it proves not to have done with us: The limit of Miller's reading is the limit of representation itself and the distinction that remains to be thought through between representation, a mode of human intervention or control (whether more or less technological), and that which is beyond all representation, within but inexpressibly other than representation: the trace…*

This has left inscriptions or inscriptions, encrypted, sometimes unconscious marks in J. Hillis Miller's *The Medium Is the Maker*, for example, when he discusses Derrida on telepathy. Referring to Derrida, Miller describes something that "turned up again, close at hand, at a time when it was too late…," a description of a ghost if there is any, creeping in this seemingly innocuous analytic formula. And then goes on: "This present fake lecture [note the apotropaic, 'fake' protective irony here], already far too long to be read in one séance [note again the protective irony, but also the scene of writing as a conjuring up of the ghost] ought to have been part of my *For Derrida,* but has been written too late for inclusion there."

> *Though I can rewind, fast forward, pause, and so on, I cannot control that return, that which can always arrive from within and overflowing the technological, the revenance in the trace of the voice.*

In a word, such experience comes too late, to use Miller's words, there is a *decalage,* or a counter-temporality at work there, my words *For Derrida* come too late for Derrida. And right after this sentence, "my For Derrida," "too late for inclusion there," Hillis writes: "The Fort/Da sequence of his losing and then refinding 'Telepathy,' says Derrida, 'remains inexplicable for me even to this day."[11] Just after *For Derrida,* seconds later, a heartbeat later, a *Fort/Da,* for Derrida, an F-D, an inscription of *Todestrieb,* of a death drive, Derrida Fort but not Da, not anymore, left to haunt Miller's work like a vacant center, a touch he cannot touch. An impossible touch of Derrida (a dubious genitive here, *je me touche toi*) which comes too late, written too late, always already too late for Derrida, but also for Miller. We will not have mourned the ghost, the spectral, in the living, never enough. And by missing the other so much he comes to the truth.

> [R]e-presentation that can always return to haunt from the future, and additionally serve to exceed and so erase or deconstruct the premise of a separation on which binaries such as "recorded/live" "dead/live," fort / da, here / there, presence / absence, and so forth are all predicated. As soon as we acknowledge the trace, there is the ghost in the machine.

Hillis is here far from "Hillis le Mal," the rugged Virginian, the almost demonic force with an untouchable, so to speak, imperturbable serenity, which Tom Cohen justly or unjustly but humorously discerns in him, "Hillis le Mal," so not Hillis le Mal, but Hillis *l'Animal,* the animal looking for the lines of escape, the evading animal frightened by the death of the other, "l'animal que *J.* suit." "I am, he is," you will notice, a confusion engulfs the writing here in a difference which cannot be heard, or touched, but which animates the scene of writing but also of filming, like an animal que je suis/t. *L'animal,* also, *qui est mal,* the wounded, hurting animal which I follow, in me, in the other, there where we wait for each other at the limit of each other's finitude and death, at the limit of truth, there where I is the other, Je (J) *est un autre.*

> *There is, in this, no absolute sequence. Speaking of a "before" or an "after" is to assume a logic that is both temporal and spatial,*

---

11 J. Hillis Miller, *For Derrida* (New York. Fordham University Press, 2009), 44.

> when what takes place is a constant interchange. Derrida is
> talking about wondering what it must be like to be, to feel like,
> to taste oneself as, to have the taste of, for J. Hillis Miller, of
> Miller's taste of, for himself. In this too there is an edit whereby
> the laptop, the technological substrate disappears, giving us in
> the illusion, through the medium by which film is filmed, that
> we are no longer watching a film on a laptop, projection within
> a film, the subject of which is no longer visible but watching
> from elsewhere, like the ghost of himself that the film would
> make of him, regardless of whether he is alive (as is Miller)
> or dead (as is Derrida). One subject, always already absent,
> assumes a supplementarity for the other subject. These are all
> provisional positions and can always change.

This countertemporality and spectrality which cannot be seen is precisely what I tried to convey or to allow to appear without appearing (not visible to me either), then, in editing with the cascading frames, but can we *see* how many? I am the one who is probably the most blind. Let's try to enumerate some of them. The scene of Derrida on the computer is preceded by the cut on Hillis's eye made by the glass frame. And where? In Irvine (which will appear shortly in Derrida's explicit mention of "the Archive") after the fall on the stairs leading to the Humanities Hall where Derrida held his seminars! The eye itself as frame; Hillis's eye held by the metonymy of the prosthetic camera eye, thus the viewer's eye, seeing the wound and the cut as frame, from which the scene flows (the water stream, the video stream…); thus, the framed, wounded, lachrymose eye (seen in the slow motion, the eye/I wading anamorphically through the ocular water), the eye wounded by the loss larger than the camera, the frame and the scene, beholding the viewer, including the "director," the "I-eye" filming it in the grip of interminable blinding melancholia. In the film, I told Hillis, jokingly: "what about that scar, what did you do to the other guy?" to which Hillis responded: "Yes, you should see the other guy." And then I proceeded to edit the entire sequence about Derrida and mourning, yes, go and see the other guy who wounded

Hillis's eye, go and see the mourning as the other that wounds the eye/I. But I only myself saw it in the end, on a big screen at the first public screening, blinded by my own wounded and lachrymose gaze and refusal to see the demise of Derrida. And Barbara Cohen's picture afterwards, framing a friendship, with J and J touching each other, the haptic in the cinematic, the ultimate ghost, and there they are both... touching each other and by that touch creating a counter-time "at the heart of the syncope, between touching and untouchable," and thus also already a prosthetic mourning, "the ageless intrusion of technics, which is to say the transplantation of the prosthesis."[12] With the voiceover and the punctuation of the piano chord: "For nothing in the world would I have passed up the chance to recall, publicly, that it has been given to me, like a benediction, to know Joseph Hillis Miller for more than thirty five years, to have had the honor of teaching at his side, [...] the honor also of having shared with him more than with any other, through I don't know how many countries, colloquia, meetings of all sorts, the intellectual adventure that signs and seals our lives" ("J," 712). And then, Hillis, "Am I on camera?" walking alone (Derrida's *I Will Now Have to Walk Alone,* Deleuze's obituary, another mournful frame, was my reference here) after posting a letter, creating the counter time of mourning, they miss each other, do they miss each other, how they miss each other! Like Romeo and Juliet, the counter time of mourning as the impossibility of *being with* is put on display or on replay here — Derrida in Hillis's solitude (the crunching of the gravel also a sound frame, the *Mittagsgespenst* of the archive fever leaving the traces in stone), more "visible" and "in picture" than ever. Where? There.

The scene of Hillis walking back to "us," to the camera ("Am I on camera?"), when he sends the letter, comes right after the analysis of the letter sent from that very same mail box on Deer Isle, the address clearly visible in the corner of the letter which

---

12 Jacques Derrida, *On Touching — Jean-Luc Nancy,* trans. Christine Irizarry (Stanford: Stanford University Press, 2005), 112.

Derrida reproduced moments earlier. The letter Hillis sent in that scene of posting the letter went to Derrida.... When? Then!

From Derrida, to a letter. From Derrida on the screen, to a letter, on the screen, by virtue of another screen, one screen on the screen inside a screen, reproduced for the screen, yet another. The "original" letter, transferred to a transparency and thus reiterated, placed on a projector, becomes yet one more in a tissue of traces, the thinnest of leaves overlaying one another, so thin, so seemingly transparent as to have no weight, no depth.

When is this letter, where is this letter? The letter sent by Hillis (the scene of Hillis sending the letter) in the film from Deer Isle arrived in time to follow Derrida's lecture eight years before the scene of sending; only to announce that Derrida's letter to Miller were not arriving to the right addressee. The letter described by Derrida seemed, in turn, "to forecast today's lecture and keynote, from more than thirty years distance" ("J," 706). Thus, the missive announces the miss and the missing, always already, from the time immemorial. I missed you, says Derrida in his lecture and in his letter, but when, where? Am I missing something here? This *destinerrance* of the letter, however, which is displayed in the film as coming after (after the long history of friendship), also comes before the film, as the traumatic space of memory of this lecture at which both Hillis and I were present. And in which scene in the film Hillis sees Derrida's demise, "he already looked old and not that well."

In conclusion: so, perhaps, and I do not say this lightly, perhaps Miller is, if not wrong exactly in his response to the tele-technological ghost, then not quite right either. For as the recording, that which can be played back is only ever a trace, it is different only in degree, rather than as one might at first believe, in kind. A prosthetized archive, memory denatured, made available through an othering, a nonhuman externalisation, the recording can always come back, but only on the condition that we understand it not as a representation, though it is

> *this of course. Instead, we must see past the merely visible, the mimicry, the mimetic tendency of tele-technology to be, in its apprehension of the trace, simply representation.*

The memory of a loss, to which Miller's writing, his postings, have subsequently tried to respond, like in the scene of mailing the letter, but also in *For Derrida*, are profoundly informed or imprinted by this spectral but non-representable division, of "the lack which does not have a place in dissemination" (*PC*, 441). The letter is thus fully (un)accounted for, both before and after, here and there, but never in the right place: "The letter might not be found, or could always possibly not be found" (*PC*, 442) dividing the scene of representation as the infinitely divisible specter haunting the frame of "representation," but also, I would claim, informing the very scene of writing in works like *The Medium Is the Maker*.

> *I have introduced a distinction to do with representation and what cannot be represented, and which distinction therefore admits the possibility of speaking about haunting beyond representation, where the visible fails, and haunting takes place all the more forcefully through memory and that which countersigns memory, always, already: loss.*

In *The Medium Is the Maker* Miller has an innovative analysis pertaining to the question of finitude in Heidegger and Derrida. For Heidegger, the finitude of being (*da-sein*) partakes in the movement of general Being, it "holds," Hillis says, "all the horizons of time with one mobile unit. [...] Heidegger's time is grounded in *Sein*, Being with a capital B. Derrida's time is created out of performative media, the media as makers [...]. On each occasion a given medium is used that creates its own ground and its own differance."[13] What this means is that each time we use a technical apparatus, flip a cell phone, type on a computer, make a film, watch a TV, we are opening a new tem-

---

13 Miller, *For Derrida*, 25.

poral ground in which our finitude is both confirmed and traversed and overcome. By using technical apparatuses, we partake in our own survival. And that happens every time I speak, teach or touch someone. "As if the word 'I' were inaugurating, in the first person, the very grammar of all spectrality, like a mask, 'I' of a revenant" ("J," 714). But it is most discernible in the usage of the technical apparatuses like recording live or life. Just like Derrida's notion of the letter in *The Post Card*, which from "the first stroke divides itself, and must indeed support partition in order to identify itself." Thus, "there are nothing but post cards, anonymous morsels without fixed domicile, without legitimate addressee, letters opened, but like crypts" (*PC*, 53). And, just like in the scene with the letter, Derrida displays, posts a post it for all to see, a piece of an open letter but also a crypt. An inscryption, the pieces (*mor*ceaux) of which are little bites (*morsures*) of death (*mort*). "Soon everyone will be there, and me, I will have to leave" (*PC*, 61).

"This too will be in the archive": the film as epitaph, cenotaph, and *cine*taph.

> *The archive, its very idea, the phantom eidolon following in the wake but also presaging the material possibility of the archive, is always already haunted by the play of the trace on which the archive relies for its somewhat uncanny existence.*

The letter sent many years ago never quite arrives, it arrives erroneously, too late, it misses its addressee. The division of the address that Derrida tried to discern in the "J" of "J. Hillis Miller" is divided between "John" and "Joseph," thus between the Old and the New Testaments. "And one of the sins that I must have committed at the origin, by substituting John for Joseph, will have been to risk evangelizing and Christianizing a name that hovered between the Old and the New Testaments" ("J," 718).

It is not hard to see in the film how bemused Derrida is by this originary confusion, and his mistake. Precisely, by a mistake of "revealing" the secret name, the name of the "secret God," and thus giving visibility to what must remain hidden. But by this mistaking Joseph for John, Derrida in fact enacts what he in *Ulysses Gramophone, the Yes Saying of Joyce* sees as an affirmative yet disruptive force of alterity in the messianic without the Messiah. Without this possibility of the non-arrival of the letter, of the wrong arrival of the letter already divided by this errant "sailing, sealing, signing," without this intrusion of the Jewish other in the Greek tradition, everything would be just the repetition of the same, it would lead to the non-arrival of Greek onto-theology to itself, and Ulysses (but not the novel, *Ulysses*), thus returning to himself/itself/themselves as the arrival of a dead letter. (The danger of such "Greek" return to itself is made evident in Heidegger's Danube, *Der Ister,* flowing *rückwertz,* from Greece, towards Schwarzwald, as to its proper destination, the origin flowing to itself, as he writes in 1942; and just like Greece itself, in a Europe programmed by the exclusion of the Greek other, by the exclusion of economic justice, which is coming back to haunt Germany, in 2012, returns to Germany as the origin coming back and imploding Europe and Germany like the return of the repressed. The danger against which Miller's *Topographies* is one of the most emphatic warnings ever written, particularly regarding Heidegger, in "Slipping, Vaulting, Crossing"[14]).

Could we hear in Derrida's bemused laughter the "eschatological tone of the yes-laughter" which is "traversed by the vowels of a completely different song," that broke out in Dublin in Joyce's *Ulysses,* in the body of Molly Bloom, "necessary in order to contrive the breach necessary for the coming of the other," whom "one can always call an Elijah, if Elijah is the name of the unforeseeable other for whom a place must be kept: [...] Elijah, the Other."[15] The amused, contagious laughter which broke out in the lecture hall with Derrida upon the revelation of this confusion, announced, in this erroneous attribution of the letter

---

14 J. Hillis Miller, *Topographies* (Stanford: Stanford University Press, 1995).
15 Jacques Derrida, "Ulysses Gramophone: Hear Say Yes in Joyce," trans. Tina Kendall and Shari Benstock, in *Acts of Literature,* ed. Derek Attridge, 253–310 (New York: Routledge, 1992), 294–95.

address and the name (Christian for Jewish), a laughing recognition and affirmation, yes, yes, that the non-arrival of the other is the very condition of something happening, taking place, as a difference or differance. The possibility of this *destinerrance* is the very condition of the arrival of the Other. This is the lesson that the "protestant" J. teaches the "Jewish" J., in a chiasmatic reversal, in the letter in which Miller teaches Derrida how to write.

Keep the place at the table for J, the Other, "the uncanniest of guests."[16]

A Coda: Ulysses, a Destinerrance of the Other

> *Within, other than the visible, the visual, beyond mere representation, the trace of the other is there, the trace in my relation to that trace remains singular. It can always arrive to touch me, because for me, if for no one else, it has about it that singularity phenomenally, by which the trace bears in it the ghost of a chance. This is most eloquently illustrated, I think, in the final scene of another film that treats of ghosts, personal and those of history, Theo Angelopoulos's Ulysses' Gaze.*

Theo Angelopoulos's *Ulysses' Gaze* (1996) narrates how a modern-day Ulysses (Harvey Keitel) seeks to find three undeveloped reels by the Manakis brothers whose first movie, which does exist, and is one of the first ever, depicts women weaving, somewhere in the Balkans. (That movie is actually shown at the beginning of *Ulysses' Gaze*). The quest for knowledge leads Ulysses through many scenes repeating the violence of history that constitutes the space known as the Balkans: in Greece, Albania, Macedonia, Romania, then Belgrade and Sarajevo. (A scene in the movie shows an insignificant village, Janina, filmed by the Manakis brothers, as the voice over narrates: "All European armies have marched through it.") It is to the Sarajevo of the last war that the teleology of his will to know takes him, and finding

---

16 J. Hillis Miller, "The Critic as Host," in *Deconstruction & Criticism* (New York: Continuum, 1979), 253.

the reels, it finds its destination, its end. The undeveloped reels are kept by a Jewish curator, to be killed with his entire family soon after he hands the movie over to Keitel. The last scenes depict Sarajevo in the fog, the only time when the city is at peace. And in that moment of peace is the time to bury the dead. And it is in this moment of suspended shared danger that the youth orchestra ("the young Serbs, Croats, Muslims, playing together," the Jewish curator explains to Keitel) can perform in the open. A sheltered gathering appears in the face of a catastrophe, during the fog, which re-orients Ulysses' heading, to the possibility of another Bosnia, another Europe.

Ulysses' Gaze subverts the entire Greek, and therefore exemplary European notion of the onto-teleology of gazing and spacing, starting at least with Plato's cave, and proposes another "dislocation of the Greek logos," a certain Greco-Jewish contamination, as Jacques Derrida has it in "Violence and Metaphysics": "a dislocation of our identity, and perhaps of identity in general; it summons us to depart from the Greek site and perhaps from the very site in general."[17] These are Derrida's words about another patient Jew, Emmanuel Levinas ("Jewgreek, greekjew" is how Joyce calls his Ulysses, and how Derrida calls Levinas[18]). This different site and sight will be motivated not by the will to know, see, or name, which can only testify to the already programmed catastrophe of history. (This "will to know" is in itself complicit in many ways with the violence taking place, as exemplified by a cynical anecdote spun in Sarajevo during the siege; one neighbor to another, as a curse, says a Serb to a Muslim: "May your house appear tonight on CNN!" CNN is therefore not where war and destruction are, war and destruction are where there is CNN. The citizens of Sarajevo understood that better than the "liberal West" or "Europe"). Rather, this alternative sight will be motivated, or imagined, by an utmost passivity: weaving, keeping the patient commemoration of danger which wards off exactly that

---

17 Jacques Derrida, "Violence and Metaphysics," in *Writing and Difference*, trans. Alan Bass (Chicago: University of Chicago Press, 1978), 82.
18 Ibid., 153.

kind of ophtalmo-phallocratic gaze of war under which the European history unravels or ruins itself. It is in weaving and keeping, in danger, that, as Levinas says, "the face of the other, in this nudity, exposed unto death […] reminds one of the very mortality of the other person."[19] The responsibility to the other will always have preceded the certainty of the name, sight, or gaze.

In one of the last scenes of the movie, the blank frames flicker in front of Ulysses' gaze.

> *A Greek-American filmmaker, having returned to Greece, journeys through the Balkans in search of three missing reels of film, thought to be the first film, the first "gaze." Finally, in Sarajevo, he finds the film. We witness the filmmaker watching the film, but we never see what he sees, by which he is moved to tears, to which he responds with words promising return, the narrative of an other, to which he gives voice. We can never witness the ghost directly.*

In the blank screen he sees, maybe, the catastrophe of history: the face of every person who died in the Bosnian war; the end of a site and of a sight, a sight/site of Europe. But in the blank flickering of the frames, an opening: the blank, undeveloped film, an unseen memory of the unprogrammed other, patience, passivity, a promise, a future. For example, an example. An example? In the meantime, Sarajevo is in fog. The world is blind.

---

19 Emmanuel Levinas, *Time and the Other*, trans. Richard A. Cohen (Pittsburgh: Duquesne University Press, 1987), 107.

Vincent W.J. van Gerven Oei

Postface

This collection of essays is an example *par excellence* of the postcard effect so extensively treated in Jacques Derrida's *The Post Card: From Socrates to Freud and Beyond*. None of these essays was ever meant to end up in my hands, being now the presumed "editor" of this volume. As if in an actual enactment of, or perhaps, better, faithfulness to the project of this publication, its original addressee returned the mail, which, poste restante on the west coast of the United States, in a locale not far away from the Jacques Derrida Papers housed at the Special Collections and Archives of UC Irvine, was forwarded to my inbox.

My own encounter with Derrida's work started with a similar form of *destinerrance,* when I stumbled across *Of Grammatology* in the philosophy of language section of the W.E.B. Du Bois library at the University of Massachusetts in Amherst. A graduate student in linguistics, I was convinced that the book was addressing me. It spoke of the origins of language, took on Saussure, and developed the notion of "trace." Freshly trained in Chomskyan linguistics, all of these seemed so familiar to me, yet I understood nothing — as if it was written in another English, an English I could pronounce but not read.

The arrival of this text in my non-comprehending hands led me through a maze that only later I came to understand as the so-called analytical–continental divide. In retrospect, it seemed silly to ask my professor in mathematical logic where to turn to gain an understanding of this seemingly inaccessible book. We don't teach this in our philosophy department, he said. Back in the Netherlands, the philosophy department of the University of Leiden told me to chase my lead at the comparative literature department. A few years later, in 2003, it became one of the first philosophy books I bought. By then, I had entered the European Graduate School.

There was a door in the linguistics wing of UMass's South College, at the end of a corridor, that was never opened. Or, more precisely, I never saw it opened. Only later, much later, I understood from a friend who had been to "the other side" what was hidden behind that door: the CompLit department. Not even once during my exchange year had I entered it. That door no longer exists; the building has been renovated, and now has a different purpose. It houses the College of Humanities and Fine Arts.

***

The fourteen essays gathered in *Going Postcard: The Letter(s) of Jacques Derrida* all respond to a single request: to provide a gloss to one or multiple phrases from *The Post Card*. That this request is not a facile demand becomes theatrically clear in the opening lines of Peggy Kamuf's contribution: "A commentary? On 'Envois'? No, really, you're joking, right?" *The Post Card,* as Kamuf argues, demonstrates that the presuppositions underlying such a request are shaky, to say the least. This is extensively proven by the contribution of J. Hillis Miller, who, providing a gloss to the preface, inquires "to what genre does 'Envois' belong?" To all genres and none at all.

Despite the wide range of topics and approaches extracted from *The Post Card* by the different contributors, several larger themes can be distinguished. Nicholas Royle, Hannah Markley, and Zach Rivers explore different aspects of telephony and other postal logics. Julian Wolfreys and Éamonn Dunne both address the theme of love, another relevant aspect of this text that *also* belongs to genre of amorous epistles. Nevertheless, it appears that being a shape-shifting, superbly elusive, and often self-defeating text, *The Post Card* resists commentary to the extent that it has managed to derail and extemporize the present volume, destining it for a form of publication that truly adheres to the "postal logic": open access — for all to read, *sans envelope*.

***

Several authors have remarked about the fact that part of the correspondence has been burned, or so Derrida tells us. Miller cites from the preface to "Envois," the first half of the larger work, that its letters are "a recently destroyed correspondence. Destroyed by fire or what figuratively takes it place, more certain of leaving nothing out of the reach of what I like to call the tongue of fire, not even the cinders if cinders there are [*s'il y a là cendre*]" (*PC*, 3), a phrase which Miller provides with an extensive gloss. He also refers to a later episode in which Derrida writes about burning the collection at the roadside in suburban Paris. Michael Naas, conversely, examines the white spaces, the 52-character "blanks," which, rather than the result of consumption by fire, are insertions standing in for erased passages of variable length. How long, we (and Derrida) no longer know, because "I have totally forgotten the rule as well as the elements of such a calculation, as if I had thrown them into the fire" (*PC*, 5).

This burning of the letters, of correspondence, but also, by extension, of philosophical texts, is explicitly thematized at several points in "Envois." One of these places is where Derrida considers Plato's Second Letter, written to the tyrant Dionysius. Towards the end of the letter, Plato asks Dionysius to "read this letter over repeatedly and then burn it up."[1] Derrida speaks of this order as "indeed the most amorous, most crazy order, which I had also given to you" (*PC*, 59). The unknown addressee of his *envois*, somehow, is thus expected to complete the task that he himself couldn't finish, or, perhaps, Derrida himself is the addressee: "This order was not an order, despite the imperative, as they believe [...]. My order was the most abandoned prayer and the most inconceivable simulacrum — for myself first of all"

---

1 Plat. *L.* 2.314c.

(*PC*, 59). Within the space of less than a page, Plato thus already starts to mirror Derrida while Dionysius becomes this elusive "you [*tu*]." This is far from the only time such a maelstrom of readdresses appears in *The Post Card*. As James Burt suggests in his contribution, it is the constant "proliferation of pronouns [...] that leaves [you] panting."

As extensively treated by Kamillea Aghtan, *The Post Card* plays with the abbreviations "S." and "p." of "Socrates" and "plato," the latter written with a lowercase letter in reference to his smaller stature on the postcard reproduction (see p. 15) from Matthew Paris's *Prognostica Socratis basilei* that Derrida found in the Bodleian library, the alleged beginning or impetus of the "Envois." Several authors have picked up on aspects of this image. Nicholas Royle ana(para)lyses the "stingray" emerging underneath S.'s buttocks, while Wen-Chuan Kao sees links the emergence of the phallus with similar imagery from Bataille, and Eszter Timár sees in it a figure of autoimmunity. Burt, imagining a philosophical relay race, speaks of a "confused baton-handover."

But S. and p. are not the two only philosophical abbreviations; there is a third: the D. of — at first — Dionysius the Younger of Syracuse, the addressee of Plato's letter. But one phrase, a page later, which initially seems to rephrase p.'s request to D. to burn the letter after reading, suddenly opens a vista upon the inaugural pyromania of philosophy. In a letter dated September 4, 1977, Derrida writes, "P. asks D. to reread before burning, so be it, in order to incorporate the letter (like a member of the resistance under torture) and to take it in him by heart. Keep what you burn, such is the demand" (*PC*, 60).

Because Dionysius was not the only D. that p. related to by means of burning, this D. — and this must have been one of Derrida's reasons to abbreviate — invokes also another philosopher, and one that p. never deigned to mention or address: Democritus. What follows is a wider reading of some of the implications of this displacement of D.

In his own words, Democritus had always been the newcomer. Whereas Plato was the established Athenian, Democritus was the stranger whom nobody in Athens knew.² Despite this anonymity, Plato is reported to have had an enormous dislike for "the laughing philosopher,"³ sometimes also the "prince of the philosophers," who managed to establish a good reputation among the Athenians. In his *Lives of the Philosophers,* Diogenes Laertius claims that Plato would have liked to see nothing more than all of Democritus's works burned:

> Aristoxenus in his Historical Notes affirms that Plato wished to burn all the writings of Democritus that he could collect, but that Amyclas and Clinias the Pythagoreans prevented him, saying that there was no advantage in doing so, for already his books were widely circulated. And there is clear evidence for this in the fact that Plato, who mentions almost all the early philosophers, never once alludes to Democritus, not even where it would be necessary to controvert him, obviously because he knew that he would have to match himself against the prince of the philosophers.⁴

Derrida projects Plato's desire to obliterate Democritus's oeuvre onto his own correspondence when he refers to his "demand of the first letter: burn everything'" (*PC,* 59). Here, the letter as the result of an abbreviation and the letter as a piece of correspondence impress upon each other, as "first letter" refers back to some previous epistle *and* the "first letter" of plato: p. "Burn everything," is the demand of both.

---

2 Hermann Diels, *Die Fragmente der Vorsokratiker,* vol. 2, ed. Walther Kranz (Berlin: Weidmannsche Buchhandlung, 1935), 165, B116: ἦλθον γὰρ εἰς Ἀθήνας καὶ οὔ τίς ἔγνωκεν. — "For I came to Athens and no one knew me" (trans. C.C.W. Taylor, *The Atomists: Leucippus and Democritus: Fragments, A Text and Translation with a Commentary* [Toronto: University of Toronto Press, 1999], D1).
3 Cf. L. Annaeus Seneca, "De Ira," in *Moral Essays,* vol. 1, ed. John W. Basore (London/New York: Heinemann, 1928), 2.10.5: "Democritum contra aiunt nunquam sine risu in publico fuisse; adeo nihil illi videbatur senum eorum quae serio gerebantur."
4 Diogenes Laertius, *Diogenis Laertii Vitae Philosophorum,* ed. H.S. Long (Oxford: Oxford University Press, 1964), IX 7.40.

Hannah Markley suggests in her contribution that the injunction to "burn everything" "appears only insofar as it haunts and recursively undoes 'the single event of understood language,'" naming the "impossibility of legibility." But the specific desire to burn Democritus's writings, and by extension any philosophical text, is also, to speak with Rick Elmore, a "troubling line" that draws the foundation of the Western metaphysical tradition, a tradition that is firmly rooted in the work of small p. and not the atomism of prince D., whose philosophy, even though the former failed in his pyromaniac plot, has been all but forgotten, with only snippets and fragments preserved here and there. Friedrich Nietzsche, two millennia later, was to become the first philosopher to cast a light upon p.'s inaugural hatred for D. and lament the fate of the latter's oeuvre: not destroyed by fire but by the steady grind of Christianity. In his early forays into pre-Platonic philosophy, Nietzsche observed:

> Bad things have happened to the writings of Democritus: although they would be characterized as full of insightful judgments, as stylistic beauties, as model writings in a philosophic presentation, they would be nonetheless destroyed because in later centuries their justification would be felt as more and more strange, and especially by Christianity as it discarded the grounds for comprehending Democritus, as Aristotle had taken exception to his rejection of teleology. All but the hardest fate had already caught up to them a half century after the death of their composer: and this is truly the reason that the Christian scholars and monastic transcribers forced their hands from Democritus, to remove him as if he were possessed, a plan which Plato had kindled, to throw the collected writings of Democritus in the fire. […] We are still very much guilty of the death sacrifice of Democritus, and only to some extent have we made good on the indebtedness to him by the past.[5]

---

5   Friedrich Nietzsche, quoted in Paul A. Swift, *Becoming Nietzsche: Early Reflections on Democritus, Schopenhauer, and Kant* (Oxford: Lexington Books,

This originary scandal has also not been left unnoticed by Derrida, who at several points in his oeuvre has hinted at the violence with which metaphysics has asserted its authority:

> [T]he Democritean tradition [...] had been subjected since its origin, and first of all under the violent authority of Plato, to a powerful repression throughout the history of Western culture. One can now follow its symptomatology, which begins with the erasure of the name of Democritus in the writings of Plato, even though Plato was familiar with his doctrine. He probably feared that one might draw some conclusion as to the proximity, or even the filiation, of some of his philosophemes.[6]

One of these philosophemes drawn by p. from D., Derrida suggests elsewhere, is *"khōra,"* the "bastardly notion" from the *Timeaus*.[7] Rivers picks up on this telephonic connection, proposing to listen to *correspondances* as *khōra*-spondances. But that's not the only leftover of the "Democritean tradition." Another, perhaps even less known notion, is *eteē*, usually translated as "reality" or "truth." It has, however, nothing to do with that quintessential Platonic and metaphysical concept, *alētheia*.[8] Besides lying at the foundation of the elusive science of etymology, *eteē* is closely (and indeed etymologically) related to the Socratic method of *exetasis*, of "examination," "testing," or "scrutiny," and belongs to a juridical semantic field that also includes *elengkhos* "interrogation" and *basanos* "torture." That which interrogation or examination is to bring out, in the Socratic method, is not so

---

2008), 76.
6 Jacques Derrida, "My Chances/*Mes chances*: A Rendezvous with Some Epicurean Stereophonies," trans. Avital Ronell, in *Psyche: Inventions of the Other*, vol. 1, eds. Peggy Kamuf and Elizabeth Rottenberg, 344–76 (Stanford: Stanford University Press, 2007), 362.
7 Jacques Derrida, "Plato's Pharmacy," in *Dissemination*, trans. Barbara Johnson, 67–168 (London/New York: Continuum, 2004), 159.
8 See Jean-Pierre Levet, *Le vrai et le faux dans la pensée grecque archaïque* (Paris: Les Belles Lettres, 1976).

much *alētheia* about the world, but the *eteē* of a person—the concordance between their words, actions, and character. This is not a trivial matter. As Socrates famously stated in the *Apology,* "The unexamined life [*anexetastos bios*] is not livable for a human."⁹

This incomplete and very tentative gloss allows us to inspect the second part of the phrase. p. is asking D. to reread his work before burning it, "in order to incorporate the letter (like a member of the resistance under torture) and to take it in him by heart." As Avital Ronell has pointed out, the theme of torture, or *basanos* (and by extension *elengkhos* and *exetasis*), is deeply anchored in Greek origins of philosophical practice; torture, especially the torturing of a slave, was thought to be a fool-proof way at arriving at the truth.¹⁰ In his contribution, Wan-Chuan Kao discusses torture in yet another context, that of ecstasy and eroticism. But the way in which Derrida invokes torture here, as a case or example in which the incorporation of a letter, of taking it by heart, which is of vital necessity in order *not* to reveal its contents to the Gestapo, suggests a different paradigm. Rather than speaking the truth after the first or repeated infliction of pain, D. is asked not to say anything—knowing that all the material evidence has been burned. Derrida thus inverts here the Greek paradigm. Rather than torture being a certain way of arriving at the content of a letter, torture here provides the context in which a letter is incorporated and taken "by heart." The Greek slave always speaks, whereas the member of the resistance never does. He therefore also highlights a contradiction within Plato's own stance toward the burning of letters. Whereas in his letter to Dionysius, the burning becomes the guarantee for memorization, the burning of Democritus's writings would be the guarantee for their oblivion.

Finally, the abbreviation D. suggests a subtext in which Derrida identifies with Democritus, albeit reversing the plot—a

---

9   Pl. *Apol.* 38a: ὁ δὲ ἀνεξέταστος βίος οὐ βιωτὸς ἀνθρώπῳ.
10 See Avital Ronell, *The Test Drive* (Urbana/Chicago: University of Illinois Press, 2005), 81–86.

reversal not unlike "S. before p." — by burning his letters, his correspondence *himself*. This reading of D. for Derrida is also offered by Dragan Kujundžić, who moreover links it to the da of the Freudian *fort–da* (and, why not, to Alan Bass's gloss in his introduction "L before K" on the "prefix of negation" *dé-* or *dé* "die"[11]). After first inverting the relation between incineration and memory, Derrida, in the third and final part of the above-cited phrase, appropriates p.'s destructive desire — by burning his own correspondence: "Keep what you burn, such is the demand."

This collection has tried to obey this impossible demand. To keep what was presumed to be destroyed, on the threshold of to gloss and to gloss over.

---

11 Allan Bass, "L before K," introduction to Derrida, *The Post Card,* xix.

About the Contributors

Kamillea Aghtan works as an independent scholar in Brisbane, Australia, and has published on regulatory and sensual ethics in a variety of contexts from medieval history to contemporary literature. She has a particular interest in the writings of Michel Serres and the ways in which his thought can expose and lodge itself within the fissures, breaches, and recuperations endemic to socio-legal, institutional, and academic structures.

James Burt is currently living and writing in Brighton, England. He is recovering from a hip injury which has stopped him from running. His website can be found at www.orbific.com.

Éamonn Dunne is a research scholar at the School of Education, Trinity College Dublin. He is currently living and teaching in Bangkok, Thailand, and working on a book on events of unlearning and the philosophy of weak pedagogy. He is the author of *J. Hillis Miller and the Possibilities of Reading: Literature after Deconstruction* (Continuum, 2010), *Reading Theory Now* (Bloomsbury, 2013) and, with Aidan Seery, *The Pedagogics of Unlearning* (punctum books, 2016). Research interests include philosophies of the event, radical pedagogies, and literature and trauma.

Rick Elmore is Assistant Professor of Philosophy at Appalachian State University. He earned his PhD in philosophy from DePaul University in 2012. He researches and teaches in 20th century French philosophy, Critical Theory, ethics, social political philosophy, environmental philosophy, and new realisms. His articles and essays have appeared in such venues as *Politics & Policy*, *Symplokē*, *The Cormac McCarthy Journal*, and *The Aesthetic Ground of Critical Theory* (Rowman and Littlefield International). He is the editor (with Anthony Paul Smith) of the *Ecotones: Ecology and Theory* book series (Rowman and Littlefield International). Elmore's work is guided by the question of how political, ethical, and environmental systems and institutions situate themselves in relation to violence, that is, to issues of inclusion, exclusion, power, force, law, policing, and normativity.

Vincent W.J. van Gerven Oei is a philologist and publisher at independent open-access publisher punctum books, where he also manages *Dotawo,* the imprint of the Union for Nubian Studies. At home he directs project bureau for the arts and humanities The Department of Eagles, organizing cultural projects in Tirana, Albania. His recent publications include *Cross-Examinations* (Gent: MER. Paper Kunsthalle, 2015), and the edited volume *Allegory of the Cave Painting* (Milan: Mousse, 2015; with Mihnea Mircan). As a translator, Van Gerven Oei works mostly with anonymous Medieval Nubian scribes and more recent authors such as Jean Daive, Hervé Guibert, Dick Raaijmakers, Avital Ronell, and Nachoem M. Wijnberg. His writings have appeared in *ArtPapers, nY, Përpjekja, Polish Archeology in the Mediterranean, postmedieval, Theory & Event,* and *tripwire,* among other venues.

Peggy Kamuf is Marion Frances Chevalier Professor of French and of Comparative Literature at the University of Southern California. She is the author, among other titles, of *Book of Addresses* (2005) and *To Follow: The Wake of Jacques Derrida* (2010). Her essays on literary theory, the university, and deconstruction have appeared in journals and anthologies in the US, Canada, Britain, and throughout Europe. She has coordinated the Derrida Seminars Translation Project and is co-editor, with Geoffrey Bennington, of the series The Seminars of Jacques Derrida at the University of Chicago Press.

Wan-Chuan Kao is an assistant professor of English at Washington and Lee University. His research interests include Chaucer, gender and sexuality, history of conduct and marriage, affect, cuteness, and whiteness studies. His work has appeared in *Studies in the Age of Chaucer, Journal of Lesbian Studies, Mediaevalia,* and *postmedieval.* Wan-Chuan is currently working on a monograph titled *White Before Whiteness,* which examines late medieval representations of whiteness across bodily and non-somatic figurations.

Dragan Kujundžić is a Professor of Jewish, Germanic and Slavic Studies, and Film and Media Studies at the University of Florida. He is the author of numerous articles in critical theory, deconstruction and literary criticism. He has edited "Deconstruction, A Merry Science" (1985), "*Khora*ographies for Jacques Derrida on July 15, 2000" (2000), "Who or What — Jacques Derrida" (2008) and two volumes on J. Hillis Miller, "J" (2005) and "Provocations to Reading" (with B. Cohen, 2005). His other publications include monographs "Critical Exercises" (Novi Sad, 1983), "The Returns of History" (New York, 1997), "Tongue in Heat" (Moscow, 2003), "Out of *Interculturality*" (Novi Sad, 2016). His documentary film, "The First Sail: J. Hillis Miller" (2011) has been released together with the book about the film (Kujundžić, Hillis Miller, et. al., London, 2015). He is currently working on the new monograph, "Cinetaphs: Encryptions of East and Central Europe in Film."

Hannah Markley is a Ph.D. candidate and fellow at the Bill and Carol Fox Center for Humanistic Inquiry at Emory University where she is completing her dissertation, "Wasting Romanticism: Melancholic Hunger and Maternal Remains Mary Shelley, Thomas De Quincey, and Emily Brontë." The project considers idiosyncratic acts of eating that not only fail to nourish the body, but systematically waste and destroy it. In addition to this project, she has published articles on Jacques Derrida in *Parallax,* Thomas De Quincey in *Essays in Romanticism,* and Samuel Taylor Coleridge in *European Romantic Review.*

J. Hillis Miller is UCI Distinguished Research Professor of English and Comparative Literature Emeritus at the University of

California at Irvine. He was educated at Oberlin College (BA 1948) and Harvard (MA 1949; PhD 1952). He taught at Johns Hopkins for 19 years. He then taught for 14 years at Yale, and in 1986 moved to UC Irvine. Over the years, Miller has lectured or taught as a visitor at many universities around the world. He has published many books and essays, primarily on 19th- and 20th-century literature and on literary theory. His recent books include *The Conflagration of Community: Fiction Before and After Auschwitz* (University of Chicago Press, 2011). A book co-authored with Claire Colebrook and Tom Cohen, *Theory and the Disappearing Future: On de Man On Benjamin,* was published by Routledge in 2011, and his *Reading for Our Time: Adam Bede and Middlemarch* appeared from Edinburgh University Press in March 2012. A book on *Communities in Fiction,* with essays on novels by Trollope, Hardy, Conrad, Woolf, Pynchon, and Cervantes, appeared in early 2015. *An Innocent Abroad: Lectures in China* (Northwestern University Press, 2015) gathers fifteen of the more than thirty lectures Miller gave at various universities in China between 1988 and 2012. A Chinese version of this book appeared in 2017 from Nanjing University Press. Miller is a Fellow of the American Academy of Arts and Sciences and a member of the American Philosophical Society.

Michael Naas is Professor of Philosophy at DePaul University. He works in the areas of Ancient Greek Philosophy and Contemporary French Philosophy. His most recent books include *The End of the World and Other Teachable Moments: Jacques Derrida's Final Seminar* (Fordham University Press, 2014) and *Miracle and Machine: Jacques Derrida and the Two Sources of Religion, Science, and the Media* (Fordham University Press, 2012). He is the co-translator of several works by Jacques Derrida, including *Rogues* (Stanford University Press, 2005), and *Learning to Live Finally* (Melville House, 2007). He is also co-editor of the *Oxford Literary Review.*

Eszter Timár is assistant professor of Gender Studies at Central European University, Budapest. Her research focuses on queer theory and Derridean deconstruction; her articles on Derridean autoimmunity and recent scientific developments in immunology appeared in *Parallax* and *InterAlia: A Journal of Queer Studies,* another is forthcoming in *Oxford Literary Review.*

Zach Rivers is a PhD candidate in Comparative Literature at New York University (Gender Studies MA, Central European University; English Literature BA, Georgia State University). His dissertation at NYU studies iterations of weaving in Ancient Greek literature and philosophy — mostly of the 4th and 5th Century BCE — as indissociable from sexual difference in order to approach such divergent topics of embodiment, the materiality of language, cultural inheritance, and cultural obliteration. By reading for embodied feminine weavers that exceed patriarchy's dream of autopoesis, his dissertation attempts to unravel disavowed yet existing threads of material subjects and objects made unintelligible by the discursive frameworks that structure and allocate social and material positioning. Indeed, the woven veils, shrouds, words, and robes that populate philosophy's most renowned metaphors helped to murder husbands, form social bonds, give voice to the tongueless, and keep menacing suitors at bay. His dissertation enacts an embodied, situated knowledge approach that affirms deconstructive feminisms as always already imbricated with intransigent yet volatile Ancient inheritances.

Nicholas Royle is Professor of English at the University of Sussex, England. His books include *Telepathy and Literature* (1991), *After Derrida* (1995), *The Uncanny* (2003), *Jacques Derrida* (2003), *How to Read Shakespeare* (2005), *In Memory of Jacques Derrida* (2009), and *Veering: A Theory of Literature* (2011). In addition he is co-author (with Andrew Bennett) of *This Thing Called Literature* (2015) and *An Introduction to Literature, Criticism and Theory* (5th edition, 2016). Royle has also published two novels, *Quilt* (2010) and *An English Guide to Birdwatching* (2017).

"W. dreams, like Phaedrus, of an army of thinker-friends, thinker-lovers. He dreams of a thought-army, a thought-pack, which would storm the philosophical Houses of Parliament. He dreams of Tartars from the philosophical steppes, of thought-barbarians, thought-outsiders. What distance would shine in their eyes!"

— Lars Iyer

www.ingramcontent.com/pod-product-compliance
Lightning Source LLC
Chambersburg PA
CBHW071739150426
43191CB00010B/1627